Introduction to Securitization

The Frank J. Fabozzi Series

Introduction to Securitization

FRANK J. FABOZZI
VINOD KOTHARI

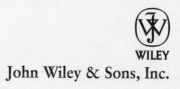

WILEY

John Wiley & Sons, Inc.

Published by John Wiley & Sons, Inc., Hoboken, New Jersey.
Published simultaneously in Canada.

For general information on our other products and services or for technical support, please
contact our Customer Care Department within the United States at (800) 762-2974, outside
the United States at (317) 572-3993, or fax (317) 572-4002.

Wiley also publishes its books in a variety of electronic formats. Some content that appears in
print may not be available in electronic books. For more information about Wiley products,
visit our web site at www.wiley.com.

Library of Congress Cataloging-in-Publication Data:

Fabozzi, Frank J.
  Introduction to securitization / Frank J. Fabozzi, Vinod Kothari.
    p. cm. — (The Frank J. Fabozzi series)
  Includes bibliographical references and index.
  ISBN 978-0-470-37190-9 (cloth)
1. Asset-backed financing. 2. Securities. I. Kothari, Vinod. II. Title.

  HG4028.A84F325 2008
  332.63'2--dc22

                          2008014508

Printed in the United States of America.

10 9 8 7 6 5 4 3 2 1

Contents

Preface

There is a choice of books on securitization, collateralized debt obligations (CDOs), and structured credit products. In fact, both of us have written other books on the subject. This book, however, was conceived as a short, handy and easy-to-comprehend guide to securitization, minus technical details. The idea originated while both of us were working on a comprehensive article on securitization: One which says it all in a limited space and serves as a curtain-raiser on the subject. As we were both very happy with the result of our efforts, we realized that practitioners as well as students need a simpler introduction to securitization than what they are being served in compendious volumes full of details that they may not need. Hence, the caption *Introduction to Securitization*.

When we were writing this book, the subprime crisis had already started erupting from various quarters. Different commentators had already started criticizing securitization for the subprime losses and consequent repercussions on the global economy. By the time we completed the book, securitization seemed to have become a hated word by several people. Though we have seen financial innovation over several years and we may easily distinguish between a temporary fad and a basic bad, we asked ourselves serious questions about the fundamental logic of securitization. Our analysis has been that securitization as a tool tries to weave a structured fabric, picking up threads from the financial assets originated by banks and others. If the underlying assets are bad, one cannot expect to weave gold out of it. We have taken up the gains and concerns in securitization at length in this book.

In short, the book is concise, comprehensive, and contemporary. Since there has been a coming together of the principles of structured finance with credit derivatives, we have included the fundamentals of structured credit products and CDOs in this book.

The book is divided into five parts. The two chapters in Part One provide the background for securitization. In Chapter 1 we explain what securitization is, the relationship between securitization and structured finance, how securitization differs from traditional forms of financing, the types of securities issued (asset-backed securities), and the parties to a securitization. We explain the six primary reasons why a corporation might prefer to use securitization as a vehicle for raising funds rather than issuing corporate bonds and the goals when a corporation structures a securitization transaction in Chapter 2.

Part Two has five chapters that look more closely at how to structure a securitization transaction. We begin in Chapter 3 with the securitization of conforming loans that result in the creation of agency mortgage-backed securities and the redistribution of cash flows to create collateralized mortgage obligations (CMOs). After explaining prepayments and prepayment conventions, we describe the different types of bond classes or tranches in a CMO structure. We begin with agency products because it allows us to clearly demonstrate how the risk of the collateral of a pool of assets is redistributed amongst the different bond classes. The risks redistributed in the case of agency CMOs is prepayment risk and interest rate risk. We then move into the structuring nonagency deals which include the securitization of prime mortgages and subprime loans in Chapter 4. In the case of nonagency deals involving residential mortgage loans, structuring involves the redistribution of prepayment and interest rate risks and credit risk. We explain the difference in structuring considerations for a prime and subprime transaction.

We cover credit enhancement mechanisms in a securitization transaction in Chapter 5. We explain that (1) the amount of credit enhancement required to obtain a targeted credit rating is set by the rating agencies, (2) the amount of credit enhancement will depend on the type of collateral, (3) some forms of credit enhancement are more suitable for certain types of assets but would be totally inappropriate for other types, and (4) all credit enhancement has a cost associated with it so an economic analysis of the cost of further enhancement of a structure versus the improved execution of the transaction must be analyzed in considering why additional credit enhancement is justified.

A securitization transaction may require the use of an interest rate derivative for asset-liability management or yield enhancement.

We describe the different types of interest rate derivatives used (interest rate swaps, interest rate caps, and interest rate corridors) in Chapter 6. Since these instruments are over-the-counter financial products, this exposes a transaction to counterparty risk. After providing the basics about interest rate derivatives, we explain how they are used in a securitization providing examples from prospectus supplements.

Operational risk refers to the various risks that any of the agents responsible for the various operations or processes that lead to transformation of the securitized assets into investors' cash flows may not do what they are supposed to do, or there might be failure of systems, equipments, or processes that may lead to leakages, costs, delays, etc. Because operational issues in securitization have attracted quite some attention in recent years, we devote Chapter 7 to this topic.

The three chapters in Part Three review the different types of assets that have been securitized. In Chapter 8, we make a distinction between the securitization of existing assets and future assets and a distinction between a cash securitization and a synthetic securitization. We then go on to discuss the two main types of retail assets that have been securitized (in addition to residential mortgage loans that we covered in Part Two): credit card receivables and auto loans. Asset-backed commercial paper conduits, structured investment vehicles, etc. have been hotly talked about lately. We discuss the structure of these conduits and how it differs from term securitization, in Chapter 9. In addition, in that chapter, we explain other structured vehicles (conduits based on liquidity support, the number of sellers, and on asset type). In Chapter 10 we cover the securitization of future cash flows, whole business securitization (also referred to as operating revenues securitization), and securitization of embedded profits in insurance businesses.

In Part Four we look at the application of securitization technology to structured credit portfolios, more specifically collateralized debt obligations (CDOs). In Chapter 11, we provide an introduction to CDOs, explaining the economic motivation for their creation, the terminology used in CDOs, the structure of CDOs, and the types of CDOs. More details about the types of CDOs, including their structure and special features, are described in Chapter 12. This includes balance sheet CDOs (cash and synthetic), arbitrage CDOs (cash and synthetic), the resecuritization or structured finance CDOs, and index trades and indexing tracking CDOs. We devote Chapter 13 to a variety of issues concerning CDOs involving structuring and their analysis. In that chapter we look at measures of pool quality (asset quality tests, diversity tests), asset and income coverage tests (overcollateralization tests and interest coverage tests), the ramp-up period, the CDO manager, investing in CDOs, and collateral and structural risk in CDO investing.

Part Five looks at the implications of securitization for financial markets and economies. We set forth the benefits of securitization in Chapter 14 and the concerns with securitization in Chapter 15.

There are two appendices. Appendix A provides the basics of credit derivatives. We provide coverage on this latest type of derivative product because of its use in creating synthetic CDOs. In Appendix B, we explain the fundamental of valuing MBS and ABS.

In order to ensure that each chapter can be condensed into key learnings, we provide a list of the key points covered in the chapter for all the chapters. We believe that these key points will allow the reader to quickly assimilate the "take home" value after reading a chapter.

We hope this book will be a valuable addition to the existing literature on the subject.

Frank J. Fabozzi
Vinod Kothari

About the Authors

Frank J. Fabozzi is Professor in the Practice of Finance and Becton Fellow in the School of Management at Yale University. Prior to joining the Yale faculty, he was a Visiting Professor of Finance in the Sloan School at MIT. Professor Fabozzi is a Fellow of the International Center for Finance at Yale University and on the Advisory Council for the Department of Operations Research and Financial Engineering at Princeton University. He is an affiliated professor at the Institute of Statistics, Econometrics and Mathematical Finance at the University of Karlsruhe (Germany). He is the editor of the *Journal of Portfolio Management* and an associate editor of the *Journal of Fixed Income* and the *Journal of Structured Finance*. He earned a doctorate in economics from the City University of New York in 1972. In 2002, Professor Fabozzi was inducted into the Fixed Income Analysts Society's Hall of Fame and is the 2007 recipient of the C. Stewart Sheppard Award given by the CFA Institute. He earned the designation of Chartered Financial Analyst and Certified Public Accountant. He has authored and edited numerous books about finance.

Vinod Kothari, chartered accountant and chartered secretary, is an established author, trainer, and consultant on asset-based financing, structured finance, and structured credit. Mr. Kothari has been a rank holder throughout his academic career and was awarded the Outstanding Young Person Award in the field of Finance and Taxation by a voluntary organization. He wrote his first book at the age of 23; he has authored books on leasing, securitization, credit derivatives, and security interests. Mr. Kothari is a visiting faculty at Indian Institute of Management, Kolkata, where he teaches structured finance, and a visiting faculty at National University of Juridical Sciences, Kolkata, where he teaches corporate insolvency.

PART
One

Background

CHAPTER 1

Introduction

What do David Bowie, James Brown, the Isley Brothers, and Rod Stewart have in common? The obvious answer is that they are all recording artists. The financial professional would go beyond this obvious commonality by adding: All of them have used a financing technique known as *securitization* to obtain funding from their future music royalties. The first was David Bowie who in 1997 used securitization to raise $55 million backed by the current and future revenues of his first 25 music albums (287 songs) recorded prior to 1990. These bonds, popularly referred to as "Bowie bonds" and purchased by Prudential Insurance Company, had a maturity of 10 years. When the bonds matured in 2007, the royalty rights reverted back to David Bowie. Despite the attention drawn to securitization by the popular press because of the deals done by these recording artists, the significance of this financial innovation is that it has been an important form of raising capital for corporations and government entities throughout the world, as well as a tool for risk management.

Prior to the 1980s, the meaning of securitization was used to describe the process of substituting the issuance of securities to obtain debt financing for bank borrowing. Economists referred to this process for fund raising as *disintermediation*. For example, the former chairman of Citicorp offered the following definition for securitization: "the substitution of more efficient public capital markets for less efficient, higher cost, financial intermediaries in the funding of debt instruments" (Kendall and Fishman, 1996). The development of the high-yield bond market in the late 1970s and early 1980s can be viewed as a securitization under this broad definition because bank loans to speculative-grade-rated corporations were replaced by the issuance of public bonds by these borrowers.

3

Today, however, the definition of securitization has taken on a more specific meaning. As stated by Lumpkin (1999, p. 1):

More recently, the term has been used to refer to so-called "structured finance," the process by which (relatively) homogeneous, but illiquid, assets are pooled and repackaged, with security interests representing claims to the incoming cash flows and other economic benefits generated by the loan pool sold as securities to third-party investors.

Admittedly, defining securitization in terms of structured finance begs the question of what is meant by *structured finance*. There is no universal definition of structure finance. Fabozzi, Davis, and Choudhry (2006) note that the term covers a wide range of financial market activity. Based on a survey of capital market participants, they provide the following working definition for structured finance:

... techniques employed whenever the requirements of the originator or owner of an asset, be they concerned with funding, liquidity, risk transfer, or other need, cannot be met by an existing, off-the-shelf product or instrument. Hence, to meet this requirement, existing products and techniques must be engineered into a tailor-made product or process. Thus, structured finance is a flexible financial engineering tool.

Structured finance by this definition would include not just securitization but also structured credits, project finance, structured notes, and leasing (large ticket leasing, particularly leveraged leases). In a survey of capital market participants, some respondents equated structured finance as securitization as in the definition by Lumpkin. In fact, a 2005 report by the Bank for International Settlements (BIS) defines structured finance as follows:

Structured finance instruments can be defined through three key characteristics: (1) pooling of assets (either cash-based or synthetically created); (2) tranching of liabilities that are backed by the asset pool (this property differentiates structured finance from traditional "pass-through" securitizations); (3) de-linking of the credit risk of the collateral asset pool from the credit risk of the originator, usually through use of a finite-lived, standalone special purpose vehicle (SPV). (BIS, 2005, p. 5)

As we discuss securitization in this book, we see the importance of the three characteristics cited in the BIS definition. Moreover, while we refer to a securitization as a means of financing, as will become clear, the end result of a transaction is that a corporation can obtain proceeds by selling assets and not borrowing funds. The asset securitization process transforms a pool of assets into one or more securities that are referred to as asset-backed securities.

The purpose of this book is to explain the fundamentals of securitization. While the focus is on securitization from the perspective of the issuer, Appendix B explains the valuation and the analysis of the interest rate risk for the securities created from a securitization transaction from the investor's perspective.

WHAT IS A SECURITIZATION?

There are some similarities between securitization and secured lending. In *secured lending*, also called *asset-based lending*, the lender requires that the borrowing firm commit specific assets of the firm as security or collateral for a lending arrangement. The assets that are used as collateral may be short-term assets such as accounts receivable or long-term assets such as equipment. For example, in accounts receivable financing the lender looks first to the accounts receivable of the borrower to fulfill the financial obligations of the lending arrangement. The amount advanced by the lender to the client firm depends on (1) what the lender deems acceptable based on the quality and nature of the receivables; (2) the type of customer the client firm sells to and the terms of the sale; and (3) the historical performance of the client firm's accounts receivables. Moreover, certain types of receivables may not be appropriate for financing via secured lending. For longer-term assets such as equipment, secured lending can be in the form of a loan or a bond. The cost of borrowing depends on the credit quality of the borrower because lenders are looking to the ability of the borrowing firm to satisfy the terms of the borrowing arrangement.

A securitization differs from these traditional forms of financing in several important ways. The key in a securitization is that the cash flow generated by the asset pool can be employed to support one or more securities that may be of higher credit quality than the company's secured debt. The higher credit quality of these securities is achieved by relying on the cash flow created by the pool of assets rather than on the payment promise of the borrowing firm, such cash flows having been isolated in a bankruptcy remote structure and "credit enhanced" using several credit enhancement techniques discussed in Chapter 5.[1] Compare this with secured lending. In the case of accounts receivable financing, while the lender looks first to the cash flow generated by the receivables, the borrowing firm is responsible for any shortfall. In the case of secured lending where the collateral is property, the lender relies primarily on the borrowing firm's ability to repay and only secondarily to the value at which the collateral can be liquidated in bankruptcy. Moreover, in relying on the liquidation value of the collateral, the lender assumes that in a bankruptcy proceeding the distribution of assets will be based on the principle of absolute priority (i.e., secured lenders are repaid before unsecured lenders and equity investors receive any proceeds). However, while this is the case in a liquidation of a corporation, the principle of absolute priority typically does not hold in a corporate reorganization.[2]

Because securitization involves the sale of assets, it is commonly compared to factoring.[3] Unlike in a secured lending arrangement such as accounts receivable financing, the client firm has sold the accounts receivables to the factor. The factor's credit risk depends on the arrangement: recourse factoring, modified recourse factoring, and nonrecourse factoring. In recourse factoring, the factor does not

---

[1] As will be explained in Chapter 5, the credit quality of the securities can also be achieved by the use of a third-party guarantor.

[2] See, for example, Meckling (1977) and Miller (1977).

[3] Another reason for the comparison is that the factor becomes the credit and collection department of the client firm; in the case of securitization, the collection and servicing function is typically either originator-retained, or transferred to independent servicers.

absorb the risk of loss for a customer account but instead obtains repayment from the client firm. In modified recourse factoring, insurance is obtained by the factor and offered to the client firm. The client firm is then not responsibile for the risk of loss for a customer account.[4] In nonrecourse factoring, all of the credit risk is transferred to the factor. In terms of cost, recourse factoring is the least expensive because the factor is not exposed to the credit risk of the customer accounts and nonrecourse factoring is the most expensive because the credit risk is transferred to the factor. Hence, unlike recourse financing, securitization slices the credit risk into several slices; the juniormost slice may be retained by the borrower, but the other slices are transferred to the "lenders." That is to say, investors buying the securities. At the option of the client firm, the factor may provide a cash advance against a portion of the accounts receivable.

Just three of the advantages of securitization compared to nonrecourse and modified recourse are that (1) there is typically lower funding cost when a securitization is used; (2) receivables that factors will not purchase may be acceptable for a securitization; and (3) proceeds from the sale in a securitization are received immediately while the firm may or may not obtain a cash advance from the factor.

As noted earlier, generally, securitization is a form of structured finance. Structured finance also encompasses project finance, the financing of some types of equipment, and some other kinds of secured financing. The common theme to all types of structured finance transactions is that the transaction is structured to modify or redistribute the risk of the collateral among different classes of investors by the use of a structure. The risks of the collateral are its credit risk, interest rate risk, prepayment risk, and liquidity risk. Securitization is primarily concerned with monetizing financial assets in such a way that the risk is tied primarily to their repayment rather than to the performance of a particular project or entity.

The assets that can be sold by an originator and then used as collateral in an asset securitization fall into two types: (1) existing assets/existing receivables and (2) assets/receivables to arise in the future. Some examples of assets that fall into the former category are

---

[4] The client firm is still responsible for the customer account if the nonpayment is due to reasons such as disputes over product specifications or quality of the product.

residential mortgage loans, commercial mortgage loans, corporate loans, automobile car loans, and student loans. Transactions with this type of collateral are referred to as *existing asset securitizations*. Transactions of asset/receivables to arise in the future are referred to as *future flow securitizations*. Examples include airline ticket receivables, oil and gas royalties, and tax revenue receivables.

ILLUSTRATION OF A SECURITIZATION

We use a hypothetical securitization to illustrate the key elements of a securitization and the parties to a transaction. Our hypothetical firm is the Ace Corporation, a manufacturer of specialized equipment for the construction of commercial buildings. Some of its sales are for cash, but the bulk are from installment sales contracts. For simplicity, we assume that the installment period is typically seven years. The collateral for each installment sales contract (sometimes loosely referred to herein as a loan) is the construction equipment purchased by the borrower. The loan specifies the interest rate the customer pays.

The decision to extend a loan to a customer is made by the credit department of Ace Corporation based on criteria established by the firm, referred to as its *underwriting standards*. In this securitization, Ace Corporation is referred to as the *originator* because it has originated the loans to its customers. Moreover, Ace Corporation may have a department that is responsible for collecting payments from customers, notifying customers who may be delinquent, and, when necessary, recovering and disposing of the collateral (i.e., the construction equipment in our illustration) if the customer fails to make loan repayments by a specified time. These activities are referred to as *servicing* the loan. While the servicer of the loans need not be the originator of the loans, in our illustration we are assuming that Ace Corporation is the servicer.

Suppose that Ace Corporation currently has $400 million in installment sales contracts (i.e., its accounts receivable). The *chief financial officer* (CFO) of Ace Corporation wants to use its installment sales contracts to raise $320 million rather than issue a traditional corporate bond. To do so, the CFO will work with its legal staff to set up a legal entity referred to as a *special purpose vehicle* (SPV), also referred to as a *special purpose entity* (SPE). The SPV is critical in a securitization transaction because it is this entity that delinks the credit of the entity seeking funding (Ace Corporation) from the creditworthiness of the securities that are created in a securitization. Assume that the SPV set up by Ace Corporate is called Financial Ace Trust (FACET). Ace Corporation sells $320 million of the loans to FACET and receives from FACET $320 million in cash, the amount the CFO wanted to raise. Since Ace Corporation is the originator of the loans and has sold these loans to FACET, Ace Corporation is referred to as the *originator/seller* in this transaction.

It is critical that the sale of the loans transferred be a *true sale* by Ace Corporation to FACET. By a true sale it is meant that the sale of the assets closely substantively resembles a commercial sale of such assets by Ace Corporation. If it is subsequently determined in a bankruptcy proceeding that the so-called sale by Ace Corporation was merely a nomenclature or a camouflage, then a bankruptcy judge can rule that the assets were never sold and were merely pledged as collateral for a financing. In that case, in the event of a bankruptcy filing by Ace Corporation, the bankruptcy judge can have the assets of FACET treated as part of the assets of Ace Corporation. This would defeat the purpose of setting up the SPV. Typically, a true sale opinion letter by a law firm is sought to provide additional comfort to the parties in the transaction.

Where does FACET obtain the $320 million to buy the assets? It does so by issuing asset-backed securities, called *bond classes* or *tranches*. A simple transaction can involve the sale of just one bond class with a par value of $320 million. The payments to the bond classes are obtained from the payments made by the obligors (i.e., the buyers of the construction equipment). The payments from the obligors include principal repayment and interest. However, most securitization transactions involve a more complex structure than simply one bond class. For example, there can be rules for distribution of principal and interest other than on a pro rata basis to different bond classes. The creation of different bond classes allows the distribution of the collateral's risk among different types of investors: investors with different appetite's for interest rate risk (i.e., price sensitivity to changes in interest rates) and credit risk.

An example of a more complicated transaction is one in which two bond classes are created, bond class A1 and bond class A2. The par value for bond class A1 is $120 million and for bond class A2 is $200 million. The priority rule set forth in the structure can simply specify that bond class A1 receives all the principal generated from the collateral until all the entire $120 million of bond class A1 is paid off and then bond class A2 begins to receive principal. Bond class A1 is then a shorter-term bond than bond class A2. This type of tranching is used to create securities with different exposures to interest rate risk.

Also, as will be explained in later chapters, in most securitizations there is more than one bond class and the various bond classes differ as to how they share any losses resulting from the obligor defaults. For example, suppose FACET issued $290 million par value of bond class A, the senior bond class, and $30 million par value of bond class B, a subordinated bond class. As long as there are no defaults by obligors that exceed $30 million, then bond class A receives full repayment of its $290 million.

SECURITIES ISSUED IN A SECURITIZATION

The term used to describe the securities issued by the SPV in a securitization are referred to as *asset-backed notes, asset-backed bonds*, or *asset-backed obligations*. When the security is short-term commercial paper, it is referred to as *asset-backed commercial paper* (or ABCP). As will be explained when we discuss the different types of securitization structures in later chapters, asset-backed securities can have different credit exposure and based on the credit priority, securities are described as *senior notes* and *junior notes* (subordinated notes).

In the prospectus for a securitization, the securities are actually referred to as *certificates*: pass-through certificates or pay-through certificates. The distinction between these two types of certificates is the nature of the claim that the certificate holder has on the cash flow generated by the asset pool. If the investor has a direct claim on all of the cash flow and the certificate holder has a proportionate share of the collateral's cash flow, the term *pass-through certificate* (or *beneficial interest certificate*) is used. When there are rules that are used to allocate the collateral's cash flow among different bond classes, the asset-backed securities are referred to as *pay-through certificates*.

KEY POINTS OF THE CHAPTER

> ➤ *Securitization is a form of structured finance.*

> ➤ *The common theme to all types of structured finance transactions is that the transaction is structured to modify or redistribute the risk of the collateral among different classes of investors by the use of a structure.*

> ➤ *Securitization involves the pooling of assets/receivables and the issuance of securities by a special purpose vehicle.*

> ➤ *The end result of a securitization transaction is that a corporation can obtain proceeds by selling assets and not borrowing funds.*

> ➤ *The asset securitization process transforms a pool of assets into one or more securities referred to as asset-backed securities.*

> ➤ *A securitization differs from traditional forms of financing in that the cash flow generated by the asset pool can be employed to support one or more securities that may be of higher credit quality than the company's secured debt.*

> ➤ *Three advantages of securitization compared to nonrecourse and modified recourse factoring are that (1) there is a typically lower funding cost when a securitization is used; (2) receivables that factors will not purchase may be acceptable for a securitization; and (3) proceeds from the sale in a securitization are received immediately while the firm may or may not obtain a cash advance from the factor.*

> ➤ *Securitization is primarily concerned with monetizing financial assets in such a way that the risks of the collateral (credit risk, interest rate risk, prepayment risk, and liquidity risk) are tied primarily to their repayment rather than to the performance of a particular project or entity.*

> ➤ *The assets used in a securitization can be either existing assets/ existing receivables in which case the transaction is referred to as an existing asset securitization or assets/receivables to arise in the future in which case the transaction is referred to as a future flow transaction.*

➤ *The parties to a securitization are the originator, the servicer, and the investors in the asset-backed securities.*

➤ *The originator (also referred to as the* originator/seller*) makes the loans based on its underwriting standards and sells a pool of loans it originates to an SPV, the sale being required to be a true sale for legal purposes.*

➤ *The SPV purchases the pool of loans from the proceeds obtained from the sale of the asset-backed securities.*

➤ *The capital structure of the SPV can involve just one bond class or several bond classes with different priorities on the cash flow from the collateral.*

➤ *While the securities issued in a securitization are commonly referred to as asset-backed securities, in the prospectus they are referred to by various names.*

CHAPTER 2

Issuer Motivation for Securitizing Assets and the Goals of Structuring

In this chapter, we explain the economic motivation for nonfinancial and financial institutions to employ securitization. One of the reasons is to reduce funding costs. (Later, in Chapter 14, we examine this often-cited reason within the context of several economic theories regarding a firm's capital structure.) The reason cited for being able to reduce funding costs is because the issuer has the ability to structure the cash flows generated by a pool of assets to create securities that are more attractive to a wide range of institutional investors. The creation of securities from a pool of assets is referred to as *structuring* a transaction. In the last section, of this chapter we explain the goals of structuring.

REASONS SECURITIZATION IS USED FOR FUNDING

Securitization appeals to both nonfinancial and financial corporations as well as state and local governments. The six primary reasons for corporations using securitization are:

1. The potential for reducing funding costs.
2. The ability to diversify funding sources.
3. The ability to manage corporate risk.
4. For financial entities that must satisfy risk-based capital requirements, potential relief from capital requirements.
5. The opportunity to achieve off-balance financing.
6. Generating fee income.

We discuss these reasons in the rest of this section.

Potential for Reducing Funding Costs

To understand the potential for reducing funding costs by issuing as-set-backed securities rather than a corporate bond, suppose that our illustration, Ace Corporation, has a single-B credit rating. This rating is referred to as a *speculative-grade rating* and if Ace Corporation is-sued corporate bonds, those bonds would be referred to as *high-yield bonds* or *junk bonds*. If the CFO of Ace Corporation wants to raise $320 million by issuing a corporate bond, its funding cost would be whatever the benchmark Treasury yield is plus a spread for single-B issuers in the industry sector in which Ace Corporation operates. (The same is true if Ace Corporation wants to raise funds via commercial paper.) Suppose, instead, that the CFO of Ace Corporation uses $320 million of its installment sales contracts as collateral for a bond issue. Despite this form of secured lending, the credit rating probably will be the same as if it issued a corporate bond. The reason is that if Ace Corporation defaults on any of its outstanding debt obligations, the bankruptcy laws may impair the ability of the secured lender to seek enforcement of security interest to liquidate the bonds.

However, suppose that Ace Corporation can create another legal entity and sell the loans to that entity. That entity is the SPV that we described in Chapter 1 in our hypothetical transaction (FACET). If the sale of the loans is done properly—that is, there is a true sale of the loans—FACET then legally owns the receivables, not Ace Corpo-ration. This means that if Ace Corporation is forced into bankruptcy, its creditors cannot recover the loans sold to the SPV because they are legally owned by FACET.

The implication of structuring a transaction by using FACET, the SPV, is that when FACET sells bonds backed by the loans (i.e., the asset-backed securities), the rating agencies will evaluate the credit risk associated with collecting the payments due on the loans inde-pendent of the credit rating of Ace Corporation. That is, the credit rating of the originator/seller (Ace Corporation) is not relevant. The credit rating that will be assigned to the bond classes issued by FACET will be whatever the issuer wants the credit rating to be! It may seem strange that the issuer (FACET) can get any credit rating it wants, but that is the case. The reason is that FACET will show the characteristics and historical performance of similar loans in the securitization transaction to the rating agencies from whom ratings for the bond classes are being sought. In turn, the rating agencies evaluating the bonds classes will tell the issuer how the transaction must be structured in order to obtain a specific rating for each of the bond classes in the structure. More specifically, the issuer will be told how much *credit enhancement* is required in the structure to be award a specific credit rating to each bond class.

By credit enhancement it is meant that there is a source of capital that can be used to absorb losses incurred by the asset pool. There are various forms of credit enhancement that we review in Chapter 5. Basically, the rating agencies will evaluate the potential losses from the collateral and determine how much credit enhancement is required for the bond classes in a proposed structure to achieve the targeted rating sought by the issuer. The higher the credit rating sought by the issuer, the more credit enhancement a rating agency will require for a given collateral. Thus, Ace Corporation, which we assumed is single-B rated, can obtain funding using the loans to its customers as collateral to obtain a better credit rating for one or more of the bond classes it issues than its own credit rating. In fact, with enough credit enhancement, bond classes backed by the collateral can be awarded the highest credit rating, triple A. The key to a corporation issuing bonds via a securitization with a higher credit rating than the corporation's own credit rating is the SPV. Its role is critical because it is the SPV that legally separates the assets used as collateral for the securitization from the corporation that is seeking financing (the originator/seller), thus insulating the transaction from the credit risk of the originator. The SPV itself is structured as a bankruptcy-remote entity. Thus, we are left with the risk of losses in the asset, or credit risk, which can be mitigated by proper credit enhancements to a point where the target rating can be achieved.

Even after factoring in the cost of credit enhancement and other legal and accounting expenses associated with a securitization, capital seeking firms have found securitization to be a less expensive than issuing corporate bonds. For example, consider the auto manufacturers. In 2001, the rating downgrades of the firms in this industry pushed Ford Motor, General Motors, and Toyota Motor to issue in early 2002 asset-backed securities backed by auto loans rather than issue corporate bonds. Ford Motor Credit, for example, issued $5 billion in the first two weeks of 2002. Since 2000, when there was the first threat of the parent company's credit rating, Ford Motor Credit reduced its exposure from $42 billion to $8 billion, substituting the sale of securitized car loans that were rated triple A. In fact, from 2000 to mid-2003, Ford Motor Credit increased securitizations to $55 billion (28% of its total funding) from $25 billion (13% of its total funding). Also, while the ratings of the auto manufacturers were downgraded in May 2005, the ratings on several of their securitization transactions were actually upgraded due to high subsisting levels of credit enhancement.

While we explained the difference between the legal preference that an investor in a securitization has compared to that of an investor in a secured debt obligation of an issuer, the question is why a corporation cannot provide this legal preference without selling the assets to an SPV. The reason is that the prevailing legal structure does not permit the isolation of specific assets that is free from the claims of the corporation's other creditors if it has financial difficulty. Hence, securitization is basically a form of "legal" arbitrage.

While we have stated that investors in a securitization are protected from the creditors of the originator/seller when there is a true sale, in the United States the truth of the sale has been directly challenged in the courts. The bankruptcy of LTV Steel Company, Inc. (LTV), filed in the United States Bankruptcy Court for the Northern District Court of Ohio on December 29, 2000, was the closest challenge. LTV argued that its two securitizations (a receivables securitization and an inventory securitization) were not true sales but instead disguised financing transactions. If this were upheld by the bankruptcy court, the creditors of LTV would have been entitled to the cash flow of the assets that LTV allegedly merely transferred but did not sell to the SPV. Based on this argument, LTV in an emergency motion to the bankruptcy court sought permission to use the cash flow of the assets that were the collateral for the two securitizations as long as it provided adequate protection to the investors in the asset-backed securities issued by the SPV. In an interim order, the bankruptcy court did allow LTV to use the cash flow from the assets that were the collateral for the securitization. However, the bankruptcy court did not have to eventually rule on this argument of whether there was a true sale of the assets because the case was settled. As part of a settlement, there was a summary finding that the securitizations of LTV were in fact a true sale. Troubling to investors in asset-backed securities is that the court decided to permit LTV to use the cash flows prior to the settlement.[1]

Diversifying Funding Sources

A corporation that seeks to raise funds via a securitization must establish itself as an issuer in the asset-backed securities market. Among other things, this requires that the issuer be a frequent issuer in the market in order to get its name established in the asset-backed securities market and to create a reasonably liquid aftermarket for trading those securities. Once an issuer establishes itself in the market, it can look at both the corporate bond market and the asset-backed securities market to determine its best funding source by comparing the all-in-cost of funds in the two markets, as well as nonquantifiable benefits associated with securitization.[2]

Managing Corporate Risk

The credit risk and the interest rate risk of assets that have been securitized are no longer risks faced by the originator/seller. Thus, securitization can be used as a corporate risk management tool. For example, consider the interest rate risk faced by a bank. A bank that originates longer-term fixed rate residential mortgage loans (i.e., long duration assets) and funds these loans by issuing short-term floating rate notes (short duration liabilities) is exposed to considerable interest rate risk because of the mismatch between the duration of the assets (the residential mortgage loans) and the liabilities (the short-term floating rate notes). By selling off the residential mortgage loans and capturing the spread from the origination process up front, the bank has eliminated the interest rate mismatch. Credit risk is also removed

---

[1] While *true sale* is a significant legal issue in securitization, it must be appreciated that the question is whether a sale is "true." This implies determination of the truth of what is apparently a sale—the question is therefore subjective. While market practitioners try to learn from past experience and construct transactions that abide by certain true sale tests, there cannot be an absolute safe harbor.

[2] For a further discussion, see Chapter 9 in Kothari (2006).

to the extent that the originator/seller has only a limited interest in the securitized structure.

The risk management capability of securitization is not limited to banks. For example, consider once again Ford Motor Credit. Since 2000, it used securitization to reduce its car loan portfolio and thereby reduce its exposure to the credit risk associated with those loans. At the end of 2001, Ford Motor carried $208 million in auto loans and realized first quarter credit losses of $912 million. By 2003, credit losses for the first quarter declined to $493 million with loans on the balance sheet down by $28 million to $180 million.

Managing Regulatory Capital

For regulated financial entities, securitization is a tool for managing risk-based capital requirements (i.e., attaining optimal capital adequacy standards) in the United States and other countries. While a complete description of mandated risk-based capital guidelines for financial institutions is beyond the scope of this chapter, several common themes that have direct implications for the strategic importance of securitization in the asset/liability management process merit discussion.

The central idea underlying risk-based capital guidelines is the regulatory requirement of a direct link between capital reserves and the credit risk associated with a regulated financial entity's portfolio of assets. The risk associated with each asset is quantified by assigning a risk weight to each asset category. Upon classifying the assets held by a financial entity into the various risk categories, the risk-weighted value for that category is determined by weighting the book value of the asset category by the risk weight. The total capital reserves required by the financial entity are then determined as a percentage of the total risk-weighted asset values. All things equal, institutions that hold a risky portfolio have to reserve a higher amount of capital. Since securitization results in lower retained risk with the originator, capital guidelines, which are risk-sensitive, require presumably lesser capital in the case of securitization than in the case of the unsecuritized portfolio of loans. As a result, frequently a regulated financial entity can lower its regulatory capital requirements by securitizing certain loans that it would normally retain in its portfolio. On the demand side, it should be noted that regulated financial entities would prefer to hold higher-rated securities backed by loans than hold the loans directly.

Achieving Off-Balance-Sheet Financing

Most securitizations transfer assets and liabilities off the balance sheet, thereby reducing the amount of the originator's on-balance-sheet leverage. The off-balance-sheet financing can help improve the securitizer's return on equity and other key financial ratios. However, many equity and corporate debt analysts now consider both reported and managed (i.e., reported plus off the balance sheet) leverage in their credit analysis of firms that employ securitization.

Moreover, the Enron bankruptcy prompted the Securities and Exchange Commission (SEC) and the Financial Accounting Standards Board (FASB) to reexamine the use of off-balance-sheet transactions. Enron used SPVs for a variety of illegal purposes. This resulted in new SEC rules and FASB accounting rules for SPVs despite the fact that the use of SPVs in securitization had nothing to do with how SPVs were used to mislead investors by Enron.

The basic issue is whether or not the SPV should be consolidated with the corporation. Pre-2003 *generally accepted accounting principles* (GAAP) for consolidation required that a corporation consolidate if it had a "controlling financial interest." The definition of *controlling financial interest* was that the firm had a majority voting interest. Hence, GAAP's pre-2003 rules set forth that a corporation could be the primary beneficiary of the activities of an SPV; but absent a majority voting interest, consolidation was not necessary.

The FASB on January 17, 2003 issued FASB Interpretation No. 46 ("Consolidation of Variable Interest Entities"), referred to as *FIN 46*, which set forth a complex set of rules and principles for consolidation of what is referred to as *variable interest entities*, one example being an SPV.[3] If an SPV is consolidated, then the fair market value of the assets is reported on the corporation's balance sheet as an asset. On the other side of the balance sheet, a fair value for the liability is recorded, as well as the fair market value of the minority interest in

---

[3] Qualifying SPEs defined in Para. 35 of FAS 140 are not required to be consolidated under FIN 46.

the SPV. While FIN 46 is complex and subject to interpretation, securitizations must comply with it in order to avoid consolidation for financial reporting purposes.[4]

With respect to SEC requirements, Section 401(a) of the Sarbanes-Oxley Act of 2002 (SOX) and its amendments deal with disclosure in periodic financial reports. With respect to off-balance-sheet transactions, SOX requires that a company in its annual and quarterly filings with the SEC disclose all material off-balance-sheet transactions, arrangements, obligations (including contingent obligations), and other relationships of the issuer with unconsolidated entities or other persons, that may have a material current or future effect on financial condition, changes in financial condition, results of operations, liquidity, capital expenditures, capital resources, or significant components of revenues or expenses.

The amendments to SOX address the lack of transparency of these transactions in a public company's financial disclosure by requiring a discussion of them in a separate section within the management discussion and analysis section in SEC filings that it is reasonable to assume will have an effect on not only the firm's financial condition but other matters material to investors. With a greater understanding of a company's off-balance-sheet arrangements and contractual obligations, investors will be better able to understand how a company conducts significant aspects of its business by using securitization, for example, and to assess the quality of a company's earnings and the risks that are not apparent on the face of the financial statements.

Generating Servicing Fee Income

Typically, the originator of a loan will be the servicer. Securitization can be used to allow the originator of loans to convert capital intensive assets to a less capital intensive source of servicing fee income.

---

[4] Basically, there are four questions that must be asked to determine if a consolidation is required: (1) Does the corporation have enough equity at risk in the SPV? (2) Is the corporation allowed to make decisions about the activities of the SPV by either voting rights or similar rights? (3) If the SPV incurs a loss, does the corporation have an obligation to absorb that loss? (4) If here are any residual economic benefits expected from the activities of the SPV, does the corporation has the right to receive them? If the answer to any of the above questions is affirmative, then consolidation is required.

By doing so, this augments its servicing and origination fees without increasing its capital base. This is accomplished by securitizing and selling the loans while retaining the rights to service the loans, with the servicing fee that is retained being like an interest-only strip of payments that compensates the servicer. In this respect, financial institutions and finance companies that are also originators of loans are uniquely positioned to take advantage of the growth of securitization since their infrastructure includes the human and technical resources required to service assets.

STRUCTURING GOALS

We have stated that securitization allows the creation from an asset pool securities that are more appealing to a wide range of investor types. Yet it is difficult to appreciate that statement if the process of structuring a transaction at the microlevel is not understood. In the next two chapters, we describe how different types of bond classes (i.e., asset-backed securities) are created.

In the structuring illustrations in the next two chapters, we use residential mortgage loans as a representative asset. It is helpful to classify securitizations in terms of the borrower's credit. The market can be broadly divided into prime borrowers and subprime borrowers. Prime borrowers are viewed as having high credit quality because they have strong employment and credit histories, income sufficient to pay the loans without compromising their creditworthiness, and substantial equity in the underlying property. The loans made to such individuals are broadly classified as *prime loans,* and have historically experienced low incidences of delinquency and default. In contrast, loans to borrowers of lower credit quality that are more likely to experience significantly higher levels of default are classified as *subprime loans* and the borrowers are referred to as *subprime borrowers.* Subprime loan underwriting typically relies on nontraditional measures to assess the borrower's credit risk, as these borrowers often have lower income levels, fewer assets, and blemished credit histories. After issuance, these loans must also be serviced by special units designed to closely monitor the payments of subprime borrowers. In the event that subprime borrowers become delinquent, the servicers move immediately to either assist the borrowers in becoming current or mitigate the potential for losses resulting from loan defaults.

The reason why this distinction between deals backed by prime and subprime borrowers is important is because of the credit enhancement that is required. The high credit quality of the loans in the prime sector makes the credit enhancement fairly straightforward. For example, residential mortgage loans that satisfy the underwriting standards of Ginnie Mae, Fannie Mae, and Freddie Mac are viewed as prime loans and the resulting securitizations are referred to as *agency deals*.[5] Credit enhancement in agency deals is obtained through the mechanism of the guaranty provided by the agency issuing the deal. This guaranty is paid for by the sponsor of the deal in the form of a guaranty fee. In the case of the securitization of the rest of the prime loan universe, the credit enhancement mechanism employed is the subordinated structure wherein there are bond classes that have different degrees of priority with respect to both cash inflows and loss write-offs. While structurers have some flexibility with respect to creating the most efficient credit enhancement in prime deals, determination of the amount of credit enhancement is often dictated by the rating agencies, and the subordination structures are fairly straightforward. What has the greatest impact on the execution of the deal is how the senior bonds are structured. Because of pooling of a large number of diversified loans, the size of the nonsenior bond classes is small in terms of par value relative to the senior bond classes. (They are zero in the case of agency deals.) The rules for the allocation of losses are fairly straightforward. (In agency deals there are no loss allocation rules.) Often, the securitizer seeks a triple-A rating for the most senior bond class in the structure.

Now let us look at the securitization of subprime loans. As with prime loans that have been securitized that are not agency deals, these securitizations will have bond classes with a range of cash flow priorities and ratings. However, compared to the securitization of prime

---

[5] Technically, only Ginnie Mae (the Government National Mortgage Association) is an agency of the U.S. government, being part of the Department of Housing and Urban Development. Fannie Mae and Freddie Mae are government-sponsored entities and the securities they issue are called conventional mortgage-backed securities. However in this chapter we refer to the securitization of these three entities as *agency deals*.

loans, the securitization of subprime loans requires a larger amount of credit enhancement in order to create senior bond classes. This fact affects what drives the cost efficiency of prime versus subprime deals. While the driving force in prime deals in order to create efficient structures is the carving up of the senior bonds, in subprime deals it is structuring the transaction so as to produce efficient credit enhancement with the overriding goal of protecting the senior bonds in the deal.[6]

For this reason, while the structuring approach is similar in terms of creating bond classes with different priorities and ratings, the credit enhancement techniques utilized for securitizing prime loans would be inefficient if applied to subprime loans, particularly if subordination is used as the only form of credit support. There are least two reasons for this. First, the subordinate bond classes would be larger relative to those in the case of prime securitizations. In addition, the incremental interest paid by the borrowers whose loans are being securitized (which typically carry high rates due to their greater credit risk) may be optimally utilized toward providing credit support for the senior bond classes. It is for this reason that in securitizing subprime loans, structurers utilize a combination of the credit enhancement mechanisms that will be described in Chapter 5. The second reason is that in establishing the rules for the allocation of cash flows in the securitization of subprime loans, they must be such that there are more tests designed to safeguard the senior bond classes compared to the securitization of prime loans. We discuss this further when we review the different types of credit enhancement mechanisms in Chapter 5.

Either acting as agents for an originator or as principals, investment bankers will structure a transaction. While it is not unusual in some securitizations to find a transaction with 70 bond classes, the maximization of the number of bond classes is not the objective in structuring. Rather, the sole economic goal of the structurer is to maximize the total proceeds received from the sale of all the bond classes that are backed by the asset pool. (In market parlance, the goal is to obtain *best execution*.) Or alternatively, for a given funding size, the goal is to attain the lowest weighted average cost. In seeking to obtain the highest prices or the lowest cost, the structurer must take into account market conditions, demand for various struc-

---

[6] See Chapter 5 in Fabozzi, Bhattacharya, and Berliner (2007) for a further discussion.

tured products, and all the costs of creating such bond classes. For example, in a steep yield curve environment, a structurer will seek to create as much par value of short-term bond classes because the yield that must be offered to sell those bond classes to the market will be less than that for intermediate-term and long-term bond classes.

Maximizing proceeds in an asset securitization can be accomplished by structuring the cash flows in two ways. First, and the purpose of the discussion in the next chapter, carving up a collateral's cash flows and tranching them so as to create bond classes that better match the specific interest rate risk (i.e., effective duration, effective convexity, and key rate durations) and return profiles or views of different investor clienteles. This type of structuring typically takes place in both agency deals and for the senior bond classes in deals with prime loans. The techniques discussed in the next chapter are employed to alter the return and risk profiles of the senior bond classes in a structure by altering how principal and/or interest are allocated to the bond classes in question. The structurer seeks to produce a combination of bond classes that maximize the proceeds received once all the bond classes are sold.[7]

The second way to maximize proceeds in an asset securitization is for the investment banker to create more cost-efficient structures, particularly for nonagency deals where the cost of credit enhancement is embedded in the transaction through the mechanism of subordination. Generally, the securitizer in such cases will realize better execution by creating the largest possible amount of senior bonds while simultaneously obtaining the greatest possible proceeds for the resulting nonsenior bond classes (i.e., subordinated bond classes and interests). As it will be explained, the nonsenior bond classes can often be complex, particularly for asset-backed securities deals that utilize the credit enhancement mechanisms of subordination and overcollateralization that will be discussed in Chapter 5.

KEY POINTS OF THE CHAPTER

> *The main reasons that corporations use securitization are (1) the*
> *potential for reducing funding costs; (2) the ability to diversify*

---

[7] Blum and DiAngelo (1998) discuss how an investment banker seeks to create an efficient structure.

funding sources; (3) the ability to manage corporate risk; (4) for financial entities that must satisfy risk-based capital requirements, potential relief from capital requirements; (5) the opportunity to achieve off-balance financing; and (6) the opportunity to generate fee income.

➤ *The key to a corporation issuing bonds via a securitization with a higher credit rating than the corporation's own credit rating is the SPV because that entity legally separates the assets used as collateral for the securitization from the corporation that is seeking financing (the originator/seller).*

➤ *The SPV is structured as a bankruptcy-remote entity, thus insulating the transaction from the credit risk of the originator/seller.*

➤ *The risk of losses in an asset pool used in a securitization transaction can be mitigated by proper credit enhancements to a point where a target rating can be achieved.*

➤ *Even after factoring in the cost of credit enhancement and other legal and accounting expenses associated with a securitization transaction, capital seeking firms have found securitization to be less expensive than issuing corporate bonds.*

➤ *By establishing itself in the securitization market, a corporation can look at both the corporate bond market and the asset-backed securities market to determine its best funding source.*

➤ *Securitization can be used as a corporate risk management tool because it removes the credit risk and the interest rate risk associated with the assets sold to the SPV.*

➤ *For regulated financial entities, securitization is a tool for managing risk-based capital requirements because, all things equal, institutions that hold a risky portfolio of loans will have to reserve a higher amount of capital than if they sold off the loans to an SPV for a securitization.*

➤ *Most securitizations transfer assets and liabilities off the balance sheet, thereby reducing the amount of the originator's on-balance-sheet leverage.*

➢ *Section 401(a) of the Saxbanes-Oxley Act of 2002 (SOX) and its amendments deal with disclosure for securitizations in periodic financial filings with the SEC.*

➢ *Securitization can be used by loan originators to convert capital intensive assets to a less capital intensive source of servicing fee income by selling the loans to an SPV while retaining the rights to service the loans.*

➢ *The servicing fee that is retained by the originator in a securitization transaction is like an interest-only strip of payments that compensates the servicer.*

➢ *The creation of securities from a pool of assets is referred to as structuring a transaction.*

➢ *Either acting as agents for an originator or as principals, investment bankers will structure a securitization transaction.*

➢ *Structuring allows the creation from an asset pool securities that are more appealing to a wide range of investor types.*

➢ *Securitizations are categorized in terms of the borrower's credit because the type of borrower dictates the amount of credit enhancement needed.*

➢ *The market can be broadly divided into prime borrowers (i.e., high-credit-quality borrowers) and subprime borrowers (i.e., low-credit-quality borrowers).*

➢ *In the case of residential mortgage loans, there are deals that are agency deals (prime loans included in the loan pool that satisfy the underwriting standards of Ginnie Mae, Fannie Mae, and Freddie Mac), prime deals that are not agency deals (prime loans included in the loan pool where the loans do not satisfy the underwriting standards of Ginnie Mae, Fannie Mae, and Freddie Mac), and subprime deals (subprime loans included in the loan pool).*

➢ *Credit enhancement in agency mortgage-backed securities deals is obtained through the mechanism of the guaranty provided by the agency issuing the deal.*

➢ *In the case of the securitization of the rest of the prime loan universe for residential mortgage loans, the credit enhancement mechanism employed is the subordinated structure with structurers having some flexibility with respect to creating the most efficient credit enhancement given the amount of credit enhancement dictated by the rating agencies.*

➤ *Compared to the securitization of prime loans, the securitization of subprime loans requires a larger amount of credit enhancement in order to create senior bond classes.*

➤ *While the driving force in prime deals in order to create efficient structures is the carving up of the senior bonds, in subprime deals it is structuring the transaction so as to produce efficient credit enhancement with the overriding goal of protecting the most senior bonds in the deal.*

➤ *The structurer's sole economic goal in a securitization is the maximization of the total proceeds received from the sale of all the bond classes that are backed by the asset pool.*

➤ *Maximizing proceeds in an asset securitization can be accomplished by structuring the cash flows in two ways: (1) carving up a collateral's cash flows and tranching them so as to create bond classes that better match the specific interest rate risk and return profiles or views of different investor groups; and (2) creating more efficient cost (i.e., credit enhancement) structures.*

PART TWO

Structuring ABS Transactions

CHAPTER 3

Structuring Agency MBS Deals

In this chapter we illustrate the structuring of agency deals backed by residential mortgage-backed securities. The resulting structures are referred to as *collateralized mortgage obligations* (CMOs).[1] Before illustrating structuring, we must briefly review the concept of prepayments, its measurement, and the convention that has developed in the marketplace for quoting the rate of prepayments (i.e., prepayment speeds).

PREPAYMENTS AND PREPAYMENT CONVENTIONS

Different types of loans may permit the borrower to prepay the loans in whole or in part at any time prior to the scheduled principal repayment date. This is certainly the case of the largest asset class that has been securitized in the United States: residential mortgage loans. The payment made by the borrower in excess of the scheduled principal payment is called a *prepayment*. Estimating the cash flow from collateral that allows prepayments requires making an assumption about future prepayments.

Why are we concerned with prepayments? With a debt obligation, nonpayment or delayed payment is an adverse economic consequence for the debt holder. In contrast, prepayment can be beneficial or harmful to the debt holder depending on the circumstances. Particularly in the case of for long-duration debt instruments such as residential mortgages, the mortgage not being allowed to continue until maturity but instead being prepaid may cause substantial loss

---

[1] More accurately, agency CMOs are backed by a pool of agency mortgage pass-through securities. Nonagency CMOs are backed by unsecuritized residential loans (whole loans).

of value to the mortgage lender, and upon securitization, to the mortgage-backed securities investor. What makes prepayment painful is that because it is an option granted to the borrower, it is always exercised to the benefit of the borrower and against the lender. For example, a fixed rate mortgage can be prepaid when mortgage rates decline below the loan rate paid by the borrower as the borrower can refinance the mortgage at the prevailing lower rate. An adjustable-rate mortgage may have a tendency to get prepaid when mortgage rates rise, making the mortgage unaffordable for the borrower. While prepayment is a risk for all debt obligations, the loss of value is particularly substantial, as mentioned before, in the case of mortgage products. Hence, prepayment is seen as a significant risk of mortgage investments.

In the residential MBS market, several conventions have been used as a benchmark for prepayment rates. Today the benchmarks used are the conditional prepayment rate and the Public Securities Association (PSA) prepayment benchmark.[2]

The *conditional prepayment rate* (CPR)[3] as a measure of the speed of prepayments assumes that some fraction of the remaining

---

[2] In the earliest stages of the development of the MBS market, cash flows were calculated assuming no prepayments for the first 12 years at which time all the mortgages in the pool were assumed to prepay. This naive approach was replaced by the "FHA prepayment experience" approach, where FHA is an abbreviation for Federal Housing Administration. The prepayment experience for 30-year mortgages derived from an FHA table on mortgage survival factors was once the most commonly used benchmark for prepayment rates. It calls for the projection of the cash flow for a mortgage pool on the assumption that the prepayment rate will be the same as the FHA experience (referred to as *100% FHA*), or some multiple of FHA experience (faster or slower than FHA experience). Despite the method's past popularity, prepayments based on FHA experience were not necessarily indicative of the prepayment rate for a particular pool, mainly because FHA prepayments are for mortgages originated over all sorts of interest rate periods. Prepayment rates are tied to interest rate cycles, however, so an average prepayment rate over various cycles is not very useful in estimating prepayments. Moreover, new FHA tables are published periodically, causing confusion about which FHA table prepayments should be based on.

[3] It is referred to as such because it is applied on the pool balance that remains after the previous period's prepayment. It is not applied on the original pool balance—hence, it is not an absolute rate.

principal in the mortgage pool is prepaid each month for the remaining term of the collateral. The CPR used for a particular deal is based on the characteristics of the collatral (including its historical prepayment experience) and the current and expected future economic environment.

The CPR is an annual prepayment rate. To estimate monthly prepayments, the CPR must be converted into a monthly prepayment rate, commonly referred to as the *single-monthly mortality rate* (SMM). The following formula is used to determine the SMM for a given CPR:

$$SMM = 1 - ((1 - CPR)^{1/12})$$

An SMM of w percent means that approximately w percent of the remaining mortgage balance at the beginning of the month, less the scheduled principal payment, will prepay that month. That is,

$$
\begin{aligned}
\text{Prepayment for month } t = \ &SMM \\
&\times (\text{Beginning mortgage balance for month } t \\
&- \text{Scheduled principal payment for month } t)
\end{aligned}
\tag{3.1}
$$

One problem with using the CPR is that it assumes a constant prepayment rate from the very outset of the origination of the loans. For example, it is not likely that prepayments might be the largest in dollar amount shortly after loans are originated than later on after loans have seasoned. Yet using a constant CPR makes that assumption. For residential mortgage loans, the PSA prepayment benchmark deals with this problem.[4] The PSA prepayment benchmark is expressed as a monthly series of annual prepayment rates. The basic PSA benchmark model assumes that prepayment rates are low for newly originated loans, then will speed up as the mortgages become seasoned, and then reach a plateau and remain at that level.

The PSA standard benchmark assumes the following prepayment rates for 30-year residential mortgages loans:

---

[4] The PSA and the CPR approaches are not mutually exclusive alternatives but are mostly used together—the PSA to explain the ramp-up of the expected CPR over the initial months of seasoning. Thereafter, the pool undergoes a constant CPR.

- A CPR of 0.2% for the first month, increased by 0.2% per year per month for the next 29 months when it reaches 6% per year.
- A 6% CPR for the remaining years.

All months above are counted with reference to origination of the pool.

This benchmark is referred to as *100% PSA*. Mathematically, 100 PSA can be expressed as follows:

$$\text{If } t \leq 30 \text{ months, then } CPR = 6\%(t/30)$$

$$\text{If } t > 30 \text{ months, then } CPR = 6\%$$

where t is the number of months since the mortgage originated.

Slower or faster speeds are then referred to as some percentage of PSA. For example, 50% PSA means one-half the CPR of the PSA benchmark prepayment rate and 165% PSA means 1.65 times the CPR of the PSA benchmark prepayment rate. A prepayment rate of 0% PSA means that no prepayments are assumed.

The PSA benchmark is commonly referred to as a *prepayment model*, suggesting that it can be used to estimate prepayment. However, it is important to note that characterizing this market convention for prepayments as a prepayment model is wrong.

With this background on prepayments conventions, we can now discuss the structuring of agency deals. To illustrate structuring and how it used to create bonds with different exposure to interest rate and prepayment risk via tranching, we will use a hypothetical pass-through security that will be the collateral for our illustrations. Let us look at the monthly cash flow for a hypothetical pass-through given a PSA assumption. We will assume the following for the underlying mortgages:

- Type: fixed rate, level payment mortgages
- *Weighted average coupon* (WAC) rate: 6.0%
- *Weighted average maturity* (WAM): 358 months
- Servicing fee: 0.5%
- Outstanding balance: $660 million

The pass-through security has a coupon rate of 5.5% (WAC of 6% minus the servicing fee of 0.5%).

This first step in structuring requires a projection of the cash flow of the mortgage pool. The cash flow is decomposed into three components:

1. Interest (based on WAC of 6% and pass-through rate of 5.5%).
2. Regularly scheduled principal (i.e., amortization).
3. Prepayments based on some prepayment assumption.

To generate the cash flow for the hypothetical pass-through we will assume a prepayment speed of 165% PSA. The cash flow is shown in Table 3.1.

Column 2 shows the outstanding mortgage balance at the beginning of the month (i.e., outstanding balance at the beginning of the previous month reduced by the total principal payment in the previous month). Column 3 gives the SMM for 165% PSA.[5] The aggregate monthly mortgage payment is reported in column 4. Notice that the total monthly mortgage payment declines over time, as prepayments reduce the mortgage balance outstanding.[6] Column 5 shows the monthly interest that is determined by multiplying the outstanding mortgage balance at the beginning of the month by the pass-through rate of 5.5% and dividing by 12. The regularly scheduled principal repayment (amortization), shown in column 6 is the difference between the total monthly mortgage payment (column 4) and the gross coupon interest for the month (6.0% multiplied by the outstanding mortgage balance at the beginning of the month, then divided by 12). The prepayment for the month is reported in column 7 and is found by using equation (3.1). The sum of the regularly schedule principal and the prepayment is the total principal payment and is shown in column 8. The projected monthly cash flow is then the sum of the monthly interest plus the total principal payment as shown in the last column of the Table 3.1.

---

[5] Notice that for month 1, the SMM shown in Table 3.1 is for a pass-through that has been seasoned two months. This is because the WAM is 358 months.

[6] In the absence of prepayments, this amount would be constant over the life of the pass-through security. The formula for calculating the total monthly mortgage payment can be found in Chapter 22 in Fabozzi (2006).

TABLE 3.1   Monthly Cash Flow for a $660 Million Pass-Through with a 5.5% Pass-Through Rate, a WAC of 6.0%, and a WAM of 358 Months, Assuming 165% PSA

(1)	(2)	(3)	(4)	(5)	(6)	(7)	(8)	(9)
Month	Outstanding Balance	SMM	Mortgage Payment	Net Interest	Scheduled Prinicipal	Prepa-ments	Total Principal	Cash Flow
1	660,000,000	0.00083	3,964,947	3,025,000	664,947	546,435	1,211,383	4,236,383
2	658,788,617	0.00111	3,961,661	3,019,448	667,718	728,350	1,396,068	4,415,516
3	657,392,549	0.00139	3,957,277	3,013,049	670,314	909,895	1,580,209	4,593,258
4	655,812,340	0.00167	3,951,794	3,005,807	672,732	1,090,916	1,763,649	4,769,455
5	654,048,691	0.00195	3,945,214	2,997,723	674,970	1,271,261	1,946,231	4,943,954
6	652,102,460	0.00223	3,937,538	2,988,803	677,025	1,450,775	2,127,800	5,116,603
7	649,974,660	0.00251	3,928,768	2,979,051	678,895	1,629,307	2,308,202	5,287,252
8	647,666,458	0.00279	3,918,910	2,968,471	680,578	1,806,703	2,487,281	5,455,752
9	645,179,177	0.00308	3,907,966	2,957,071	682,070	1,982,813	2,664,883	5,621,955
10	642,514,294	0.00336	3,895,943	2,944,857	683,372	2,157,486	2,840,858	5,785,715
11	639,673,436	0.00365	3,882,847	2,931,837	684,480	2,330,573	3,015,053	5,946,890
12	636,658,383	0.00393	3,868,685	2,918,018	685,394	2,501,927	3,187,320	6,105,338
13	633,471,062	0.00422	3,853,466	2,903,409	686,111	2,671,401	3,357,511	6,260,921
14	630,113,551	0.00451	3,837,198	2,888,020	686,630	2,838,851	3,525,482	6,413,502
15	626,588,069	0.00480	3,819,891	2,871,862	686,951	3,004,137	3,691,088	6,562,950
16	622,896,981	0.00509	3,801,557	2,854,944	687,072	3,167,117	3,854,189	6,709,134
17	619,042,792	0.00538	3,782,207	2,837,279	686,993	3,327,655	4,014,648	6,851,928
18	615,028,144	0.00567	3,761,853	2,818,879	686,712	3,485,618	4,172,330	6,991,209
19	610,855,814	0.00597	3,740,509	2,799,756	686,230	3,640,872	4,327,102	7,126,858
20	606,528,712	0.00626	3,718,190	2,779,923	685,546	3,793,290	4,478,836	7,258,760
21	602,049,876	0.00656	3,694,909	2,759,395	684,660	3,942,748	4,627,408	7,386,803
22	597,422,468	0.00685	3,670,684	2,738,186	683,572	4,089,123	4,772,695	7,510,881
23	592,649,773	0.00715	3,645,531	2,716,311	682,282	4,232,298	4,914,580	7,630,892
24	587,735,193	0.00745	3,619,467	2,693,786	680,791	4,372,159	5,052,950	7,746,736
25	582,682,243	0.00775	3,592,511	2,670,627	679,100	4,508,595	5,187,695	7,858,322
26	577,494,549	0.00805	3,564,681	2,646,850	677,208	4,641,501	5,318,709	7,965,560
27	572,175,839	0.00835	3,535,997	2,622,473	675,117	4,770,776	5,445,894	8,068,367
28	566,729,945	0.00865	3,506,479	2,597,512	672,829	4,896,323	5,569,152	8,166,664
29	561,160,793	0.00865	3,476,148	2,571,987	670,344	4,848,172	5,518,516	8,090,503
30	555,642,277	0.00865	3,446,080	2,546,694	667,869	4,800,459	5,468,328	8,015,021

TABLE 3.1 (Continued)

(1) Month	(2) Outstanding Balance	(3) SMM	(4) Mortgage Payment	(5) Net Interest	(6) Scheduled Prinicipal	(7) Prepay- ments	(8) Total Principal	(9) Cash Flow
100	272,093,325	0.00865	1,875,944	1,247,094	515,478	2,349,114	2,864,592	4,111,686
101	269,228,733	0.00865	1,859,718	1,233,965	513,574	2,324,352	2,837,926	4,071,891
102	266,390,806	0.00865	1,843,631	1,220,958	511,677	2,299,821	2,811,498	4,032,456
103	263,579,308	0.00865	1,827,684	1,208,072	509,788	2,275,518	2,785,306	3,993,378
104	260,794,002	0.00865	1,811,875	1,195,306	507,905	2,251,442	2,759,347	3,954,653
105	258,034,655	0.00865	1,796,203	1,182,659	506,029	2,227,590	2,733,620	3,916,278
200	86,170,616	0.00865	786,913	394,949	356,060	742,285	1,098,345	1,493,293
201	85,072,271	0.00865	780,106	389,915	354,745	732,796	1,087,541	1,477,455
202	83,984,730	0.00865	773,358	384,930	353,435	723,400	1,076,835	1,461,765
203	82,907,896	0.00865	766,669	379,995	352,129	714,097	1,066,226	1,446,221
204	81,841,669	0.00865	760,037	375,108	350,829	704,886	1,055,714	1,430,822
205	80,785,955	0.00865	753,463	370,269	349,533	695,765	1,045,298	1,415,567
300	16,829,401	0.00865	330,091	77,135	245,944	143,445	389,388	466,523
301	16,440,012	0.00865	327,235	75,350	245,035	140,085	385,120	460,470
302	16,054,892	0.00865	324,405	73,585	244,130	136,761	380,891	454,476
303	15,674,001	0.00865	321,599	71,839	243,229	133,474	376,703	448,542
304	15,297,298	0.00865	318,817	70,113	242,330	130,224	372,554	442,667
305	14,924,744	0.00865	316,059	68,405	241,436	127,009	368,444	436,849
350	1,876,871	0.00865	213,790	8,602	204,405	14,467	218,872	227,474
351	1,657,999	0.00865	211,940	7,599	203,650	12,580	216,230	223,829
352	1,441,769	0.00865	210,107	6,608	202,898	10,716	213,614	220,222
353	1,228,154	0.00865	208,290	5,629	202,149	8,875	211,024	216,653
354	1,017,131	0.00865	206,488	4,662	201,402	7,056	208,458	213,120
355	808,672	0.00865	204,702	3,706	200,659	5,259	205,918	209,624
356	602,755	0.00865	202,931	2,763	199,917	3,484	203,402	206,165
357	399,353	0.00865	201,176	1,830	199,179	1,731	200,911	202,741
358	198,442	0.00865	199,436	910	198,444	0	198,444	199,353

At 165% PSA the average life for this pass-through security is 8.6 years. We will use average life in our illustrations because the computation of the duration, more specifically effective duration, is much more complicated to compute. The average life is a weighted average of the principal cash flows divided by the par value where the weight is the month when the projected principal is expected to be received.

SEQUENTIAL PAY STRUCTURES

We begin with the simplest form of time tranching of the collateral in order to create bond classes in a transaction that will have average lives and durations that will appeal to a wider range of investors than the collateral itself. To see this, we will use the $660 million, 5.5% pass-through security (which is comprised of residential mortgage loans that confirm to the underwriting standards of Ginnie Mae, Fannie Mae, and Freddie Mac) to create a simple structure. The structure is given below and we refer to this structure as "Structure 1."

Bond Class	Par Amount ($)	Coupon Rate (%)
A	$320,925,000	5.5%
B	59,400,000	5.5%
C	159,225,000	5.5%
D	120,450,000	5.5%

In structuring an agency deal, there are only rules specified for the distribution of principal and interest. There are no rules for deals with defaults and delinquencies because payments are guaranteed by the issuer. In Structure 1 we will use the following rules:

- *Interest.* The monthly interest is distributed to each bond class on the basis of the amount of principal outstanding at the beginning of the month .
- *Principal.* All monthly principal (i.e., regularly scheduled principal and prepayments) is distributed first to bond class A until it is completely paid off. After bond class A is completely paid off its par amount, all monthly principal payments are made to bond class B until it is completely paid off. After bond class B is com-

pletely paid off its par amount, all monthly principal payments are made to bond class C until it is completely paid off its par amount. Finally, after bond C is completely paid off, all monthly principal payments are made to bond class D.

Based on these rules for the distribution of interest and principal, Table 3.2 shows the cash flows for each bond class assuming one prepayment speed, 165% PSA. Note that bond class A is fully paid off in month 78 and in that month principal payments begin for bond class B, which is fully paid off in month 98. Bond class C starts receiving principal payments in month 98. Before we explain what we have accomplished in Structure 1, a few comments are in order. First, the total par value of the four bond classes in the structure is equal to $660 million which is equal to the par value of the collateral (the pass-through security). In any structure, the par value of the bond classes cannot exceed that of the value of the collateral.[7] In agency deals, the two values are equal. As explained later, in asset-backed transactions where there is credit risk, the value of the collateral can exceed the par value of the bond classes and this is a form of credit enhancement referred to as overcollateralization. Second, we have simplified the illustration by assuming that all bond classes have the same coupon rate. In actual deals, the coupon rate would be determined by prevailing market conditions (i.e., the yield curve) and would not necessarily be equal to each bond class. A condition that must be satisfied is that the total interest to be paid to all the bond classes in a month may not exceed the interest from the collateral otherwise an interest shortfall will occur. Equivalently, the weighted average coupon rate for the bond classes in the structure may not exceed the coupon rate for the collateral (6% in our illustration). Finally, although the payment rules for the distribution of the principal payments are known, the exact amount of monthly principal is not. The monthly principal will depend on the principal cash flows generated by the collateral, which in turn depends on the actual pre-

---

[7] If the par value of the bonds exceeds the par value of the collateral, it would mean the excess spread inherent in the assets has been capitalized. This presupposes that there will not be any prepayment and the excess spread will be realized. As this assumption is impractical, transactions structures mostly do not allow monetization of the excess spread up-front.

TABLE 3.2 Monthly Cash Flows for Selected Months for Structure 1 Assuming 165% PSA

Month	A			B		
	Beginning Balance	Principal	Interest	Beginning Balance	Principal	Interest
1	320,925,000	1,211,383	1,470,906	59,400,000	0	272,250
2	319,713,617	1,396,068	1,465,354	59,400,000	0	272,250
3	318,317,549	1,580,209	1,458,955	59,400,000	0	272,250
4	316,737,340	1,763,649	1,451,713	59,400,000	0	272,250
5	314,973,691	1,946,231	1,443,629	59,400,000	0	272,250
6	313,027,460	2,127,800	1,434,709	59,400,000	0	272,250
7	310,899,660	2,308,202	1,424,957	59,400,000	0	272,250
8	308,591,458	2,487,281	1,414,378	59,400,000	0	272,250
9	306,104,177	2,664,883	1,402,977	59,400,000	0	272,250
10	303,439,294	2,840,858	1,390,763	59,400,000	0	272,250
11	300,598,436	3,015,053	1,377,743	59,400,000	0	272,250
12	297,583,383	3,187,320	1,363,924	59,400,000	0	272,250
75	14,039,361	3,614,938	64,347	59,400,000	0	272,250
76	10,424,423	3,581,599	47,779	59,400,000	0	272,250
77	6,842,824	3,548,556	31,363	59,400,000	0	272,250
78	3,294,268	3,294,268	15,099	59,400,000	221,539	272,250
79	0	0	0	59,178,461	3,483,348	271,235
80	0	0	0	55,695,114	3,451,178	255,269
81	0	0	0	52,243,936	3,419,293	239,451
82	0	0	0	48,824,643	3,387,692	223,780
83	0	0	0	45,436,951	3,356,372	208,253
84	0	0	0	42,080,579	3,325,330	192,869
85	0	0	0	38,755,249	3,294,564	177,628
95	0	0	0	7,149,734	3,001,559	32,770
96	0	0	0	4,148,175	2,973,673	19,012
97	0	0	0	1,174,502	1,174,502	5,383
98	0	0	0	0	0	0

TABLE 3.2 (Continued)

	C			D		
Month	Beginning Balance	Principal	Interest	Beginning Balance	Principal	Interest
1	96,500,000	0	442,292	73,000,000	0	334,583
2	96,500,000	0	442,292	73,000,000	0	334,583
3	96,500,000	0	442,292	73,000,000	0	334,583
4	96,500,000	0	442,292	73,000,000	0	334,583
5	96,500,000	0	442,292	73,000,000	0	334,583
6	96,500,000	0	442,292	73,000,000	0	334,583
7	96,500,000	0	442,292	73,000,000	0	334,583
8	96,500,000	0	442,292	73,000,000	0	334,583
9	96,500,000	0	442,292	73,000,000	0	334,583
10	96,500,000	0	442,292	73,000,000	0	334,583
11	96,500,000	0	442,292	73,000,000	0	334,583
12	96,500,000	0	442,292	73,000,000	0	334,583
95	96,500,000	0	442,292	73,000,000	0	334,583
96	96,500,000	0	442,292	73,000,000	0	334,583
97	96,500,000	1,073,657	442,292	73,000,000	0	334,583
98	95,426,343	1,768,876	437,371	73,000,000	0	334,583
99	93,657,468	1,752,423	429,263	73,000,000	0	334,583
100	91,905,045	1,736,116	421,231	73,000,000	0	334,583
101	90,168,928	1,719,955	413,274	73,000,000	0	334,583
102	88,448,973	1,703,938	405,391	73,000,000	0	334,583
103	86,745,035	1,688,064	397,581	73,000,000	0	334,583
104	85,056,970	1,672,332	389,844	73,000,000	0	334,583
105	83,384,639	1,656,739	382,180	73,000,000	0	334,583
175				71,179,833	850,356	326,241
176				70,329,478	842,134	322,343
177				69,487,344	833,986	318,484
178				68,653,358	825,912	314,661
179				67,827,446	817,911	310,876
180				67,009,535	809,982	307,127

TABLE 3.2   (Continued)

	C			D		
Month	Beginning Balance	Principal	Interest	Beginning Balance	Principal	Interest
181				66,199,553	802,125	303,415
182				65,397,428	794,339	299,738
183				64,603,089	786,624	296,097
184				63,816,465	778,978	292,492
185				63,037,487	771,402	288,922
350				1,137,498	132,650	5,214
351				1,004,849	131,049	4,606
352				873,800	129,463	4,005
353				744,337	127,893	3,412
354				616,444	126,338	2,825
355				490,105	124,799	2,246
356				365,307	123,274	1,674
357				242,033	121,764	1,109
358				120,269	120,269	551

payment rate of the collateral. Thus, in order to project monthly cash flows, a prepayment assumption must be made.

Now let us look at Structure 1. To see what has been accomplished, a summary of the average life (in years) of the collateral and the four bond classes under a range of prepayment assumptions is shown:

	100%	125%	165%	250%	400%	500%
Collateral	11.2	10.1	8.6	6.4	4.5	3.7
Bond class						
A	4.7	4.1	3.4	2.7	2.0	1.8
B	10.4	8.9	7.3	5.3	3.8	3.2
C	15.1	13.2	10.9	7.9	5.3	4.4
D	24.0	22.4	19.8	15.2	10.3	8.4

Notice the substantial variance of the average life for the collateral. Is this a short-term security that would fit the needs of an institutional investor such as a bank or an intermediate-term security that might be suitable for an insurance company? Basically, the collateral was unappealing to institutional investors concerned with contraction or extension risk given their liability structure. Look at the average life for the four bond classes. They have average lives that are both shorter and longer than the collateral, thereby attracting institutional investors who have a preference for an average life different from that of the collateral. For example, a depository institution interested in shorter-term paper and concerned with extension risk would find bond class A more appealing than the collateral because within a reasonable range of prepayment speeds, bond class A's average life will be less than five years under slow prepayment speeds while the collateral's average life can extend to a little more than 11 years.[8] At the other end of the maturity preference spectrum, consider a defined benefit pension plan that is seeking longer-term investments and is concerned with contraction risk. That institutional investor would prefer bond class D to the collateral. While bond class D has considerable variance in its average life, the concern of contraction risk is greater for the collateral than for bond class D. To see that, notice in the table above that at the fastest prepayment speed shown in the table (500 PSA) the average life for the collateral can contract to 3.7 years but bond class D to only 8.3 years.

Consequently, we can see that the rules for distribution of principal among the bond classes in this structure, referred to as a sequential pay structure, have redistributed the prepayment risk (i.e., exposure to extension and contraction risk) of the collateral among the bond classes. As a result, an unattractive asset or collateral from the prospective of institutional investors can be used to create securities that better match the needs of those investors, a point that we have stated, but not demonstrated until now.

PLANNED AMORTIZATION CLASS BONDS AND SUPPORT BONDS

There are institutional investors who seek securities (bond classes) that have even greater protection against prepayment risk. Investment bankers have created a product for such investors. To under-

---

[8] Note that the average life is not the expected maturity. Assuming 100% PSA, for example, while bond class A's average life is 4.7 years, it might still take roughly 10 years for bond class A to be completely repaid.

stand how this was done by structurers for investment banking firms, look at Table 3.3. The table shows the total principal payment for selected months for our $660 million, 6% collateral assuming a prepayment speed of 100% PSA (column 2) and 250% PSA (column 3). The last column in Table 3.3 shows the minimum total principal payment for each month. That is, if the prepayment speed is constant over the life of the collateral and that constant prepayment speed is

TABLE 3.3 Total Principal Payments at 100% PSA and 250% PSA and Creation of PAC Schedule for Selected Months

Month	100% PSA	250% PSA	PAC Schedule
1	995,525	1,494,837	995,525
2	1,108,446	1,774,008	1,108,446
3	1,221,042	2,052,351	1,221,042
4	1,333,255	2,329,510	1,333,255
5	1,445,026	2,605,129	1,445,026
6	1,556,298	2,878,852	1,556,298
7	1,667,013	3,150,323	1,667,013
8	1,777,113	3,419,190	1,777,113
9	1,886,540	3,685,100	1,886,540
10	1,995,237	3,947,708	1,995,237
11	2,103,149	4,206,667	2,103,149
12	2,210,219	4,461,641	2,210,219
13	2,316,391	4,712,295	2,316,391
14	2,421,610	4,958,303	2,421,610
15	2,525,823	5,199,344	2,525,823
16	2,628,975	5,435,106	2,628,975
17	2,731,013	5,665,285	2,731,013
18	2,831,885	5,889,586	2,831,885
101	2,577,230	2,709,199	2,577,230
102	2,563,858	2,669,922	2,563,858
103	2,550,555	2,631,198	2,550,555
104	2,537,320	2,593,019	2,537,320
105	2,524,154	2,555,377	2,524,154

TABLE 3.3   (Continued)

Month	100% PSA	250% PSA	PAC Schedule
211	1,451,822	516,114	516,114
212	1,444,240	508,066	508,066
213	1,436,697	500,136	500,136
346	712,694	48,340	48,340
347	708,916	47,342	47,342
348	705,158	46,360	46,360
349	701,419	45,394	45,394
350	697,699	44,444	44,444
351	693,998	43,509	43,509
352	690,317	42,591	42,591
353	686,654	41,687	41,687
354	683,010	40,798	40,798
355	679,385	39,924	39,924
356	675,779	39,065	39,065
357	672,191	38,220	38,220
358	668,622	37,388	37,388

between 100% PSA and 250% PSA, then the monthly total principal will be as shown in the last column. If the total of the principal in the last column is summed, it is equal to $470,224,580.

The amounts in the last column allows a structurer to create a bond class, referred to as a *planned amortization class bond* (more popularly referred to as a PAC), which has priority over all other bonds classes in the structure with respect to receiving the scheduled principal repayment.[9] For example, for our hypothetical $660 mil-

---

[9] The PAC structure was first introduced in the mortgage-backed securities market in March 1987. The M.D.C. Mortgage Funding Corporation CMO Series 0 included a class of bonds referred to as *stabilized mortgage reduction term bonds* or "SMRT" bonds; another class in its CMO Series P was referred to as *planned amortization class bonds* or *PAC bonds*. The Oxford Acceptance Corporation III Series C CMOs included a class of bonds referred to as a *planned redemption obligation bonds* or *PRO bonds*. The name PAC is now used to describe these structures.

lion, 5.5% pass-through security, using a lower prepayment speed of 100% PSA and an upper speed of 250% PSA, the PAC schedule would be shown in the last column. The upper and lower prepayment speeds are referred to as the *structuring speeds* and the range of 100% to 250% PSA is referred to as the *structuring bands*. The non-PAC bond classes in the structure are referred to as the *support bonds* or *companion bonds,* a name given because of their function in the structure as will be explained shortly.

The key in this structure is that the support bonds accept the contraction risk if actual prepayment speeds are fast and accept the extension risk if actual prepayments are slow. Hence, unlike in the sequential pay structure illustrated by Structure 1, where the bond classes are afforded some protection against extension risk or contraction risk but not both, PAC bonds offer prepayment protection against both extension risk and contraction risk.

The prepayment protection in a PAC structure comes from the support bonds. It is the support bonds that receive any excess principal payments beyond the scheduled amount to be paid to the PAC bond classes and must wait to receive principal if there is a principal short-fall—hence, the term *support bonds* to describe this bond class.

To understand the rules for distribution in a PAC structure, consider the following hypothetical structure below that we identify as "Structure 2":

Bond Class	Bond Type	Par Amount ($)	Coupon Rate (%)
P	PAC	$470,224,580	5.5%
S	Support	$189,775,420	5.5%

Notice that the par amount in Structure 2 is the total for a PAC created with a structuring band band of 100% to 250% PSA.

Table 3.3 shows how this is done. Columns 2 and 3 show the monthly principal payments based on prepayment speeds of 100% and 250%, respectively. The last column shows the minimum principal payment for each month. The last column is the schedule of payments to the PAC bond class. It is this schedule, referred to as the PAC schedule, that would be shown in the prospectus.

To understand how the principal payment rules work for a PAC bond class, look at look at month 12. The PAC schedule indicates that for that month the payment to be made to the PAC bond class is $2,210,219. Suppose that actual principal payments for that month are $3,200,000. Then $2,210,219 is paid to the PAC bond class (P) and the balance, $989,781, is distributed to the support bonds.

The following table shows the average life at the time of issuance for the two bond classes:

	PSA Speed					
	50	75	100	165	250	400
P	10.21	8.62	7.71	7.71	7.71	5.52
S	24.85	22.71	20.00	10.67	3.28	1.86
Collateral	14.42	12.68	11.24	8.56	6.44	4.47

Notice that the average life is unchanged for the PAC bond class prepayment speeds from 100% to 250% PSA, the structuring band. Also notice the considerable variation in the average life of the support bond class. Its variability is much greater than that of the collateral for the prepayments speeds shown. This is to be expected because the support bond class is providing prepayment protection for the PAC bond class.

Sequential Pay PAC Structure

In practice, a typical structure may have more than one class of PAC bonds. That is, there may be a series of PAC bonds. For example, consider the following structure that we will refer to as "Structure 3":

Bond Class	Par Amount
P-A	$38,308,710
P-B	153,808,875
P-C	36,116,850
P-D	73,544,130
Bond Class	Par Amount
P-E	107,941,020
P-F	60,505,005
S	189,775,410

The first six bond classes are PAC bonds and their total par value is $470,224,580, the same as the single PAC bond in Structure 2. The rules for the distribution of principal payments is in sequence as follows:

- Pay principal payments received from the collateral to P-A up to its scheduled amount and if there is any excess principal payments, then, if such excess principal payments do not exceed expected principal payments at 250 PSA, distribute them to S or else distribute them to P-A.
- After P-A is fully paid off, pay principal payments received from the collateral to P-B up to its scheduled amount and if there is any excess principal payments, then, if such excess principal payments do not exceed expected principal payments at 250 PSA, distribute them to S, or else, distribute them to P-B.
- After P-B is fully paid off, pay principal payments received from the collateral to P-C up to its scheduled amount and if there is any excess principal payments, then, if such excess principal payments do not exceed expected principal payments at 250 PSA, distribute them to S or else distribute them to P-C.
- And so on.

The average life for each PAC bond assuming various prepayment speeds is provided below:

| | PSA Speed | | | | | |
	50%	75%	100%	165%	250%	400%
P-A	1.3	1.1	1.0	1.0	1.0	1.0
P-B	5.1	4.1	3.5	3.5	3.5	3.1
P-C	8.8	7.1	5.9	5.9	5.9	4.3
P-D	11.1	9.0	7.5	7.5	7.5	5.2
P-E	15.1	12.5	10.9	10.9	10.9	7.3
P-F	19.9	18.5	18.3	18.3	18.3	12.5

Note that the average life is stable for the structuring band for all PAC bonds. This is as to be expected. But note further that the shorter-term PAC bonds such as P-A and P-B have stability over a wider range of prepayment speeds. The reason has to do with the support bonds. In Structure 2, there is $189,775,410 par value of support bonds protecting $470,224,580 par value of a single PAC bond. In Structure 3, since P-A has first priority on the principal payments, this means that from the perspective of P-A, there is $189,775,410 par value of support bonds protecting only $38,308,710 par value of P-A. Hence, there is greater prepayment protection beyond the structuring band. Similarly, for P-B, there is $189,775,410 par value of support bonds protecting only $192,117,585 (sum of par value of P-A and P-B). While the prepayment protection of P-B is provided for a wider range of prepayment speeds compared to the structuring bands, that range is less than for P-A, but greater than for P-C and P-D.

Types of Support Bonds

Because of their role in providing protection for PAC bond classes in a structure, support bonds have the greatest prepayment risk in a structure. Investors must be particularly careful in assessing the cash flow characteristics of support bonds to reduce the likelihood of adverse portfolio consequences due to prepayments. Unfortunately, in the early years of the CMO markets, too often buyers of these types of bond classes were not aware of their investment characteristics and were attracted to them because of their high yield based on some specified prepayment assumption rather than analyzing them on an option-adjusted basis.

In the PAC-support structure given by Structure 2, there is only one support bond. In actual deals, the support bonds are often divided into different bond classes. For example, a structurer can create support bonds that payoff in sequence. To provide some support bonds with greater prepayment protection than the other support bonds in a structure, a structurer can even carve up the support bonds to create support bonds with a schedule of principal repayments. That is, support bonds that are PAC support bonds can be created. In a structure with a PAC bond and a support bond with a PAC schedule of principal repayments, the former is called a PAC I bond or Level I PAC bond and the latter a PAC II bond or Level II PAC bond. While PAC II bonds have greater prepayment protection than the support bonds without a schedule of principal repayments, the prepayment protection is less than that provided PAC I bonds.

TARGETED AMORTIZATION CLASS BONDS

In certain market environments, institutional investors may be concerned more with one type of prepayment risk, say contraction risk, rather than the other type (extension risk). To accommodate investors with such concerns, a bond class known as a *targeted amortization class bond* (TAC bond) was developed. A TAC bond resembles a PAC bond in that both have a schedule of principal repayment. The difference is that in structuring a PAC bond, a relatively wide structuring band (i.e., PSA range) is used in order to provide protection against both contraction risk and extension risk. In contrast, a TAC bond has a single prepayment speed from which the schedule of principal repayment is protected. As a result, the prepayment protection provided to investors in a TAC bond is less than for PAC bond investors and results in protection against contraction risk but not extension risk. Hence, while PAC bonds are said to afford an investor two-sided prepayment protection, investors in TAC bonds are provided one-side prepayment protection.

TAC bond have been used in different ways in structures. TAC bonds are used in some deals as an alternative to PAC bonds and given the highest cash flow priority within the deal. In other deals, a TAC bond is carved out of a support bond in order to give it better protection from contraction risk than a standalone support bond.

ACCRUAL BONDS AND ACCRETION-DIRECTED BONDS

Accrual bonds, also referred to as *Z-bonds*, are bond classes where for a specified period of time (refereed to as the lockout period) the bond coupon is accrued by adding the interest to the par value of the bond. The interest that is deferred during the lockout period is added to the accrual bond's par value in a process called *accretion*. The deferred interest is then directed to a different bond class in the structure. This directed cash flow can either form the principal for an entirely new tranche or be combined with an existing tranche to smooth the cash flow profile. Bond classes created from the directed interest are called *accretion-directed bonds*.

The motivation for a structurer to carve up normal interest-paying bonds into accrual bonds and an accretion-directed class is that overall deal execution can be improved by either creating very stable bonds (which can be sold in the market at a lower yield than otherwise) or using the accreted interest to improve the profile of existing bond classes to make them more marketable (and ultimately have them trade at a lower yield than otherwise). The creation of an accrual bond class which has a long duration has a natural clientele: It appeals to investors such as defined benefit pension plans and insurance companies seeking a fixed income security to satisfy their longer-dated liabilities. Moreover, making them even more attractive to such investors, these bond classes eliminate reinvestment during the lockout period. The appeal of the accretion-directed bonds is that they have very stable average life and duration profiles because of the characteristics of the interest cash flows generated when the accrual bond class is in the lockout period.

In creating accretion-directed bond classes, the size of the accrual bond class which the interest will be deferred to must be large enough to create a marketable bond class. The size of the accrual bond class depends on (1) the size of the bond class from which the accrual bond class will be created (referred to as the parent bond); (2) the coupon rate of the parent bond; and (3) the number of months that the accrual bond will be locked out. Letting

P_a = par value of the accrual bond class

P_p = par value of the parent bond class

C_p = parent bond's monthly coupon rate (i.e., annual coupon rate divided by 12)

T = lockout period in months

then the par value of the accrual bond class is

$$P_a = \frac{P_p}{(1+C_p)^T}$$

For example, suppose that the parent bond class is $80 million par value ($P_p$), the coupon rate on the parent bond is $5.5% so that C_p is 0.004583, and the lockout, T, is 60 months. Then the par value of the accrual bond is $60,803,960.

Let us compare a structure with an accrual bond class to that of Structure 1. To do so, we use the following structure that we refer to as Structure 4, where Z denotes the accrual bond class in the structure:

Bond Class	Par Amount ($)	Coupon Rate (%)
A	340,748,100	5.5%
B	76,398,300	5.5%
C	184,347,900	5.5%
Z	58,505,700	5.5%

The rules for the allocation of interest and principal in this structure are as follows:

- *Interest.* Disburse monthly coupon interest to bond classes A, B, and C on the basis of the amount of principal outstanding at the beginning of the period. For bond class Z, accrue the interest based on the principal plus accrued interest in the previous period. The interest for bond class Z is to be paid to the earlier bond classes as a principal paydown.
- *Principal.* Disburse principal payments to bond class A until it is completely paid off. After bond class A is completely paid off, disburse principal payments to bond class B until it is completely paid off. After bond class B is completely paid off, disburse principal payments to bond C until it is completely paid off. After bond C is completely paid off, disburse principal payments to bond classe Z until the original principal balance plus accrued interest is completely paid off.

Structure 4 is the same as Structure 1 in that there are four bond classes with a coupon rate of 5.5% and that pay off in sequence. The difference is the par amount of each bond class and the treatment of the last bond class in the sequential pay structure. The following table shows the average life for Structure 1 (no accrual bond) and Structure 4 (with accrual bond) for various PSA speeds

		100%	125%	165%	250%	400%	500%	600%
Bond class A	No accrual bond	4.7	4.1	3.4	2.7	2.0	1.8	1.6
	With accrual bond	4.5	4.0	3.4	2.7	2.0	1.8	1.6
Bond class B	No accrual bond	10.4	8.9	7.3	5.3	3.8	3.2	2.8
	With accrual bond	9.9	8.7	7.3	5.5	3.9	3.4	3.0
Bond class C	No accrual bond	15.1	13.2	10.9	7.9	5.3	4.4	3.8
	With accrual bond	14.1	12.7	10.9	8.3	5.9	4.9	4.3

Look at the average life for the three bond classes A, B, and C at the pricing speed for the deal at 165% PSA. The average lives are unchanged. What has been accomplished by including the accrual bond in the structure? Look at the principal balances of each bond class in the two structure as summarized in the following table:

		Par Value ($)
Bond class A	No accrual bond	320,925,000
	With accrual bond	340,748,100
Bond class B	No accrual bond	59,400,000
	With accrual bond	76,398,300
Bond class C	No accrual bond	159,225,000
	With accrual bond	184,347,900
Bond class D	No accrual bond	120,450,000
Bond class Z	With accrual bond	58,505,700

Notice that the par value of bond classes A, B, and C is greater when there is the accrual bond in the structure ($601,494,300 in Structure 4 versus $539,550,000 in Structure 1). Of course, this means that the par value of the accrual bond in Structure 4 will be less than the par value of the bond class Z in Structure 1. Effectively, part of the balance of the parent sequential bond has been pushed forward to the shorter bonds in the structure ($61,944,300). This means that in an upward sloping yield curve environment, almost

$62 million more of the shorter bonds can be offered at a lower yield, thereby increasing the proceeds from the structure. There is another benefit of including the accrual bond class. In the earlier table we see that the average life profile of bond classes A, B, and C has less variability in Structure 4 compared to Structure 1.

While the accrual bond class in our illustrative structures is structured from sequential pay bond classes, it can be structured from PAC bonds or support bonds. The advantage of accrual bond classes created from support bonds is that the structures are more complex and, as a result, often offered substantially below par value. A bond class with this attribute appeals to investors such as hedge funds who seek highly leveraged bets on fast prepayments.

There is special type of accretion-directed bond class that has even greater appeal to institutional investors, the VADM bond class (VADM being an acronym for "very accurately dated maturity"). This bond class is a standalone accretion-directed bond that is structured so as to be free from extension risk even in the absence of prepayments; that is, even if the prepayment speed is 0% PSA, the VADM bond classes will not extend. Under any scenario these bonds have relatively short "legal final maturities," which is the last possible date for principal to be paid. VADM bonds are attractive to investors that have no tolerance for extension risk and to depository institutions who for regulatory reasons seek bond blasses with short legal final maturities.

To illustrate a VADM, consider the Structure 5 below that has a VADM bond class (V) and an accrual bond class (Z):

Bond Class	Par Amount ($)	Coupon Rate (%)
A	$320,925,000	5.5%
B	59,400,000	5.5%
C	159,225,000	5.5%
V	65,343,300	5.5%
Z	55,106,700	5.5%

The rules for the distribution of interest and principal are:

- *Interest.* Disburse monthly coupon interest to bonds classes V, A, B, and C based on the amount of principal outstanding at the beginning of the period. The interest earned by bond class Z is to be paid to bond class V as a paydown of principal and accrued as interest to bond class Z.

■ *Principal*. Disburse principal payments to bond class V until it is completely paid off. The interest from bond class Z is to be paid to bond class V as a paydown of principal. After bond class V is completely paid off, disburse principal payments to bond class A until it is completely paid off. After tranche A is completely paid off, disburse principal payments to bond B until it is completely paid off and so then to bond class C. After bond class C is completely paid off, disburse principal payments to bond class Z until the original par value plus accrued interest is completely paid off.

Structure 5 has the same bond classes A, B, and C as Structure 1 with the same coupon rate and the same par values. However, instead of bond class D in Structure 5, there are two bond classes, V and Z, whose total par value is equal to bond class D. The average life for bond class V, the VADM bond class, for various PSA speeds is shown below:

0%	100%	165%	200%	400%	500%	600%
8.1	8.1	8.1	8.0	6.1	5.3	4.6

Notice that the average life at the structuring speed is 165% is 8.1 years. However, even if the prepayment speed declines to 0% PSA, the average life does not extend but remains at 8.1 years.

FLOATING RATE BOND CLASSES

Thus far we have seen how redirecting the principal payments among different bond classes can be used to create bond classes appealing to different types of investors in the bond market and thereby improve the execution of a transaction. The same can be done by redirecting interest payments so as to create bond classes with different exposures to changes in interest rates and prepayment risk. The first bond class type we will discuss is floating rate bond classes.

The structures discussed thus far offer a fixed coupon rate for all bond classes. If only fixed rate coupon bond classes can be created, the market for CMOs would be limited. Because many participants in the financial markets are funded on a floating rate basis, they prefer floating rate assets so as to avoid an asset-liability mismatch.

Can a floating rate tranche be created from fixed rate collateral? As explained when we discuss nonagency CMOs and ABS, it is possible to do so by using interest rate derivatives. Without the use of such derivatives, it would extremely difficult to do so. The reason is that if a bond class is created with a floating rate and the reference rate for that floating rate bond class exceeds the interest rate on the collateral, there would be an interest shortfall for the months where this occurs. One way to handle this problem is to create a floating rate bond class that has an interest rate cap. An interest rate cap is common in the floating rate market. While structures can be created with at least one floating rate bond class with an interest rate cap rate, the interest rate would be so low that it made the floating rate bond class unattractive to investors seeking a floating rate bond.[10] In addition, with upward fluctuations in the reference rate, the bond class with a floating rate will attract more interest payments, thus reducing the available interest for the other class bonds.

To tackle this drawback, structurers created bond classes that had both a floating rate bond class (i.e., floater) and an inverse floating rate tranche (i.e., inverse floater). The coupon rate on an inverse floater changes in the opposite direction from the reference rate used to reset the coupon rate for the corresponding floater. Inclusion of an inverse floater with a floater bond class allows a higher interest rate cap for the floater bond class. The floater's interest rate cap is determined by the floor (the minimum coupon rate) on the inverse floater.

The economic rationale for creating a floater/inverse combination in a structure is to improve deal execution by taking advantage of the relatively lower yields that can be offered on floaters, particularly when the yield curve is steep. The inverse floater appeals to leveraged investors who want to bet on a decline in interest rates or as touted by Wall Street firms seeking to sell this product as a hedge against declining interest rates. Unfortunately, some buyers of inverse floaters have discovered there substantial exposure to interest rate risk too late, the classic example being the one-time treasurer of Orange

---

[10] In the early days of the CMO market, floating rate bond classes were sold as part of the residual interest bond class in a structure.

County, California, Robert Citron. The decline of inverse floaters when interest rate rose was a primary factor in the bankruptcy of that municipality—in fact, the largest municipal bankruptcy on record.[11]

We illustrate the creation of a floater and inverse floater combination using Structure 4, which is a sequential pay structure four bond classes one of which is an accrual bond class. We can select any of the bond classes from which to create a floater and an inverse floater. The bond class selected is referred to as the parent bond class. Structure 6 below shows a structure with a floater and inverse floater created from bond class A (i.e., this bond class is the parent bond):

Bond Class	Par Amount ($)	Coupon Rate (%)/Reset Formula
FL	234,264,319	One-month LIBOR + 50 basis points
IFL	106,483,781	16.5% – (One month LIBOR × 2.2)
B	76,398,300	5.5%
C	184,347,900	5.5%
Z	58,505,700	5.5%

The payment rules are as follows:

- *Interest.* Disburse monthly coupon interest to bond classes FL, IFL, B, and C on the basis of the amount of principal outstanding at the beginning of the period. For bond class Z, accrue the interest based on the principal plus accrued interest in the previous period. The interest for tranche Z is to be paid to the earlier tranches as a principal paydown. The maximum coupon rate for FL is 8%; the minimum coupon rate for INV is 0%.
- *Principal.* Disburse principal payments to bond classes FL and IFL until they are completely paid off. The distribution to the bond classes should be 68.75% to bond class FL and 31.25% to bond class IFL After bond classes FL and IFL are completely paid off, disburse principal payments to bond class B until it is completely paid off. After bond B is completely paid off, disburse principal payments to bond class C unil it is completely paid off. After bond C is completely paid off, disburse principal payments to bond class Z until the original principal balance plus accrued interest is completely paid off.

---

[11] See Jorion (1995) for a description of the Orange Country bankruptcy.

Notice the following about this structure:

- The total par value of FL and IFL is equal to the par value of the parent bond from which they were created (bond class A with a par value of $340,748,100 in Structure 4).
- Bond class FL is the floater and has the typical coupon reset formula of a reference rate plus a quoted margin. The quoted margin is 50 basis points and is a market-determined number.
- The interest rate cap for the floater is 8% and is determined as follows. When bond class IFL has a coupon rate of zero, all the interest from the parent bond class goes to bond class IF. Since the par value of the parent bond class is $340,748,100 and the coupon rate for the parent bond class is 5.5%, the interest is $18,741,146. If all of that interest goes to bond class FL and the par value is $234,264,319, the maximum interest rate for that bond class is $18,741,146/ $234,264,319 or 8%.
- Bond class IFL is the inverse floater.
- The coupon reset formula for the inverse floater is 16.5% – (One month LIBOR × 2.2) and, therefore, as one-month LIBOR falls, the coupon rate for bond class IFL declines.
- The 2.2 in the inverse floater's coupon reset formula is called the *multiple* or *coupon leverage*.[12]
- The maximum coupon rate for the inverse floater is 16.5% should one-month LIBOR all to zero.
- The interest rate floor on the inverse floater is zero.
- When principal payments are allocated between FL and IFL is based on their relative size. Since FL is 68.75% of the par value of the parent bond class ($234,264,319/$340,748,100), that is its share of the principal payment distributed. IFL receives 31.25% ($106,483,781/$340,748,100). Consequently, if some month prior to these two bond classes being paid off the principal from the collateral is $1 million, then bond class FL receives $687,500 and bond class IFL receives $312,500.

---

[12] Inverse floaters with a wide variety of coupon leverages are available in the CMO market. Participants refer to low-leverage inverse floaters as those with a coupon leverage between 0.5 and 2.1; medium-leverage as those with a coupon leverage higher than 2.1 but not exceeding 4.5; and high-leverage as those with a coupon leverage higher than 4.5. The issuer develops the coupon leverage according to the desires of investors.

The total interest paid on the floater and inverse floater can be supported by the parent bond class which has a coupon rate of 5.5%. To see this, the weighted average coupon of the floater and inverse floater is

$$0.6875 \text{ (One-month LIBOR} + 0.5\%) + 0.3125$$
$$(16.5\% - (\text{One month LIBOR} \times 2.2) = 5.5\%$$

and this is the coupon rate for the parent bond class.

The interest rate cap for the floater and the inverse floater, the floor for the inverse floater, the coupon leverage, and the floater's quoted margin are not determined independently. Any cap or floor imposed on the coupon rate for the floater and the inverse floater must be selected so that the weighted average coupon rate does not exceed the coupon rate of the parent bond class. The relationships among the parameters for the parent bond class, floater, and inverse floater are summarized below assuming that the floor for the inverse floater is zero:

Floater coupon rate = Reference rate + Floater quoted margin

$$\text{Floater par value} = \frac{\text{Coupon leverage} \times \text{Par value for parent bond class}}{(1 + \text{Coupon leverage})}$$

Inverse floater par value = Par value for parent bond class
$$- \text{Floater par value}$$

Inverse floater interest
= (Par value for parent bond class × Coupon rate for parent bond class)
− (Floater par value × Coupon rate for floater)

$$\text{Floater interest rate cap} = \frac{\text{Coupon interest for parent bond class}}{\text{Floater par value}}$$

Inverse floater interest rate cap
$$= \frac{\text{Par value for parent bond class} \times \text{Coupon rate for parent bond}}{\text{Inverse floater par value}}$$

NOTIONAL INTEREST-ONLY BOND CLASSES

In all of the structures discussed thus far, the coupon rate for all of the fixed rate bond classes was set at 5.5%. Unless the yield curve is flat, it is unlikely that every bond class will have the same coupon rate. For example, consider Structure 1. Suppose that the yield curve is such that the shorter term bond class in the structure, bond class A, can be offered at par value with a coupon rate of 4.5%. This means that if the structurer creates a 5.5% coupon rate for bond class A, the bond must be sold at a premium to par. It is well known that investors are reluctant to purchase newly issued MBS at a premium above par. The reason is that early prepayments will result in an immediate capital loss. Hence, structurers are reluctant to create premium bond classes. Instead, structurers will strip off the excess interest (that is, the interest that exceeds the amount necessary to create a bond class to sell at par) and can create an interest-only bond class as follows.

Suppose in Structure 1 a 4.5% coupon rate would be required to sell bond class A at par. Since the par value of bond class A is $320,925,000 and the coupon rate from the collateral is 5.5%, the interest for bond class A is $17,650,875. However, if bond class A is issued with a coupon rate of 4.5%, then the total interest to be paid to the holders of bond class A is $14,441,625. The excess interest is $3,209,250 ($17,650,875 − $14,441,625). From this excess interest an interest-only bond class, referred to as a *notional IO* or *structured IO*, can be created. The notional IO created would have a par value equal to the size of bond class A. So, from the collateral of $320,925,000 having a coupon rate of 5.5%, we have size of class A bonds having par value of $320,925,000 carrying coupon of 4.5%, and IO strip having a notional value of $320,925,000 and a coupon rate of 1%. Over time, as the collateral value comes down due to amortization and prepayment, the par value of class A bonds and the notional value of the IO strip will keep coming down. Note that when determining the par value for the structure, the par value of the notional IO is not included because that par value is never paid out. Rather, it is used to benchmark the interest payments (hence it is referred to as *notional*) to be made to the holder of the notional IO. Quite obviously, there is no principal payment to the IO class.

An alternative is to combine the excess interest for several bond classes to create a notional IO. Returning to Structure 1, suppose that bond class B could be offered at 5% to be sold at par value. Then the excess interest for bond class B would be the difference between the 5.5% from the collateral and the 5% that would have to be offered to sell the bond class B at par multiplied by the par value for bond class B. Since the par value for bond class B in Structure 1 is $59,400,000, the excess interest is $297,000. To create a notional IO with a coupon rate of 5.5%, for example, the par value would be $5,400,000. Instead of creating two separate notional IOs, a structurer can combine the notional IO created from bond class A and the notional IO created from bond class B.

Investors in notional IOs include investors who are looking for a highly leveraged vehicle with which to bet on interest rates. A notional IO is attractive in an environment of slow prepayments. In a fast prepayment environment, the principal is repaid faster and therefore there is less par value and therefore less interest. Other investors argue that notional IOs, if properly used, can be employed to hedge positions in mortgage-backed securities because when interest rates rise, the value of an MBS portfolio will decline but the value of a notional IO will increase.

KEY POINTS OF THE CHAPTER

➤ *In structuring agency mortgage-backed securities it is necessary to understand prepayment risk.*

➤ *Different types of loans may permit the borrower to prepay the loans in whole or in part at any time prior to the scheduled principal repayment date.*

➤ *A prepayment is a payment made by the borrower in excess of the scheduled principal payment.*

➤ *Prepayment risk means that there is uncertainty in the cash flow because the rate of future prepayments is unknown.*

➤ *Prepayment risk can be divided into extension risk and contraction risk.*

➤ *In order to estimate the cash flow from collateral that allows prepayments an assumption about future prepayments is required.*

➤ *In the agency mortgage-backed securities market, the prepayment benchmarks used are the conditional prepayment rate and the Public Securities Association (PSA) prepayment benchmark.*

➤ *The* conditional prepayment rate *(CPR) as a measure of the speed of prepayments assumes that some fraction of the remaining principal in the mortgage pool is prepaid each month for the remaining term of the collateral.*

➤ *The CPR is an annual prepayment rate and its corresponding monthly rate is called the* single monthly mortality *(SMM) rate.*

➤ *The PSA prepayment benchmark is expressed as a monthly series of annual prepayment rates that assumes that prepayment rates are (1) low for newly originated loans; (2) will then speed up as the mortgages become seasoned; and (3) reach a plateau and remain at that level.*

➤ *Slower or faster speeds are then referred to as some percentage of PSA (e.g., 150% PSA or 75% PSA).*

➤ *The average life of a mortgage-backed security is a weighted average of the principal cash flows divided by the par value where the weight is the month when the projected principal is expected to be received based on some prepayment assumption.*

➤ *Structuring agency pass-through securities to create* collateralized mortgage obligations *(CMOs) is an illustration of how a pool of loans with unattractive interest rate risk attributes can be used to create bond classes that appeal to a wide range of investors.*

➤ *The creation of CMOs involves redistributing the prepayment risk and interest risk of the loan pool to the different bond classes.*

➤ *In an agency CMO, only prepayment risk and interest risk are redistributed since no credit risk is assumed.*

➤ *The structuring of an agency CMO involves time tranching of the collateral's cash flow by establishing rules for how interest and principal from the collateral are to be distributed to the different bond classes in the structure.*

➤ Time tranching of the collateral is done in order to create bond classes in a transaction that will have average lives and durations that will appeal to a wider range of investors than the collateral.

➤ The simplest form of time tranching is a sequential pay structure wherein bond classes in a structure are paid off in sequence.

➤ In a sequential pay structure extension risk and contraction risk are redistributed among the bonds classes in the structure.

➤ In a planned amortization class (PAC) structure, a class of bonds (referred to as the PAC bonds) have a schedule that is specified and have priority over all other bond classes in the structure with respect to payments to satisfy the scheduled payments.

➤ In a PAC structure, the PAC bonds have protection under certain prepayment scenarios against both extension and contraction risk (i.e., have a constant average life).

➤ The support bonds in a PAC structure are the bond classes that do not have a schedule of principal payments.

➤ The key in a PAC structure is that the support bonds accept the contraction risk if actual prepayment speeds are fast and accept the extension risk if actual prepayments are slow.

➤ Unlike a sequential pay structure where the bond classes are afforded some protection against extension risk or contraction risk but not both, PAC bonds offer prepayment protection against both extension risk and contraction risk.

➤ A PAC structure typically has a sequential pay PAC structure.

➤ Support bonds have the greatest prepayment risk in a structure.

➤ Some support bonds can have a PAC schedule giving them greater prepayment protection than other support bonds in the structure and are referred to as PAC II bonds or Level II PAC bonds.

➤ A targeted amortization class (TAC) bond resembles a PAC bond in that both have a schedule of principal repayments but differs in that a PAC bond has a relatively wide structuring band in order to provide protection against both contraction risk and extension risk while a TAC bond has a single prepayment speed resulting in far less prepayment protection.

➤ *A TAC bond is structured such that it provides protection against contraction risk but not extension risk, unlike a PAC bond which has protection against both types of risk.*

➤ *Accrual bonds or Z-bonds are bond classes where during the lockout period the bond coupon is accrued by adding the interest to the par value of the bond and the interest not paid out is directed to another bond class.*

➤ *Bond classes created from the directed interest from an accrual bond are called* accretion directed bonds.

➤ *While the bond classes created from collateral that has a fixed interest rate typically pay a fixed rate, floating rate bond classes can be created.*

➤ *In an agency CMO structure, when a floating rate bond class is created, it is typically necessary to create an accompanying bond class called an inverse floating rate bond class.*

➤ *The coupon rate for an inverse floating rate bond class moves in the opposite direction of the change in the reference rate.*

➤ *A notional interest-only or structured interest-only bond class is created by stripping off excess interest from one or more bond classes.*

CHAPTER 4

Structuring Nonagency Deals

The discussion of structuring agency deals in the previous chapter gave us our first look at how securitization can be used to create bond classes that appeal to a greater number of investor types. The collateral for agency transactions is agency pass-through securities which are in turn backed by residential mortgage loans that conform to the underwriting standards of Ginnie Mae, Fannie Mae, and Freddie Mac.

The creation of agency CMOs is different in its motivation than for corporate entities using asset securitization. Agency deals are basically arbitrage transactions. Fannie Mae and Freddie Mac purchase a pool of pass-through securities and create bond classes so as to generate proceeds that exceed the cost of the pool of pass-through securities purchased as collateral. For corporations seeking funding using receivables and loans, securitization provides access to the capital markets and is a funding tool. The securitization process is different in an agency deal. In this chapter, we identify the basic structuring elements that differ from agency deals and the considerations in the securitization process.

One can think of a securitization transaction as a standalone profit-seeking corporation. Consider the basic features of a corporation. It has a balance sheet consisting of assets and liabilities. The structure of the liabilities and the mix between liabilities and equity is the capital structure decision. The difference between the cash flow generated by the corporation's assets and the cash flow paid to satisfy all obligations accrues to the benefit of the equity holders. That residual cash flow, called profits, can either be withdrawn from the corporation or retained by the corporation as support in the future if there is a negative cash flow. How the earnings will be handled by management is referred to as the *dividend decision*. The initial equity in a corporation is provided by investors. Over time, the book value of the equity changes. Moreover, the board of directors can repurchase shares. Even in a profitable corporation, there may be periods where there is a short-term liquidity problem and as a result a corporation must have backup facilities to meet temporary needs. The corporation has a perpetual life.

Now let us consider a securitization structure and discuss the similarities and differences. The corporation is basically the SPV. While it has no employees nor management,[1] the SPV has assets, the pool of loans or receivables. The financing of the SPV is obtained primarily from the asset-backed securities issued, some of which are senior and some junior, and the junior-most serves the same economic purpose as equity in a corporation. For each month, the difference between the cash flow generated by the pool of loans and receivables and the interest paid to the holders of the asset-backed securities and the fees paid (primarily for servicing) is in effect the monthly profit. In securitization terminology, it is referred to as the *excess spread*. The excess spread can either be distributed to the equity investors or retained. The decision as to how it will be handled is not left up to the board of directors since no such body exists in an SPV. Rather, it is determined by the structure's rules. The originator/seller would like to withdraw the excess spread. However, the creditors (i.e., investors in the asset-backed securities) would prefer that the excess spread be retained as a form of credit support to absorb losses that are likely to occur in the future. In a securitization, there are various devices by which the originator/seller can remove any residual profit (i.e., excess spread) from the transaction. There devices are referred to as profit extraction devices and they can have different consequences on the legal structure, accounting treatment, and the credit support level. In structuring the transaction, a certain level of credit support is required and it can come from the retention or "trapping" of the excess spread.

Also, as with a corporation, there is equity. The equity may come either in form of subordinated, first-loss liabilities referred to above, or, as it happens with some deals, the par value of the pool of loans and receivables may exceed the par value of the asset-backed securi-

---

[1] The exception is collateralized debt obligations that we discuss in Part Four of this book.

ties issued. This is referred to as *overcollateralization* and is another form of credit support. Effectively, there is initial equity in the SPV and the equity owner is often the originator/seller. While a corporation can repurchase shares at the board's discretion, equity cannot be withdrawn from the SPV except by the rules set forth at the inception of the transaction. (These are rules for the release of collateral and called *step-down triggers*.)

Unlike a corporation, an asset securitization does not have a perpetual life. After the last debt obligation is paid off, the SPV is terminated and any assets remaining are transferred to the holder of the residual certificates. Finally, there will be instances where the timing of the cash flow from the asset pool will require the SPV to borrow funds on a short-term basis. Hence, as with a corporation a backup facility for short-term borrowing is needed—we will call this *liquidity facility*.

What should be evident from this brief comparison of a corporation and a structure resulting from a securitization transaction is that the major difference between the two is that for the latter major decisions are completely nondiscretionary. While management discretion and board action are features of corporations, securitization transactions do not rely on either but on the assets and the mechanisms/devices established in the structure. As a result of this distinguishing feature of securitization transactions, several factors become important when structuring a transaction.

First is the need to identify risk at the very outset of the transaction. In a securitization, these risks include credit risk, liquidity risk, and other risk factors that affect the securitization such as the failure of the servicer. While is true that corporations undertake risk management, when a corporation is started, corporate governance typically allows the board to establish future policies for risk management. That responsibility is then typically delegated to either a risk management committee or the chief risk officer. Corporate risk management is an ongoing policy. In contrast, since there is no management nor discretion given to the SPV, the structure must be established so as to identify all the risks and clearly specify mechanisms for how to handle them. Basically, the entire transaction is preformulated like a computer program. In fact, the documents for the structure are coded and used by the rating agencies, accounting firm providing the comfort letter for the transaction, and service providers to generate the cash flows under different assumptions about prepayments, default rates, and recovery values.

There have been many types of assets that have been securitized. While it is not possible to go through the variables that affect the structuring of each, there are many variables that are common to traditional securitizations. In this chapter, we discuss some of the important structuring considerations.

IDENTIFICATION OF THE ASSET POOL

After a corporation has decided it wants to create a securitization, the first step is to identify the assets that are to be securitized. Careful attention must be given to the following four factors in identifying the asset pool. First, the size of the pool is fixed. This is done while keeping in mind the corporation's funding needs; in turn this is based on the intended application of the funding. For originators engaged in a regular business of originating loans and receivables, the proceeds generated from the securitization are then utilized in funding further originations. The size of funding must be a trade off between the cost of repeat securitization issuance, and the negative carry that invariably happens between the date of securitization and the reinvestment of the funding raised into creating further assets.

Second, the type of assets to be securitized (e.g., assets with high-spread or low-spread, prime assets or subprime assets) must be addressed and the resolution can only be made with reference to the objective of the originator/seller. As an example, the objective for the originator/seller may be to capture the excess spread and maximize the gain on sale.[2] Given that objective and the fact that subprime assets have the larger excess spread than prime assets, the corporation may decide to securitize subprime assets.

The third important structuring issue with respect to the collateral is whether the asset pool should be a static or dynamic pool. If

---

[2] Accounting standards such as FAS 140 permit recognition of the excess profit as a gain on sale, subject, of course, to netting of all liabilities created in the process of securitization. Related international accounting standard IAS 39 also permits recognition of gain on sale where the transaction qualifies for off-balance-sheet treatment.

the transaction specifies that principal payments over a specified time period is reinvesting in new assets, the structure is said to be a *revolving structure*. This time period is referred to as the *revolving period* (or *lockout period*) and the pool is essentially dynamic. The limitation of a revolving structure is that it is difficult to use when the pool assets have a long duration.

The fourth significant consideration in pool selection may be capital relief—either regulatory or economic. Regulatory capital relief is a function of the banking regulations on minimum capital that banks and financial intermediaries need to maintain, and the international treaty for such capital norms is commonly referred to as Basel I or Basel II. Since these capital requirements are based on risk-weighted assets, securitization involving putting assets off the balance sheet also results into *regulatory capital relief*. As different assets may have different risk weights, as also there might be different regulatory capital consequences for each securitization,[3] an originator may be motivated to securitize assets where the resulting capital relief is maximized, a tendency called *regulatory capital arbitrage*. Likewise, leading banks may have their own economic capital models, that is, models to allocate capital to different business segments commensurate with the volatility of returns, and securitization may be used as a device of economic capital management as it normally caps the downside risk of the originator.

SELECTION OF THE ASSETS

Once the type of assets to be securitized is determined, the selection of the specific assets in the pool must be made. To do so, selection criteria are established. One essential criterion in selecting assets is the assembling of an asset pool so as to provide a balanced spread of constituents with maximum possible diversity. For example, in the selection of the loans for a residential mortgage-backed securities, geographical diversification of the properties is sought. This criterion is an important factor used by rating agencies in determining the amount of credit support for a securitization transaction.

---

[3] For instance, providing for capital for the first-loss risk retained by the originator/seller, or below-investment-grade securities bought by the seller, or liquidity risk in case of revolving securitizations.

Other selection criteria are the amount of seasoning of the assets (the amount of time since origination), the current performance of the assets (performing versus nonperforming assets), and historical performance. It is typically preferable to have a seasoned pool rather than a newly originated pool, currently performing assets, and assets with no overdue balances or more than a certain number of overdue days. The assets selected for the pool should have the same average characteristics of the pool. Significant deviations of assets selected from the average defining features of the pool quality are not ideal.

Depending on the collateral type, detailed selection criteria such as *loan-to-value* (LTV) ratio, debt-to-income ratio, property type, and the like are laid down.

IDENTIFICATION OF RISKS

The next task after the selection of the assets to be included in the asset pool is the analysis of the risks associated with the pool and the proposed structure. These risks include credit risk, interest rate risk, prepayment risk, delayed payment risk, exchange-rate risk, servicing risk, legal risk, and tax risks.

Credit risk is the risk that the obligor will default by either refusing to pay or declaring bankruptcy. The end result of the investigation of credit risk is to develop based on empirical analysis a cumulative loss percentage of the pool, referred to as the *expected loss*[4]. The investigation begins with an examination of what happens in the case of the failure of an obligor to pay. If the delinquency is treated as a default, the procedure for recovery is set forth in the servicing agreement and depends on the nature of the asset. For example, the process for recovery as set forth in the servicing agreement may require that the delinquent receivables be sold to a specialized servicer (who may be the originator, his affiliate, or a third party) at a particu-

---

[4] Expected loss or base case loss is a sort of average loss, or a loss if the future is as predicted with maximum likelihood. The deviations from the average, that is, future loss rates exceeding the expected loss rates, lead to computation of the *unexpected loss*. In most pools that have an excess spread, the excess spread level should at least be expected to absorb the expected losses. Credit enhancements are normally put in place to absorb the unexpected losses. For a further discussion, see Chapter 5.

lar value, or a foreclosure action may be followed. To estimate the expected loss the following must be quantified (1) the default rate (i.e., the percentage of loans that go into default); (2) the timing of the defaults or default rate over time; (3) the recovery rate; and (4) the recovery delay (i.e., the time between recognition of a default and actual recovery).

When assets are included in a securitization interest rate risk will exist when there is a mismatch between the cash flow characteristics of the assets and the nature of the liabilities that the structurer elects to issue. More specifically, all or some of the assets may have a fixed interest rate while the liabilities or some of the liabilities have a floating interest rate. Or, it could be that in a transaction the assets or some of the assets have a floating interest rate while the liabilities or some of the liabilities have a fixed interest rate. Even when both the assets and liabilities have a floating interest rate, there will be interest rate risk when the reference rate for the assets and the liabilities is not the same. For example, the reference rate for the assets may be based on the one-month commercial paper rate while the liabilities are based on one-month LIBOR or the reference rate for the assets may be six-month LIBOR while the reference rate for the liabilities is one-month LIBOR. This form of interest rate risk is referred to as basis risk. To deal with this mismatch, the securitizer will use interest rate swaps or interest rate caps. These derivative instruments and how they are used in a securitization are explained in Chapter 6.

Prepayment risk, a risk related to interest rate risk, is the risk that the unscheduled repayment of principal will have an adverse impact on the performance of the asset in a declining interest rate environment. For example, for example, bond classes selling at premium have three potential adverse affects resulting from prepayments. First, the prinicipal repayment will be at par value, resulting in a loss if the bond class is selling at a premium. Second, the price appreciation of the bond class is truncated because of the negative convexity feature of bonds with embedded options. Finally, there is reinvestment risk when principal is repaid and must be reinvest at a lower interest rate.

There is the risk of a timing mismatch between the asset's cash flow and when the liability payments are due to the bond classes. This risk, referred to as *delinquency risk*, occurs even though the assets are not actually in default. Rather, delinquency risk is simply due to a temporary delay in payments by obligors. This risk is quantified by dividing delinquencies of the pool of assets into time buckets such as 30 days, 60 days, 90 days, and so on.

When either some of the assets or the liabilities are denominated in different currencies, there is exchange rate or currency risk in the transaction. Finally, servicer risk, legal risk, and tax risk are risks associated with the structure rather than the asset pool.

In investigating these risks, recognition must be given to whether the asset pool is a static pool or dynamic pool. For the former, each of the risk attributes will be examined for a fixed number of assets throughout their repayment cycle. In contrast, for a dynamic pool, the risk attributes will be examined with reference to the relevant portfolio of the originator. The chief difference in the analysis of a static pool and a dynamic pool is that the former seasons over time while the latter largely remains unaffected by aging as new assets are continuously added to the pool. For example, if a pool is comprised of 4,000 assets at the time of the securitization and the rate of prepayment is 3%, that rate is applied on a static portfolio over time. Therefore, default rates and prepayment rates become time vectors when they are applied to static pools.

DETERMINATION OF THE SOURCES AND SIZE OF CREDIT SUPPORT

Credit support is needed in a nonagency securitization in order to absorb credit losses. The sources of credit enhancement may include excess spread, overcollateralization, subordination, and third-party guarantees. The costs associated with each of these have different consequences on the economics of the transaction and require a careful economic analysis to evaluate the best combination of sources to achieve the required level of credit support.

The most significant structuring variable for any securitization is the size of the credit support because it determines the economics of the transaction The estimation of the default rate and expected loss for an asset pool provides information that is needed to estimate the size of credit support that will be required to absorb the expected losses. Ultimately, the determination of the amount of credit support will be specified by the rating agencies given the target rating sought for each bond class by the securitizer. The credit enhancement decision; that is, the mix of the credit enhancement used in a transaction, is the same as the capital structure decision for a corporation.

DETERMINATION OF THE BOND CLASSES

The decision of the bond classes to be included in a transaction (or equivalently the classes of liabilities) involves establishing the priority order of the different bond classes. The bond classes include senior, mezzanine, and junior classes. This decision is related to the credit enhancement decision because the liabilities are part of the credit enhancement structure. The key factor to be considered is what credit support level is required to protect the most senior bonds in the structure. As noted earlier, the key in subprime structures is protecting the senior bonds. Another factor is obviously what is the lowest-rated bond class that can be sold in the market.

To illustrate the structuring of the bond classes, let us assume that the securitizer has the following information:

- Investment bankers indicate that the lowest-rated bond class that can be sold is triple B (BBB).
- The rating agency that will rate the bonds indicated that the level of support required to achieve the following ratings is:

Triple A (AAA)	8%
Double A (AA)	6%
Single A (B)	5%
Triple B (BBB)	4%

Consider first the most senior bond class to be issued with a triple A rating and which we refer to as bond class A. Absent any other credit support, since an 8% credit support is required, this means that bond class A can only be 92% of the size of the transaction. For example, if the pool of assets is $500 million, only $460 million of bond class A can be issued. The balance of $40 million can be issued with a rating below triple A.

Now the structurer has a choice. A two-bond class structure can be created, bond classes A and B, where B would be an unrated bond class. The reason bond class B would have to be unrated is that it has no credit support and is subordinated to bond class A. Because bond class B is unrated, it will have to be retained by the originator/seller and represents the equity in the structure at inception. The disadvantage with such a structure is that the originator/seller wants to minimize the amount of the unrated class it must retain; that is, it wants to minimize the amount of equity that it must put into the transaction. The cost of equity in the capital structure of a securitization is much like the cost of equity in a corporation: It is the most expensive form of capital.

For this reason, the structurer would select an alternative to the two-bond class structure. Armed with the information that the rating agency will require a 6% credit support level for a double-A rated bond class, the structurer can do the following. Given that 8% is the required credit support level for the most senior bond but 6% for a bond class with a double-A rating, then a bond class rated double A can be created with a size of 2% of the transaction. For example, if the transaction is for $500 million, there will be $40 million as credit support for the $460 million bond class A. Bond class B with a par value of 2% of $500 million or $10 million can be created with a double-A rating. In this case, there would be three bond classes in the structure: bond class A, bond class B, and an unrated bond class C. The unrated bond class would have a par value of $30 million ($500 million less $460 million for bond class A and $10 million for bond class B).

However, there is no reason for the structurer to stop with three bond classes. The 8% credit support level for bond class A can be sliced up to provide more bond classes in order to make the unrated bond class smaller. In fact, more rated bond classes can be created given the required credit support levels assumed above that were specified by the rating agency. Given the above assumptions, the transaction's structure would be:

Bond Class	Rating	Required Credit Support	Size of the Class
A	AAA	8%	92%
B	AA	6%	2%
C	A	5%	1%
D	BBB	4%	1%
E	Unrated	None	4%

Notice that the greater the required credit support level for the most senior bond class, the greater the number of bond classes with a lower rating that can be created. So, for example, while we have limited in our illustration bond classes with ratings of triple A, double A, single A, and double BBB, there is no reason that bond classes with finer ratings (notches) assigned by rating agencies cannot be created. However, the trade-off is the creation of many very small bond classes that would be difficult to market.

TIME TRANCHING OF BOND CLASSES

The determination of the bond classes in a structure with the same level of credit priority is nothing more than time tranching. In our illustration of agency CMOs, we demonstrated the time tranching for the purpose of creating bond classes that are more attractive to institutional investors and thereby reducing the weighted average cost for the transaction, particularly in an upward sloping yield curve environment.

What is done in agency CMOs with respect to time tranching can in principle be done for the senior, mezzanine, and subordinated bond classes in a nonagency deal. However, in practice, only the senior most bond classes are time tranched. For example, in our hypothetical structure above, bond class A might be time tranched. For example, a sequential-pay structure with say bond classes A-1, A-2, and A-3 can be created. In this case, all the principal that would be distributed to bond class A in our hypothetical structure would be distributed to bond class A-1 until that bond class is retired. Then all the principal that would be distributed to bond class A would go to bond class A-2 until it is retired. Finally, bond class A-3 receives all the principal that would have gone to bond class A. How many such bond classes are created is a question of the yield differences and investor preferences for senior bond classes of different durations. Typically, there is at least one bond class that pays off in just one year in order to qualify that bond class as a money market instrument that can be purchased by money market mutual funds.

SELECTING THE PAY-DOWN STRUCTURE FOR THE BOND CLASSES

The credit enhancement structure is a decision that is made at the inception of the transaction. The liability structure, however, changes over time depending on the pay down structure that is selected by the securitizer. The pay-down structure is the rules that deal with how the principal generated by the asset pool will be distributed to the bond classes when the liabilities are amortized over time.[5] In turn, it affects the capital structure of the transaction at different points in time, and therefore the weighted average cost of the structure. So, the pay-down structure decision can be almost as important as the credit enhancement structure decision made at the outset of the transaction.

There are four general types of pay-down structures with combinations thereof:

- Sequential
- Pro rata
- Fast-pay/slow-pay
- Step-up

In a sequential pay-down structure, the bond classes are paid down sequentially, highest credit rated bond class down to the unrated bond class. For our hypothetical five-bond class structure, this means first paying off bond class A and paying nothing to any of the other four bond classes. Once bond class A is completely retired, all principal payments are made to bond class B until it is fully retired and so on with bond classes C, D, and E.[6] Effectively, a sequential pay-down structure of the liability classes reduces the leverage in the structure because it is the higher rated classes that are the lowest cost bond classes. From a credit perspective, because a sequential pay-down structure means retirement of the highest-rated bond class first, this increases the protection available to the senior bond class as the relative size (i.e, percentage) of the rated bond classes to the equity (unrated bond classes) is reduced. At the same time, because it is the cheapest class that will

---

[5] If, for instance, the transaction provides for a bullet repayment of the liabilities, the pay-down sequence does not just matter.

[6] Note that in time tranching we explained what a sequential-pay structure is: paying off the most senior bond classes in sequence.

be retired first, the weighted average cost of the transaction increases. The significance of this is that the cost may increase to the extent that another source of credit enhancement to be discussed in Chapter 5, the excess spread, may decline materially. In practice, however, because the senior bond class is typically the largest portion of the structure, this adverse impact on the excess spread may not be that great.

In a pro rata pay-down structure (or proportional pay-down structure), the principal payments are distributed among the various bond classes in proportion to their respective share in the original capital structure. For example, in our hypothetical structure, for every $1 of principal received from the asset pool, 92% is paid to bond class B, 2% to bond class B, 1% each to bond classes C and D, and 4% to bond class E. However, there are triggers in structures that will modify these payments. This occurs when due to faster than expected prepayments or the poor performance of the collateral the credit support level for the senior bond classes deteriorate.

A fast-pay/slow-pay structure seeks to mitigate the concern that the credit support level for the senior bond classes may deteriorate. In this structure, both the senior and the junior bond classes receive principal payments as with a pro rata pay-down structure, but more is paid to the senior bond classes and less to the junior classes. Therefore, the senior bond class is the fast-pay bond class and the junior class bond is the slow-pay bond class.

In a step-up, pay-down structure the level of credit enhancement is, as the name indicates, stepped up. For example, suppose that at the inception of a transaction the credit support for bond class A is 8% but the objective is that over time the credit enhancement level is to be increased to 10%. If so, principal payments must be made to bond class A until that bond class becomes 90% of the total liabilities. Once that credit support level is reached, principal payments are made proportionally as long as it stays at the increased level.

DETERMINATION OF THE AMOUNT AND SOURCES FOR LIQUIDITY SUPPORT

There will be periods where due to a temporary shortfall in collections or some other disruption in the collection process (e.g., change-over from a normal servicer to a backup servicer) there is a need for short-term financing in order to satisfy the liabilities on a timely basis. Because of this, liquidity support or liquidity enhancement is needed; it is only intended as a temporary cash facility. The securitizer needs to determine the amount of liquidity that may be needed and arrange for a facility.

In determining the amount of liquidity, it is important to recognize that in some structures there may be internally generated liquidity. For example, in some structures there may be an accumulation payment period to retire a bullet liability. During that period, liquidity is available.

In terms of the economics of the transaction, the securitizer must realize that liquidity creation has an implicit or explicit cost. For example, if liquidity is provided by internal sources such as a cash reserve, the cost is the opportunity cost associated with reinvestment of the cash. Consequently, the structurer will seek to establish just the required amount of liquidity.

Typically, there are three sources of liquidity enhancements: bank facilities, cash reserves, and servicer advances. A servicer typically agrees to provide periodic advances to the structure so as to maintain a regular flow of payments due to the bond classes. These amounts, referred to as *servicer advances*, are typically for the amount of the delinquencies for the period. The advances are limited to amounts that the servicer expects can be collected in the future. In evaluating the liquidity enhancement provided by the servicer, rating agencies examine the servicer's financial condition.

Cash reserve is normally created either at the inception of the transaction by retaining a part of the funding raised, or by trapping the excess profit. As in the case of credit enhancements, the size of the cash reserve is also typically reset to a higher level if the transaction starts witnessing any predefined adverse material change or hits *triggers*, in which case the excess spread otherwise flowing through the transaction is arrested to increase the size of the cash reserve. As may be clear, cash reserve serves both as a credit and liquidity enhancer.

DETERMINING IF ANY PREPAYMENT PROTECTION IS NEEDED

In the illustration of agency CMOs, we explained how certain bond classes can be provided with different levels of protection against certain types of prepayment risk (i.e., contraction risk or extension risk). When the asset pool consists of long-term assets, the securitizer must decide on whether to create bond classes that have prepayment protection. The economics here is based on spreads offered in the market on different types of prepayment-protected bond classes. Consider, for example, two alternative structures. The first has a PAC and support bonds while the second has only sequential pay bonds. Depending on spreads in the market, which in turn depends on the market's expectations regarding prepayment speeds for the collateral, the weighted average cost will dictate which structure will be selected. Remember that in the PAC structure, the spreads at which protected bonds can be offered will be less than that for the sequential-pay structure. However, the wider spread that must be offered to pay the support bond classes will determine which of the two structures has the higher cost.

INCLUSION OF STRUCTURAL PROTECTION TRIGGERS

Structural protection triggers are basically preventive provisions in a structure to take care of imminent weaknesses in the transaction. As emphasized earlier, there is no management that might deal with problems that may occur after the transaction is completed. Therefore, the mechanisms/procedures for dealing with problems that might arise over the life of the structure must be specified at the time of issuance. A structural protection trigger provides that if certain pre-specified weaknesses arise in the transaction, the structure of the transaction will be modified in a certain manner. Here are three examples of structural protection triggers:

- If the cumulative losses reach or exceed a level of $x\%$, then the excess spread available to the originator will be not be distributed to the originator but be trapped to either create or increase the cash reserve.
- If the cumulative losses reach or exceed a level of $x\%$, then to increase the credit enhancement to the senior bond classes the pay-down method will be altered from proportional to sequential.

▪ If the cumulative losses reach or exceed a level of $x\%$, to increase the credit enhancement to the senior bond classes there will be a lockout on the coupon payments to the subordinated classes.

It should be noted that protective triggers in a structure are similar to the dividend suspension, acceleration, or similar covenants found in loan agreements.

KEY POINTS OF THE CHAPTER

➤ *The creation of agency collateral mortgage obligations (CMOs) is different in its motivation than for corporate entities using asset securitization.*

➤ *For corporations seeking funding using receivables and loans, securitization provides access to the capital markets and is a funding tool and hence the basic structuring elements differ from agency deals and the considerations in the securitization process.*

➤ *While there have been many asset types that have been securitized and therefore variables that affect the structuring of each asset type, there are many variables that are common to traditional securitizations.*

➤ *Factors that are important structuring considerations are (1) identification of the asset pool; (2) selection of the assets; (3) identification of the risks; (4) determination of the sources and size of credit support; (5) determination of the bond classes, (6) time tranching of bond classes; (6) selecting the pay down structure of the bond classes; (7) determination of the amount and sources for liquidity support; (8) determination if any prepayment protection is needed; and (9) inclusion of structural protection triggers.*

➤ *The first consideration in a securitization is the identification of the asset that are to be securitized.*

➤ *The following four factors are considered in identifying the asset pool: (1) the size of the pool is fixed; (2) the type of assets to be securitized must be addressed taking into account the objective of the originator/seller; (3) whether the asset pool should be a static* pool or a dynamic pool; and (4) whether regulatory or economic capital relief is being sought.

➤ Once the type of assets to be securitized is determined, the selection of the specific assets in the pool must be made based on some selection criteria established by the originator/seller.

➤ Selection criteria include (1) the assets to be included so as to provide a balanced spread of constituents with maximum possible diversity (an important factor used by rating agencies in determining the amount of credit support needed in a securitization transaction); (2) the amount of seasoning of the assets; (3) the current performance of the assets; (4) the historical performance of the assets; and (5) the asset characteristics based on the specific collateral type.

➤ Given the selection of the assets to be included in the asset pool, the risks associated with the pool and the proposed structure (credit risk, interest rate risk, prepayment risk, delayed payment risk, exchange-rate risk, servicing risk, legal risk, and tax risks) must be analyzed.

➤ In investigating risks associated with the asset pool and the proposed structure, recognition must be given to whether the asset pool is a static pool or dynamic pool.

➤ With respect to the analysis of credit risk, expected losses must be estimated which requires quantification of (1) the default rate; (2) the timing of the defaults or default rate over time; (3) the recovery rate; and (4) the recovery delay.

➤ Interest rate risk will exist in a securitization transaction where there is a mismatch between the cash flow characteristics of the assets and the nature of the liabilities that the structurer elects to issue.

➤ To deal with interest rate risk mismatch, the securitizer must select the appropriate hedging instrument, typically either an interest rate swap or an interest rate cap.

➤ Prepayment risk is the risk that the unscheduled repayment of principal will have an adverse impact on the performance of the asset in a declining interest rate environment.

➤ *Delinquency risk in a securitization is the risk of a timing mismatch between the asset's cash flow and when the liability payments are due to the bond classes even though the assets are not actually in default.*

➤ *Delinquency risk is measured by dividing delinquencies of the pool of assets into time buckets based on the number of days of delinquency.*

➤ *Exchange rate or currency risk exists in a securitization transaction when either some of the assets or the liabilities are denominated in different currencies,*

➤ *There are risks associated with the structure rather than the asset pool and they include servicer risk, legal risk, and tax risk.*

➤ *All nonagency securitization transactions require credit support (i.e, credit enhancement) in order to absorb credit losses.*

➤ *The potential sources of credit enhancement for a securitization are excess spread, overcollateralization, subordination, and third-party guarantees with each of these sources having an associated cost and consequences for the economics of the transaction.*

➤ *Analysis of the alternative sources of credit support requires a careful economic analysis to evaluate the best combination of sources to achieve the required level of credit support.*

➤ *The most significant structuring variable for any securitization is the size of the credit support because it determines the economics of the transaction.*

➤ *Estimation of the amount of credit support requires the estimation of the default rate and expected loss for an asset pool needed to absorb the expected losses.*

➤ *It is the rating agencies that ultimately specify the amount of credit support required to obtain the target rating sought for each bond class by the securitizer.*

➤ *The decision of the bond classes to be included in a securitization transaction (senior, mezzanine, and junior classes) involves establishing the priority order of the different bond classes.*

➤ *The factors considered in determining the bond classes are (1) the credit support needed to protect the most senior bonds and (2) the lowest rated bond class that it is expected that investors are willing purchase in the structure.*

➤ *The determination of the bond classes in a structure that have the same level of credit priority is an example of time tranching.*

➤ *While the credit enhancement structure is a decision that is made at the inception of the transaction, the liability structure changes over time depending on the pay-down structure that is selected by the securitizer.*

➤ *The pay-down structure decision, which can be almost as important as the credit enhancement structure, is simply the structure's rules with respect to how the principal generated by the asset pool will be distributed to the bond classes when the liabilities are amortized over time.*

➤ *There are four general types of pay-down structures with combinations of each type: (1) sequential, (2) pro rata, (3) fast-pay/slow-pay, and (4) step up.*

➤ *There will be periods over the life of a structure when the trust will need short-term financing to make payments to the bondholders because of a temporary shortfall in collections or some other disruption in the collection of payments from the obligors.*

➤ *The securitizer must estimate the amount needed for liquidity support or liquidity enhancement and arrange for a liquidity facility (three potential sources being bank facilities, cash reserves, and servicer advances) taking into account that liquidity support has a cost.*

➤ *When the asset pool for a securitization transaction exposes bond classes to prepayment risk, the structurer must decide if and how to protect designated bond classes against that risk.*

➤ *Structural protection triggers are included at the time of issuance of a transaction that set forth mechanisms/procedures for handling problems that might arise over the structure's life.*

➢ *A structural protection trigger provides that if over time certain prespecified weaknesses arise in the transaction, the structure of the transaction will be modified in a certain manner.*

CHAPTER 5

Credit Enhancements

While there are various types of credit enhancement, the nature and extent of credit enhancement required in a transaction is specific to the type of asset securitized and the type of investor targeted. There are some forms of credit enhancement that are more suitable for certain types of assets but would be totally inappropriate for other types. All credit enhancement has a cost associated with it. An economic analysis of the cost of further enhancement of a structure versus the improved execution of the transaction will be performed by the structurer.

The amount or size of credit enhancement needed to obtain a specific credit rating is specified by the rating agencies from which a rating is sought. A rating agency does the sizing of the credit enhancement and the structurer determines the best mix of credit enhancements to achieve the amount specified by the rating agency. The factors considered by rating agencies in sizing a transaction are (1) the obligor's incentives to default; (2) the credit quality of the obligors; (3) the likely loss scenario and the potential variability of loss; and (4) the diversification of the asset pool.[1]

The credit enhancement level for every bond class in a structure to be rated is based on the target rating sought for that bond class. For instance, for a rating agency to award a triple-B rating to a bond class, the probability of any losses in the portfolio impacting the triple-B bond class must not be more than the standard historical probability of a triple-B rated investment defaulting. The probability of loss has to be lower the higher the target rating sought for a bond class; hence, a higher level of credit enhancement is required for a higher target rating.

---

[1] For a more detailed discussion, see Silver (2000).

In this chapter, we discuss the various credit enhancement mechanisms and how the needed credit enhancement for a transaction is sized.

CREDIT ENHANCEMENT MECHANISMS

The mechanisms for credit enhancement can be classified into three categories: (1) originator-provided, (2) structural, and (3) third-party provided. *Originator-provided credit enhancement* refers to credit support where a part of the credit risk of the asset pool is assumed by the originator/seller. *Structural credit enhancement* refers to the redistribution of credit risks among the bond classes comprising the structure, so that one bond class provides credit enhancement to the other bond classes. *Third-party credit enhancement* refers to the assumption of credit risk by parties other than the originator and the other bond classes in the structure. We discuss each type of credit enhancement in the rest of this section.

Originator-Provided Credit Enhancements

Originator-provided credit enhancement essentially involves the originator/seller injecting an equity contribution into the transaction. This can come in the form of cash, assets in excess of the liabilities, or retained profits. In addition, typically the originator/seller will invest in the subordinated bond class. The form of equity contributed does have implications for the securitizer.

Excess Spread or Profit

Excess spread is the most natural form of enhancement and the one that is least burdensome to the originator/seller. The idea of excess spread is simple: Whatever is available from the income of the transaction (after meeting senior expenses) to meet losses on the assets is credit-enhancing excess spread. More specifically, the excess spread is equal to the interest paid by the asset pool (which is based on the note rate of the obligors in the asset pool) reduced by (1) the expenses of the transaction such as trustee fees; (2) senior servicing fees; and (3) the payments made to the bond classes (which is based on the weighted average funding cost). For example, assume a pool of loans that has a weighted average note rate of 9.5% and the originator receives a servicing fee of 1.5%. If the weighted average funding cost is 5.0%, then the excess spread is 3% (9.5% − 1.5% − 5%).

If the excess spread is not paid to the originator/seller either up-front[2] or over a specified period, it is retained by the SPV in a spread account. When it retained in a spread account, the excess spread is said to be "trapped." The advantage of retaining the excess spread is that it can be used to offset losses in future periods. In contrast, if the excess spread is distributed to the originator/seller, it can only be used to protect against losses in the current period. The structure might provide for withdrawal of the retained spread either (1) on a periodic basis; (2) after the last liability is paid off; or (3) after the retained cash builds a reserve of a particular amount.[3]

In every structure, there should be sufficient excess spread at least to absorb the expected losses. Credit enhancement goes further by providing for unexpected losses as well. If things turn bad and the losses exceed the expected loss level, will there be a default on the outstanding classes? Credit enhancement, consistent with the rating of the transaction, indicates the ability of the structure to withstand unexpected losses.

Because the excess spread cannot be relied upon as a definitive source of support, it is referred to as *soft credit enhancement*. Due to changes in the asset pool over time, the dollar amount of the excess spread varies over time; therefore, one cannot measure the excess spread as a percentage of the total liabilities of the structure at the inception of the transaction. Nor can excess spread be measured as a percentage of the outstanding asset balance. A reduction in excess spread over time may arise as a result of prepayments and defaults.

---

[2] A structure would rarely pay the excess spread up-front because the up-front payment of excess spread would imply capitalization of the expected profits. Leaving aside default rates, even prepayments can affect the expected losses—hence, transactions that pay excess spreads up-front may be left with principal losses due to prepayments.

[3] There are various forms in which the originator/seller can receive this excess profit: as excess servicing fees; as super profits on the subordinated debts acquired by the originator itself; as interest on a subordinated loan; or the redemption price of a zero-coupon bond. For a discussion of these forms, see Kothari (2006).

A major concern is that the better quality obligors in the asset pool prepay and exit the asset pool, leaving only the low credit quality obligors. As a result, this increases the credit risk of the structure. Moreover, within an asset pool there are low-spread contracts and high-spread contracts. Faster prepayments of the latter contracts will reduce the amount of future excess spread (i.e., reduce the weighted average spread of the collateral).

Rating agencies are well aware that the excess spread is soft in that it cannot be relied upon as a form of excess spread. Consequently, in giving allowance for the amount of the credit enhancement needed to obtain a target rating, rating agencies will not give a dollar-for-dollar allowance. Rather, in its modeling of the structure, it will penalize the credit enhancement based on the target rating. For example, suppose a securitizer is seeking a triple-B rating for a bond class. The rating agency might in its modeling of the structure give an 85% allowance for the excess spread in computing the credit enhancement. In contrast, if a triple-A rating is sought for a bond class, the same rating agency might only give a 40% allowance. The lower allowance is due to the risk that we just described: prepayments and defaults, particularly on high spread contracts.

Cash Collateral

A *cash collateral* or *cash reserve* to meet principal losses can be created in a structure in one of three ways.

First, the originator/seller can create a cash collateral account at the initiation of the transaction and the cash in that account is subject to withdrawal in the event of losses that exceed the amount provided by other forms of credit enhancement. At the termination of the transaction, any balance in the cash collateral account is returned to the originator/seller.

Second, the originator/seller can make a *subordinated loan* to the SPV. Both the cash collateral payment at inception and the subordinated loan are referred to as *hard credit enhancement* because the amount of the credit enhancement is known.

The third form of cash collateral is the retention of the excess spread discussed earlier.

While cash is the best form of credit enhancement, retention of cash leads to a problem of *negative carry*. The so-called cash collateral is actually reinvested in some passive financial assets of a very high quality—hence, obviously at very low rates of return. Because the rate of return is less than the coupon rates paid to investors, the result is holding assets in cash form that leads to losses.

Credit-Enhancing Interest-Only Strip

Another form of originator-provided credit enhancement is a *subordinated interest-only* (IO) *strip bond class.* This bond class has no principal but does have a notional amount on which interest payments are based. If this interest claim is subordinated and may be deferred or waived in order to protect against losses, this is also a form of credit enhancement. In economic terms, it serves the same purpose as retained excess spread and has the same risks as a form of credit enhancement. However, in contrast to excess spread, an IO strip bond class can be transferred/sold to another party by the originator/seller.

Overcollateralization

Overcollateralization is one of the most common forms of credit enhancement in certain asset classes such as future flows described in Chapter 10. It is a form of originator-provided credit enhancement because the originator/seller transfers an asset pool that has a market value that exceeds the amount paid by the SPV. The amount of the overcollateralization is a form of equity and is equal to the difference between the par value of the assets transferred and the price paid. For example, suppose that an SPV purchases $400 million from an originator/seller, $440 million is transferred to the SPV, and the SPV issues $400 million in bond classes. The additional $40 million is the amount of overcollateralization.

From the originator/seller perspective, the extra $40 million (i.e., the overcollateralization) transferred to the SPV is a transfer for the sake of security, not a legal transfer. From an accounting perspective, the overcollateralization is treated as a deposit for security, not a transfer of ownership.

As a form of credit support, overcollateralization differs from cash collateral in four noteworthy ways. First, because overcollateralization results in a collateral in kind, while cash collateralization results in a collateral in cash, the negative carry problem inherent in cash collateral does not apply to overcollateralization. Second, if it assumed that the cash collateral is invested for a fixed time, the percentage size of the cash collateral increases over time as the pool is paid down. In contrast, over time the percentage size of overcollateralization does not increase because the size of the overcollateralized assets also simultaneously declines. Third, with overcollateralization there is both excess interest and excess principal in the structure because the principal is collected on assets worth more than the liabilities. Finally, excess spread is not reduced as a result of overcollateralization because the in-kind assets generally have the same note rate as the other assets in the pool. In the case of cash reserve, the rate of return that can be earned on the cash can be significantly less than the coupon payable on the bond classes.

When there is overcollateralization, there may be *early amortization triggers*. These provisions provide that if the performance of the pool worsens as gauged by the one or more specified tests, then instead of the subordinated interest in the principal being paid off to the originator/seller, the principal is redirected to pay off the other bond classes.

Structural Credit Enhancements

As noted earlier, when various bond classes are issued with different priorities—such as bond classes A, B, and C—the subordination of bond class C provides a credit enhancement to bond class B, and both bond classes B and C provide enhancement to bond class A. Because this credit enhancement is created from the structure of the liabilities, it is referred to as structural enhancement. The most common form of credit enhancement for securitization transactions is the stratification of the bond classes into senior, mezzanine, and junior (or subordinated) bond classes.

The meaning of *senior-subordinate structure* is similar to the prioritization of claims in corporate funding—senior secured debt has a prior claim over unsecured debt, while the latter has a prior claim over subordinated debt, preferred stock or equity. In the same way, senior noteholders have a prior claim over the cash flows and the junior liabilities will pick up the losses first until they survive. Because the senior bond classes have the lowest credit risk in the structure, they are offered the lowest spread to Treasuries. The subordinated bond classes are those that have subordinated claims on the assets. Just like equity holders, investors in these bond classes stand a greater probability of realizing a loss of principal and interest. For a given duration or average life, the spread to Treasuries increases as one goes down the ladder of the liabilities.

In terms of ratings, as explained in Chapter 4, the stratification of liabilities is done so as to have a triple-A rating awarded for the senior-most bond class. The rating for the juniormost-rated bond class is what is sellable in the market. The unrated class is typically retained by the originator.

Third-Party Credit Enhancements

Third-party credit enhancement is a guarantee of some form from a party other than the SPV. There are numerous types of third-party credit enhancements available and they include monoline insurance companies, letters of credit, and related-party guarantees such as that of the originator/seller. In the case of mortgage assets, there is a special form of credit enhancement, pool insurance.

It is important to note that third-party credit enhancements are subject to *third-party credit risk*. This is the risk that the third-party guarantor may be either downgraded and, depending on the performance of the asset pool, the bond classes guaranteed made be downgraded, or the third-party may be unable to satisfy its commitment. In addition, third-party enhancements are a cost to the transaction.

Monoline Insurance

Unlike a traditional insurance company, a monoline insurance company is limited by charter to provide only financial guarantees. In the state of New York, for example, insurance law specifies:

(a)(1) 'Financial guaranty insurance' means a surety bond, a surety bond, insurance policy or, when issued by an insurer or any person doing an insurance business as defined in paragraph one of subsection (b) of section one thousand one hundred one of this chapter, an indemnity contract, and any guaranty similar to the foregoing types, under which loss is payable, upon proof of occurrence of financial loss, to an insured claimant, obligee or indemnitee as a result of any of the following events:

(A) failure of any obligor on or issuer of any debt instrument or other monetary obligation (including equity securities guarantied under a surety bond, insurance policy or indemnity contract) to pay when due to be paid by the obligor or scheduled at the time insured to be received by the holder of the obligation, principal, interest, premium, dividend or purchase price of or on, or other amounts due or payable with respect to, such instrument or obligation, when such failure is the result of a financial default or insolvency or, provided that such payment source is investment grade, any other failure to make payment, regardless of whether such obligation is incurred directly or as guarantor by or on behalf of another obligor that has also defaulted. . . .

In securitization transactions, a *financial guarantee* is employed to credit enhance a bond class in a structure to the investment-grade level of the insurer. Basically, regardless of the performance of the asset pool, a financial guarantee (also referred to as a *surety bond* or *bond insurance*) guarantees that the investors in the bond classes covered by the policy receive timely payment of principal and interest.[4] In addition to their use for providing credit enhancement for long-term assets such mortgage loans, financial guarantees have been a particularly important form of credit enhancement both for new asset classes that have been securitized and for novel structures.

In the U.S. asset-backed securities market, as of early 2008 the major monoline insurance companies were Ambac Assurance Corporation, Financial Guaranty Insurance Company (FGIC), Financial Security Assurance (FSA), and MBIA.[5] These insurers have also been responsible for insuring a significant amount of asset-backed securities outside the United States. There are major concerns with the

---

[4] For a further discussion see Kotecha (1998).
[5] Warrent Buffett's Berkshire Hathaway Assurance is licensed to provide financial guarantees (i.e., provide bond insurance).

credit risk of monoline insurers as highlighted by the subprime mortgage meltdown and its impact on these insurers.

Letter of Credit

A *letter of credit* (LOC) credit enhances a structure by substituting the credit risk of the bank providing the LOC for the performance of the asset pool. The bank issuing the LOC is paid a fee. Typically, LOCs provide coverage of credit losses on the asset pool for less than the full amount of the asset pool but an amount sufficient to obtain a triple-A rating for the senior bond classes.

The use of a LOC as a credit enhancement vehicle has declined since they are obtained from top-rated banks but the number of such banks has declined. Moreover, due to risk-based capital requirements, the economic benefit for banks to issue a LOC has declined. Hence, LOCs have become a more costly form of credit enhancement.

Pool Insurance

In securitizations involving residential mortgage loans, *pool insurance policies* cover losses that are a result of defaults and foreclosures. The policy is typically written for a dollar amount of coverage that continues in force throughout the life of the asset pool. However, some policies are written so that the dollar amount of coverage declines as the pool seasons as long as two conditions are met: (1) the credit performance is better than expected and (2) the rating agencies that rated the issue approve. Because only defaults and foreclosures are covered, additional insurance must be obtained to cover losses resulting from bankruptcy (i.e., court-mandated modification of mortgage debt), fraud arising in the origination process, and special hazards (i.e., losses resulting from events not covered by a standard homeowner's insurance policy).

SIZING OF CREDIT ENHANCEMENTS

The size of the credit enhancement is one of the most critical factors in driving the economics of the transaction. The size of credit enhancement depends on the target rating sought for the bond classes in the proposed structure. In this section, we review how the "sizing" of the credit enhancement is determined by the rating agencies.

In quantifying the credit enhancement, the rating agencies analyze the sources available to absorb losses and keep the rated bond classes protected against losses. The losses for the asset pool are first quantified based on assumptions that the rating agencies have validated based on their historical experience with a similar statistical static pool. Then the rating agencies stress test the assumptions over a particular range of probable scenarios based on the ratings sought for the bond classes.

For every rated bond class, there will be some probability of default over time. The highest credit rating means highest safety in terms of risk of default, not absolute safety against default. Rating agencies have ample empirical evidence regarding the performance of their ratings on corporate bonds. It has only been in the past few years or so where enough empirical evidence on the performance of their ratings on asset-backed securities has become available.

Rating agencies publish two types of tables. One is the probability of default over time by rating category and is sometimes referred to as a *mortality table*. The second type is a *rating transition matrix*. This table shows how over a period of time the rating has changed for each rating category.

Let look at how information about the historical mortality table is used in sizing the credit enhancement. Suppose a rating agency is considering a five-year transaction and that the rating agency's mortality table for a five-year probability of default by rating is as follows:

	Probability of Default (mortality rate)	Survival Rate (confidence level)
AAA	0.03%	99.97%
AA	0.50%	99.50%
A	0.28%	99.72%
BBB	7.64%	92.36%
BB	12.17%	87.83%
B	28.32%	71.68%
CCC	47.30%	52.70%

For example, for a BBB rated bond class, the mortality rate is 7.64%, or alternatively, there is a 92.36% probability that the bond class will survive (not necessarily with the same rating) at the end of five years. Consequently, in order for a bond class to be rated BBB, for example, there has to be sufficient credit enhancement to cover 92.36% of the probable loss scenarios.

Suppose that the collateral is a pool of retail loans. It is assumed that there is a very low to no correlation as between the different obligors in the asset pool and further assume that the probability of default for each obligor is the same. The rate of default for a pool of retail loans is like a hazard rate commonly used in engineering applications for the rate of failure over a time period. In finance, it is used to estimate the number of defaults per unit of time. In the analysis of a pool of retail loans, historical hazard rates can be estimated; the probability that the actual rate will be higher or lower than several multiples of the historical rate can be assessed.

The key in sizing is to stress test the default rate so as to reach the confidence levels required for the target rating level sought for a bond class by the securitizer. In the case of a pool of retail loans, rating agencies use the following process to stress test the multiples to the cumulative losses implied by the asset pool data. First, the expected loss for the asset pool is estimated. This is done by first projecting the asset pool data based on normal assumptions of scheduled payments, prepayments, and defaults. From that projection, the cumulative loss for the entire term of the asset pool is computed.[6] Then the cumulative loss is the *expected loss* or *base case loss*, that is, the loss without applying any stress testing. Second, given the expected loss, the stress tests are then applied. The stress tests may be applied by multiplying the default rate, or by multiplying the expected loss, by multiples based on the required confidence levels established by the rating agency. Rating agencies use these multipliers to apply to the expected loss number. The typical multipliers used by Standard and Poor's in the case of auto loan transactions, for example, are as follows by rating category:

---

[6] Note that the cumulative loss for the asset pool cannot be found by the product of the annual default rate and the number of years. This is because due to amortization and prepayments, the loss rate is applied on an ever-reducing size of the asset pool.

AAA	4–5× base case losses
AA	3–4×
A	2–3×
BBB	1.75–2×
BB	1.5–1.75×

Note that rating agencies will use different multiplies for different asset types. When there is a lack of data available for an asset type or any other relevant factor, the multipliers may be increased.

As an example, assume the following for an asset pool:

Default rate per annum: 0.5%
Base case loss for the asset pool: 1.68%

Suppose that a proposed structure will have a bond class with each rating shown in the previous table and an unrated bond class. Using the higher multiples for each rating category in the table above for purposes of this example, the sizing of credit enhancements for each category rating is:

Rating	Multiplier	Required Support	Size of Liabilities
AAA	5	8.40%	91.60%
AA	4	6.72%	1.68%
A	3	5.04%	1.68%
BBB	2	3.36%	1.68%
BB	1.75	2.94%	0.42%
Unrated			2.94%

The required support for a given rating in the above table has been worked out by multiplying the base case loss by the corresponding multiplier shown. For example, because a rating of AAA requires a credit support of 8.4%, the size of a AAA rated bond is 91.6% (1 – 8.4%). Likewise, the size of each class is computed by deducting from the enhancement required at one level above, the enhancement required at the class level.

The sizing of credit enhancement may be done by using more elaborate statistical techniques. One such technique applied in the case of retail loans uses the lognormal distribution. This technique assumes that default rates are lognormally distributed, with a certain mean and standard deviation. The mean and the standard deviation are obtained from historical data. The required enhancement levels are then worked out, being the area under the lognormal probability distribution curve that gives the required confidence level for the target rating. The higher the standard deviation, the higher will be the required enhancement level. In case of wholesale loan pools, the size of the enhancement may be worked out using a binomial distribution or simulation approaches.

KEY POINTS OF THE CHAPTER

➤ *Credit enhancements are mechanisms for providing credit support for a securitization transaction.*

➤ *The type of asset securitized and the type of investor targeted dictates the nature and extent of credit enhancement required in a transaction.*

➤ *The credit enhancement level for every bond class in a structure to be rated is based on the target rating sought for that bond class.*

➤ *Because all credit enhancement has a cost associated with it, in creating the structure the structurer will perform an economic analysis of the cost of further enhancement versus the improved execution of the transaction.*

➤ *The amount of credit enhancement needed to obtain a specific credit rating is specified by the rating agencies from which a rating is sought and is referred to as the sizing of the transaction.*

➤ *The mechanisms for credit enhancement can be classified into three categories: (1) originator-provided, (2) structural, and (3) third-party provided.*

➤ *Originator-provided credit enhancement refers to credit support where a part of the credit risk of the asset pool is assumed by the originator/seller and includes cash, assets in excess of the liabilities, and retained profits.*

➤ Excess spread, the most natural form of originator-provided credit enhancement and the one that is least burdensome to the originator/seller, is the interest not paid to the bondholders nor used to pay fees.

➤ If the excess spread is not paid to the originator/seller either up-front or over a specified period, it is retained by the SPV (said to be "trapped") in a spread account to meet future losses from the asset pool.

➤ Excess spread is a soft credit enhancement because the amount of credit enhancement available from the asset pool changes over time due to prepayments and defaults and hence full credit is typically not given by the rating agencies when it is used as a form of credit enhancement.

➤ A cash collateral or cash reserve to meet losses can be created in a structure by the originator/seller in one of the following ways: (1) at the inception of the transaction with the cash in the account being subject to withdrawal in the event of losses that exceed the amount provided by other forms of credit enhancement; (2) from a subordinated loan to the SPV; or (3) the trapping of the excess spread.

➤ Unlike excess spread which is a soft credit enhancement, cash collateral provided at the inception of the transaction and a sub-ordinated loan are forms of hard credit enhancement because the amount of the credit enhancement is known.

➤ Overcollateralization is one of the most common forms of origi-nator/seller credit enhancement wherein the originator/seller transfers an asset pool that has a market value that exceeds the amount paid by the SPV.

➤ The amount of the overcollateralization in a securitization trans-action is equal to the difference between the par value of the assets transferred and the price paid for the assets by the SPV.

➤ When overcollateralization is used as form of credit enhancement, there may be early amortization triggers that provide for the early repayment of principal of the bond classes if the performance of the pool worsens as gauged by the one or more specified tests.

➢ *Structural credit enhancement refers to credit enhancement cre-ated by the redistribution of credit risks among the bond classes comprising the structure, such that one bond class provides credit enhancement to the other bond classes.*

➢ *The most common form of structural credit enhancement for securitization transactions is the stratification of the bond classes into senior, mezzanine, and junior (or subordinated) bond classes which is done so as to achieve a triple-A rating for the senior-most bond class and a rating for the juniormost-rated bond class that is sellable in the market.*

➢ *Third-party credit enhancement refers to the assumption of credit risk by parties other than the originator and the other bond classes in the structure.*

➢ *Third-party credit enhancements are available from monoline insurance companies, letters of credit, and pool insurance poli-cies.*

➢ *Third-party credit enhancements are subject to third-party credit risk, the risk that the third-party guarantor may be either down-graded and, depending on the performance of the asset pool, the bond classes guaranteed may be downgraded, or the third-party may be unable to satisfy its commitment.*

➢ *The size of the credit enhancement is one of the most critical factors driving the economics of a securitization transaction, the amount depending on the target rating sought for the bond classes in the proposed structure.*

➢ *The rating agencies analyze the sources available to absorb losses and still keep the rated bond classes protected against losses when they size a securitization transaction.*

➢ *The expected losses or base case losses are quantified based on assumptions that the rating agencies have validated based on the historical experience with a similar statistical static pool and then the expected losses are stress-tested over a particular range of probable scenarios based on the ratings sought for the bond classes.*

➤ *The stress tests utilized by the rating agencies may be applied by multiplying the default rate, or by multiplying the expected loss, by multiples based on the required confidence levels established by the rating agency.*

CHAPTER 6

Use of Interest Rate Derivatives in Securitization Transactions

In this chapter, we explain the use of interest rate derivatives in securitization transactions for hedging and yield enhancement. Three types of over-the-counter interest rate derivatives commonly used in securitizations are interest rate swaps, interest rate caps, and interest rate corridors. Because they are over-the-counter instruments, they expose the trust (the *special-purpose vehicle* (SPV)) to counterparty risk.

INTEREST RATE SWAPS

An *interest rate swap* provides a vehicle for market participants to transform the nature of cash flows and the interest rate exposure of a portfolio, balance sheet, particular asset or liability, or structured transaction.

In an interest rate swap, two parties (called *counterparties*) agree to exchange periodic interest payments. The dollar amount of the interest payments exchanged is based on some predetermined dollar principal, which is called the *notional amount*. The dollar amount each counterparty pays to the other is the agreed-upon periodic interest rate times the notional amount. The only dollars that are exchanged between the parties are the interest payments, not the notional amount. Accordingly, the notional principal serves only as a scale factor to translate an interest rate into a cash flow. In the most common type of swap, one party agrees to pay the other party fixed interest payments at designated dates for the life of the contract. This party is referred to as the *fixed rate payer*. The other party, who agrees to make interest rate payments that float with some reference rate, is referred to as the *fixed rate receiver*.

The reference rates that have been used for the floating rate in an interest rate swap are various money market rates: Treasury bill rate, London interbank offered rate, commercial paper rate, bankers acceptances rate, certificates of deposit rate, federal funds rate, and prime rate. The most common is the *London Interbank Offered Rate* (LIBOR). LIBOR is the rate at which prime banks offer to pay on eurodollar and other currency deposits available to other prime banks for a given maturity. There is not just one rate but a rate for different maturities. For example, there is a one-month LIBOR, three-month LIBOR, and six-month LIBOR. Similarly, there are various Treasury bill rates, bankers acceptances rates, certificates of deposit rates, and so forth with different maturities quoted by different financial institutions. Interest rate swap agreements and other financial agreements define exactly which rates are used and how they are set.

An interest rate swap between two counterparties is illustrated in Figure 6.1. We assume that for the next five years party X agrees to pay party Y 10% per year, while party Y agrees to pay party X six-month LIBOR (the reference rate). Party X is the fixed rate payer, while party Y is the fixed rate receiver. Assume that the notional amount is $50 million, and that payments are exchanged every six months for the next five years. This means that every six months, party X (the fixed rate payer) will pay party Y $2.5 million (10% times $50 million divided by 2). The amount that party Y (fixed rate receiver) will pay party X will be six-month LIBOR times $50 million divided by 2. If six-month LIBOR is 7%, party Y will pay party X $1.75 million (7% times $50 million divided by 2). Note that we divide by two because one-half year's interest is being paid.

FIGURE 6.1 Diagram of Interest Rate Swap Between Two Counterparties

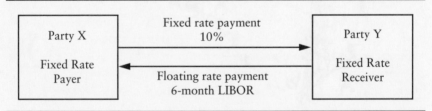

Interest rate swaps are over-the-counter instruments. This means that they are not traded on an exchange. Consequently, the risks that each party takes when it enters into a swap is that the other party will fail to fulfill its obligations as set forth in the swap agreement. That is, each party faces default risk, known in this case as *counterparty risk*. In any agreement between two parties that must perform according to the terms of a contract, counterparty risk is the risk that the other party will default. With futures and exchange-traded options the counterparty risk is the risk that the clearinghouse will default. Market participants view this risk as small. In contrast, counterparty risk in a swap can be significant.

Interpreting a Swap Position

There are two ways that a swap position can be interpreted: (1) a package of forward/futures contracts and (2) a package of cash flows from buying and selling cash market instruments.

Package of Forward Contracts

Consider the hypothetical interest rate swap used earlier to illustrate a swap. Let us look at party X's position. Party X has agreed to pay 10% and receive six-month LIBOR. More specifically, assuming a $50 million notional amount, X has agreed to buy a commodity called "six-month LIBOR" for $2.5 million. This is effectively a six-month forward contract where X agrees to pay $2.5 million in exchange for delivery of six-month LIBOR. The fixed rate payer is effectively long a six-month forward contract on six-month LIBOR. The floating rate payer is effectively short a six-month forward contract on six-month LIBOR. There is therefore an implicit forward contract corresponding to each exchange date.

Consequently, interest rate swaps can be viewed as a package of more basic interest rate derivative instruments—forwards.

Package of Cash Market Instruments

To understand why a swap can also be interpreted as a package of cash market instruments, consider an investor who enters into the transaction below:

- Buy $50 million par value of a five-year floating rate bond that pays six-month LIBOR every six months.
- Finance the purchase by borrowing $50 million for five years at a 10% annual interest rate paid every six months.

The cash flows for this transaction are set forth in Table 6.1. The second column of the exhibit shows the cash flows from purchasing the five-year floating rate bond. There is a $50 million cash outlay and then 10 cash inflows. The amount of the cash inflows is uncertain because they depend on future levels of six-month LIBOR. The next column shows the cash flows from borrowing $50 million on a fixed rate basis. The last column shows the net cash flows from the entire

TABLE 6.1　Cash Flows for the Purchase of a Five-Year, Floating Rate Bond Financed by Borrowing on a Fixed Rate Basis
Transaction:

- Purchase for $50 million a five-year floating rate bond:
  Floating rate = LIBOR, semiannual pay

- Borrow $50 million for five years:
  Fixed rate = 10%, semiannual payments

6-Month Period	Cash Flow (in millions of dollars) from:		
	Floating Rate Bond[a]	Borrowing Cost	Net
0	$-\$50$	$+\$50.0$	$\$0$
1	$+ (LIBOR_1/2) \times 50$	-2.5	$+ (LIBOR_1/2) \times 50 - 2.5$
2	$+ (LIBOR_2/2) \times 50$	-2.5	$+ (LIBOR_2/2) \times 50 - 2.5$
3	$+ (LIBOR_3/2) \times 50$	-2.5	$+ (LIBOR_3/2) \times 50 - 2.5$
4	$+ (LIBOR_4/2) \times 50$	-2.5	$+ (LIBOR_4/2) \times 50 - 2.5$
5	$+ (LIBOR_5/2) \times 50$	-2.5	$+ (LIBOR_5/2) \times 50 - 2.5$
6	$+ (LIBOR_6/2) \times 50$	-2.5	$+ (LIBOR_6/2) \times 50 - 2.5$
7	$+ (LIBOR_7/2) \times 50$	-2.5	$+ (LIBOR_7/2) \times 50 - 2.5$
8	$+ (LIBOR_8/2) \times 50$	-2.5	$+ (LIBOR_8/2) \times 50 - 2.5$
9	$+ (LIBOR_9/2) \times 50$	-2.5	$+ (LIBOR_9/2) \times 50 - 2.5$
10	$+ (LIBOR_{10}/2) \times 50 + 50$	-52.5	$+ (LIBOR_{10}/2) \times 50 - 2.5$

[a] The subscript for LIBOR indicates the six-month LIBOR as per the terms of the floating rate bond at time t.

transaction. As the last column indicates, there is no initial cash flow (the cash inflow and cash outlay offset each other). In all 10 six-month periods, the net position results in a cash inflow of LIBOR and a cash outlay of $2.5 million. This net position, however, is identical to the position of a fixed rate payer/floating rate receiver.

It can be seen from the net cash flow in Table 6.1 that a fixed rate payer has a cash market position that is equivalent to a long position in a floating rate bond and a short position in a fixed rate bond—the short position being the equivalent of borrowing by issuing a fixed rate bond.

What about the position of a floating rate payer? It can be easily demonstrated that the position of a floating rate payer is equivalent to purchasing a fixed rate bond and financing that purchase at a floating rate, where the floating rate is the reference rate for the swap. That is, the position of a floating rate payer is equivalent to a long position in a fixed rate bond and a short position in a floating rate bond.

Terminology, Conventions, and Market Quotes

Here we review some of the terminology used in the swaps market and explain how swaps are quoted. The *trade date* for a swap is the date on which the swap is transacted. The terms of the trade include the fixed interest rate, the maturity, the notional amount of the swap, and the payment bases of both legs of the swap. The date from which floating interest payments are determined is the *reset* or *setting date*, which may also be the trade date. The rate is fixed two business days before the interest period begins. The second (and subsequent) reset date will be two business days before the beginning of the second (and subsequent) swap periods. The *effective date* is the date from which interest on the swap is calculated, and this is typically two business days after the trade date. In a *forward-start swap* the effective date will be at some point in the future, specified in the swap terms. The floating interest rate for each period is fixed at the start of the period, so that the interest payment amount is known in advance by both parties (the fixed rate is known of course, throughout the swap by both parties).

While our illustrations assume that the timing of the cash flows for both the fixed rate payer and floating rate payer will be the same, this is rarely the case in a swap. An agreement may call for the fixed rate payer to make payments annually but the floating rate payer to make payments more frequently (semiannually or quarterly). Also, the way in which interest accrues on each leg of the transaction differs. Normally, the fixed interest payments are paid on the basis of a 30/360 day count. Floating rate payments for dollar and euro-denominated swaps use an actual/360 day count similar to other money market instruments in those currencies. Sterling-denominated swaps use an actual/365 day count.

Accordingly, the fixed interest payments will differ slightly owing to the differences in the lengths of successive coupon periods. The floating payments will differ owing to day counts as well as movements in the reference rate.

The terminology used to describe the position of a party in the swap markets combines cash and futures market jargons, given that a swap position can be interpreted either as a position in a package of cash market instruments or a package of futures/forward positions. As we have said, the counterparty to an interest rate swap is either a fixed rate payer or floating rate payer.

The fixed rate payer receives floating rate interest and is said to be "long" or to have "bought" the swap. The long side has conceptually purchased a floating rate note (because it receives floating rate interest) and issued a fixed coupon bond (because it pays out fixed interest at periodic intervals). In essence, the fixed rate payer is borrowing at fixed rate and investing in a floating rate asset. The fixed rate receiver is said to be "short" or to have "sold" the swap. The short side has conceptually purchased a coupon bond (because it receives fixed rate interest) and issued a floating rate note (because it pays floating rate interest). A fixed rate receiver is borrowing at a floating rate and investing in a fixed rate asset.

The convention that has evolved for quoting swaps is that a swap dealer sets the floating rate equal to the reference rate and then quotes the fixed rate that will apply. To illustrate this convention, consider the following 10-year swap terms available from a dealer:

- Fixed rate receiver:
  Pay floating rate of three-month LIBOR quarterly.
  Receive fixed rate of 8.75% semiannually.

■ Fixed rate payer:
Pay fixed rate of 8.85% semiannually.
Receive floating rate of three-month LIBOR quarterly.

The offer price that the dealer would quote the fixed rate payer would be to pay 8.85% and receive LIBOR flat. (The word *flat* means with no spread.) The bid price that the dealer would quote the floating rate payer would be to pay LIBOR flat and receive 8.75%. The bid offer spread is 10 basis points.

The swap will specify the frequency of settlement for the fixed rate payments. The frequency need not be the same as for the floating rate payments.

Assume that the frequency of settlement is quarterly for the fixed rate payments, the same as with the floating rate payments. The day count convention is the same as for the floating rate payment, actual/360. The equation for determining the dollar amount of the fixed rate payment for the period is

$$\text{Notional amount} \times (\text{Swap rate}) \times \frac{\text{No. of days in period}}{360}$$

It is the same equation as for determining the floating rate payment except that the swap rate is used instead of the reference rate (three-month LIBOR in our illustration).

For example, suppose that the swap rate is 4.98% and the quarter has 90 days. Then the fixed rate payment for the quarter is

$$\$100,000,000 \times 0.0498 \times \frac{90}{360} = \$1,245,000$$

If there are 92 days in a quarter, the fixed rate payment for the quarter is

$$\$100,000,000 \times 0.0498 \times \frac{92}{360} = \$1,272,667$$

Note that the rate is fixed for each quarter but the dollar amount of the payment depends on the number of days in the period.

Nongeneric Interest Rate Swaps Used in Securitizations

The swap market is very flexible and instruments can be tailor-made to fit the requirements of a structured transaction. A wide variety of swap contracts are traded in the market. The types most often used in securitizations are amortizing swaps and basis swaps.

In a plain vanilla swap, the notional principal remains unchanged during the life of the swap. However, in securitization transaction where the collateral amortizes, to avoid overhedging an amortizing swap can is used. In an *amortizing swap* the notional amount declines over time based on a predetermined amortization schedule, actual collateral balance, or the actual bond balance.

In a conventional swap, one leg comprises fixed rate payments and the other floating rate payments. In a *basis swap* both legs are floating rate, but linked to different money market indices. One leg is normally linked to LIBOR, while the other might be linked to the commercial paper rate.

Use in Securitizations[1]

An interest rate swap can be used to alter the cash flow characteristics of the assets (liabilities) to match the characteristics of the liabilities (assets). For example, suppose a transaction has a pool of fixed rate, monthly payment loans but the bond classes that are supported by the collateral have floating rate, monthly payment characteristics. A generic or plain vanilla swap can be used to convert the monthly, fixed rate cash flows to monthly, floating rate cash flows based on the reference rate and margin owed to the covered classes of bonds. For example, the prospectus supplement of the Toyota Auto Receivables 2003-B Owner Trust, $554,000,000 Floating Rate Asset Backed Notes, Class A-3 states:

> In order to issue the Class A-3 Notes bearing interest at a floating rate when the Receivables bear fixed interest rates, the Trust will enter into the Swap Agreement with the Swap Counterparty. Pursuant to the Swap Agreement, on each Payment Date the Trust is obligated to pay to the Swap Coun-

---

[1] This section and the discussion on the application of caps and corridors to securitizations draw from Fabozzi, Morel, and Grow (2005).

terparty in respect of the Class A-3 Notes an amount equal to the amount deemed to accrue on a notional amount equal to the outstanding principal balance of the Class A-3 Notes as of the preceding Payment Date at a fixed rate of interest of 2.295% (the "Class A-3 Notional Rate") calculated on an 30/360 basis (the "Class A-3 Swap Interest Amount"). The amount to be paid by the Swap Counterparty in respect of the Class A-3 Notes on any Payment Date will be the amount of interest that accrued thereon at the related floating interest rate from the preceding Payment Date to such current Payment Date (the "Class A-3 Interest Amount").

Any net amounts payable by the Trust to the Swap Counterparty on any Payment Date will be deducted from Collections for the related Collection Period prior to making any payments of interest or principal of the Notes.

In the above example, the trust pays a fixed rate to the counterparty in exchange for a floating rate. In other securitizations, the payments are reversed and the trust pays a floating rate to the counterparty in exchange for a fixed rate. For example, in the Citibank Credit Card Issuance Trust, $500,000,000, 4.75%, Class 2003-A10 Notes of December 2013 transaction, the class-A notes are paid a fixed rate of interest, but the assets (credit card receivables in this example) generate a floating rate of interest. This mismatch is hedged through the use of an amortizing swap where the trust pays LIBOR plus a margin to the counterparty in exchange for a fixed rate that is passed on to the ABS noteholders. The following language is taken from the related prospectus supplement:

Under the interest rate swap, the issuer will pay interest monthly to the swap counterparty on the notional amount based on a floating rate of interest equal to one-month LIBOR plus a margin not greater than 0.21% per annum and the swap counterparty will pay interest monthly to the issuer on the notional amount based on the rate of interest applicable to these Class A notes.

The issuer's net swap payments will be paid out of funds available in the interest funding subaccount for these Class A notes. Net swap receipts from the swap counterparty will be deposited into the interest funding subaccount for these Class A notes and will be available to pay interest on these Class A notes.

An amortizing swap is used in certain types of securitizations when the collateral amortizes over time. Hence, the fixed notional amount for a plain vanilla swap when a hedge is initially placed will become overhedged as the pool pays down and an amortizing swap mitigates this exposure. For example, the notional amount depends on the actual collateral balance in the KeyCorp Student Loan Trust 2003-A, Asset-Backed Notes transaction. The related prospectus supplement states:

> In accordance with the terms of the Group I Interest Rate Swap, on each Distribution Date, the Trust will owe the Swap Counterparty the sum of the following amounts for each of the monthly periods in the related Collection Period, beginning with the monthly period commencing September 1, 2003 (each, a "Net Trust Swap Payment"): (I) the product of:
>
> 1. the Commercial Paper Rate as determined as of the first day of the related monthly period;
> 2. the aggregate principal balance of the Commercial Paper Rate Loans as determined as of the first day of the related monthly period; and
> 3. a fraction, the numerator of which is the actual number of days in the related monthly period and the denominator of which is 360.

And, in accordance with the terms of the Group I Interest Rate Swap, on each Distribution Date, the Swap Counterparty will owe the Trust an amount equal to the sum of the following amounts for each of the monthly periods in the related Collection Period beginning with the monthly period commencing September 1, 2003 (each, a "Net Trust Swap Receipt"): (II) the product of:

> 1. Three-Month LIBOR (calculated in the same manner and on such dates as such index is calculated for the Notes for the related interest period) less 0.15%;

2. the aggregate principal balance of the Commercial Paper Rate Loans as determined as of the first day of the related monthly period; and

3. a fraction, the numerator of which is the actual number of days in the related monthly period and the denominator of which is 360.

Payments will be made on a net basis with respect to each of the Group I Interest Rate Swap between the Trust and the Swap Counterparty, in an amount equal to the excess of (I) over (II) above for the related Collection Period, in the case of a Net Trust Swap Payment, or the excess of (II) over (I) above for the related Collection Period, in the case of a Net Trust Swap Receipt.

Similarly, issuers of notes backed by credit card receivables use amortizing swaps where the notional amount is tied to the principal amount of the liability. The following excerpt taken from the prospectus supplement related to the Citibank Credit Card Issuance Trust, $500,000,000, 4.75%, Class 2003-A10 Notes of December 2013 issue, demonstrates this feature:

The interest rate swap will have a notional amount equal to the outstanding dollar principal amount of these Class A notes and will terminate on the expected principal payment date of these Class A notes.

Basis Risk

Interest rate derivatives are also used in securitizations to hedge against interest rate scenarios where the benchmark index for the liabilities may rise more rapidly than the asset benchmark index. This mismatch in indexes is called *basis risk*. The trust's interest liability to bondholders, subject to credit enhancement, is limited to the amount of interest generated by the collateral. This basis risk shortfall is a risk to investors that can be mitigated by incorporating interest rate derivatives into the transactions.

Transactions can mitigate interest rate and basis risk for different collateral payment characteristics by utilizing multiple interest rate derivatives. For example, the prospectus of the GE Commercial Equipment Financing LLC, Series 2003-1, $376,946,000 Asset-Backed Notes states:

> The DB Swap Agreement will include confirmations for three separate swap transactions, under which the Issuer will receive amounts based on LIBOR and pay amounts based upon a fixed rate of interest, an index based upon commercial paper rates ("CP"), and a constant treasury maturity index ("CMT"), as applicable.
>
> The GECS Swap Agreement will include one confirmation for a swap transaction under which the Issuer will receive amounts based on LIBOR and pay amounts based on an index based upon the interest rate on the Hybrid Loans.
>
> Under each Swap Agreement only the net amount due by the Issuer or by the applicable Swap Counterparty, will be remitted on each Payment Date. All net amounts received by the Issuer will be included in the Available Amounts on the Payment Date such net amounts are received.
>
> "CMT Rate" means, with respect to any Interest Accrual Period, a rate based upon the one-year constant treasury maturity index applicable to the CMT Loans.
>
> "CP Rate" means, with respect to any Interest Accrual Period, a rate based upon the rate listed for "1-Month" Commercial Paper (NonFinancial) as stated in the Federal Reserve Statistical Release H.15 (519).
>
> "Hybrid Rate" means, with respect to any Interest Accrual Period, a rate based upon a weighted average of the interest rate index applicable to the Hybrid Loans.

Use of Proceeds

From a credit perspective, the rating agencies consider interest rate derivatives to be cash flow neutral. This means that interest rate derivatives are not expected to cover loss nor build overcollateralization. Just as it is possible if the transaction is in the money and extra cash flow from the derivatives can be used to cover loss and pay down bonds, it is equally possible that when the transaction is out of the money, cash has to be diverted from covering loss and paying down bonds.[2] However, provisions must be made for how proceeds from interest rate derivatives will be used if there are any excess proceeds.

The proceeds from interest rate derivatives are utilized in the waterfall for one or more of the following three purposes:

1. Cover losses on the collateral.
2. Build overcollateralization by paying off bond principal.[3]
3. Cover basis risk shortfall.

Proceeds are directed to these purposes in the waterfall and can be prioritized in any order. It is important to understand the use of the proceeds when analyzing the impact of the derivative on bond cash flows.

In securitizations backed by residential mortgage loans that utilize excess interest and overcollateralization as credit support, proceeds from the typical swap will be used to cover losses and build overcollateralization prior to being applied to basis risk shortfall (the difference between the certificate coupon and the available funds cap).[4] Following is an example from the Structured Asset Investment Loan Trust Mortgage Pass-Through Certificates, Series 2005-4 issue, which demonstrates this priority of payments:

> (1) to the Swap Counterparty, any Net Swap Payment owed to the Swap Counterparty pursuant to the Swap Agreement for such Distribution Date;
>
> (2) to the Swap Counterparty, any unpaid Swap Termination Payment not due to a Swap Counterparty Trigger Event owed

---

[2] As a matter of fact, the negative cash flow impact of the swap payments on pre-2001 CBO transactions, and pre-9/11 aircraft ABS transactions are examples of how such derivatives can be a burden to these deals.

[3] Using interest to pay down the principal of a bonds prior to the scheduled repayment date is referred to as "turboing" bonds.

[4] An available funds cap is included in transactions backed by adjustable-rate residential mortgage loans because the loans are typically benchmarked to six-month LIBOR and the securities issued by the SPV are benchmarked to one-month LIBOR (hence there is basis risk). Hence, for any month the available interest from the loans may be less than the amount due the bondholders. The available funds cap restricts the amount due to the bondholders to the interest available.

to the Swap Counterparty pursuant to the Swap Agreement; (3) to the Offered Certificates, Current Interest and any Carryforward Interest for each such class for such Distribution Date, for application in accordance with the same priorities set forth in clauses A(ii) through (iv) and B(ii) through (iv) under "—Interest Payment Priorities" above, to the extent unpaid pursuant to such clauses; (4) to the Offered Certificates, any amount necessary to maintain the Targeted Overcollateralization Amount specified in clauses (1) and (2) under "—Credit Enhancement—Application of Monthly Excess Cashflow" above for such Distribution Date, for application pursuant to the priorities set forth in such clauses, after giving effect to distributions pursuant to such clauses; (5) to the Offered Certificates, any Basis Risk Shortfalls and Unpaid Basis Risk Shortfalls for each such class and for such Distribution Date, for application pursuant to the priorities set forth in clauses (3)(a) and (b) under "—Credit Enhancement—Application of Monthly Excess Cashflow" above, to the extent unpaid pursuant to such clauses;

On the other hand, some securitization transactions backed by residential mortgage loans use the swap proceeds to cover basis risk shortfall prior to covering losses and building overcollateralization. This type of waterfall is a deviation from the distribution waterfall that caps certificate interest payments at the available funds cap. Since the total swap proceeds is reduced by the basis risk shortfall payment prior to covering losses and building overcollateralization in this structure, the swap will provide less credit enhancement for the certificates, but will help reduce basis risk. Following is an excerpt from the prospectus supplement for the Bear Stearns Asset Backed Securities I Trust 2005-HE5 Asset-Backed Certificates, Series 2005-HE5 issue, which demonstrates this type of structure:

. . . the Swap Administrator will withdraw the following amounts from the Swap Account to remit to the trustee for distribution to the certificates in the following order of priority:

first, to each class of Class A Certificates, on a pro rata basis, to pay accrued interest and any Interest Carry Forward Amount to the extent due to the interest portion of a Realized Loss with respect to the related mortgage loans, in each case to the extent not fully paid as described under "Description of the Certificates—Distributions on the Certificates—Interest Distributions" above;

second, sequentially to the Class M-1, Class M-2, Class M-3, Class M-4, Class M-5, Class M-6, Class M-7 and Class M-8 Certificates, in that order, to pay accrued interest, in each case to the extent not fully paid as described under "Description of the Certificates—Distributions on the Certificates—Interest Distributions" above, and any Interest Carry Forward Amount to the extent due to the interest portion of a Realized Loss with respect to the related mortgage loans;

third, to pay, first to the Class A Certificates, on a pro rata basis, and second, sequentially to the Class M-1, Class M-2, Class M-3, Class M-4, Class M-5, Class M-6, Class M-7 and Class M-8 Certificates, in that order, any Basis Risk Shortfall Carry Forward Amounts for such distribution date; and

fourth, to pay as principal to the Class A Certificates and Class M Certificates to be applied as part of the Extra Principal Distribution Amount to the extent that the Overcollateralization Amount is reduced below the Overcollateralization Target Amount as a result of Realized Losses and to the extent not covered by Excess Spread distributed in the same manner and priority as the Principal Distribution Amount; and as described under "Description of the Certificates—Excess Spread and Overcollateralization Provisions" above.

CAPS AND FLOORS

Caps are agreements between two parties, whereby one party for an up-front fee agrees to compensate the other if a designated interest rate (called the *reference rate*) exceeds a predetermined level. For a floor the payment is made if the reference rate is below a predetermined level. The party that benefits if the reference rate exceeds (in the case of a cap) or falls below (in the case of a floor) a predetermined level is called the *buyer*, and the party that must potentially make payments is called the *seller*. The predetermined interest rate level is called the *strike rate*. An interest rate cap specifies that the seller agrees to pay the buyer if the reference rate exceeds the strike rate. An interest rate floor specifies that the seller agrees to pay the buyer if the reference rate is below the strike rate.

The terms of an interest rate agreement include: (1) the reference rate; (2) the strike rate that sets the cap or floor; (3) the length of the agreement; (4) the frequency of reset; and (5) the notional amount (which determines the size of the payments). If a cap or a floor is in the money on the reset date, the payment by the seller is typically made in arrears.

A *cap* is essentially a strip of options. A borrower with an existing interest rate liability can protect against a rise in interest rates by purchasing a cap. If rates rise above the cap, the borrower will be compensated by the cap payout. Conversely, if rates fall the borrower gains from lower funding costs and the only expense is the up-front premium paid to purchase the cap. The payoff for the cap buyer at a reset date if the value of the reference rate exceeds the cap rate on that date is as follows:

Notional amount × (Value of the reference rate – Cap rate)
× (Number of days in settlement period/Number of days in year)

Naturally, if the reference rate is below the cap rate, the payoff is zero.

It is possible to protect against a drop in interest rates by purchasing a floor. This is exactly opposite of a cap in that a floor pays out when the reference rate falls below the strike rate. For the floor buyer, the payoff at a reset date is as follows if the value of the reference rate at the reset date is less than the floor rate:

Notional amount × (Floor rate – Value of the reference rate)
× (Number of days in settlement period/Number of days in a year)

The floor's payoff is zero if the reference rate is higher than the floor rate.

The combination of a cap and a floor creates a *collar*, which is a *corridor* that fixes interest payments or receipt levels. A collar is sometimes advantageous for borrowers because it has a lower cost than a straight cap. A collar protects against a rise in rates, and provides some gain if there is a fall down to the floor rate. The cheapest structure is a collar with a narrow spread between cap and floor rates.

Use in Securitizations

An interest rate cap can be used to hedge against a rise in interest rates. The buyer of the cap pays the seller of the cap an up-front fee for this right at closing. An interest rate corridor is an interest rate cap where the liability of the seller is limited to a specified maximum rate (ceiling) and naturally the cost to the buyer is reduced accordingly. As with an interest rate cap, the seller is compensated via a single up-front fee. For example, the prospectus of the Park Place Securities Inc., Asset-Backed Pass Through Certificates, Series 2004-WCW2 states:

> The following Certificates will have the benefit of an interest rate corridor: (i) the Class A-1 Certificates; (ii) the Group II Certificates; and (iii) the Mezzanine Certificates (collectively, the "Cap Contracts"). Pursuant to the Cap Contracts, Swiss Re Financial Products Corporation (together with any successor, the "Counterparty" or "Cap Provider") will agree to pay to the Trust a monthly payment in an amount equal to the product of: (1) for the Distribution Date in November 2004 through the Distribution Date in July 2008, the excess, if any, of one-month LIBOR over the rate set forth in the related Cap Contract, up to a maximum rate set forth in the related Cap Contract; (2) the lesser of (i) the notional amount for such interest accrual period set forth in the related Cap Contract and (ii) the aggregate Certificate Principal Balance of the related Certificates; and (3) a fraction, the numerator of which is the actual number of days in the related Interest

Accrual Period, and the denominator of which is 360. The notional amount declines in accordance with a schedule set forth in the related Cap Contract. The Cap Contracts will terminate after the final Distribution Date set forth above.

Another use for an interest rate cap or corridor is yield maintenance. This is seen quite often in *mortgage-backed securities* (MBS) *net interest margin* (NIM) transactions. NIM securities, discussed later in this chapter, are bonds structured to receive cash flows from excess spreads to the extent there are any. A typical MBS NIM transaction is a short-term principal and interest instrument with three primary sources of funds, including any prepayment penalties, residual released from an underlying MBS transaction (usually certificated as class X and class P), and payments from a cap or corridor (also called a *yield maintenance agreement*). The NIM usually pays a fixed or floating interest rate, which is paid first in the NIM distribution waterfall, and all remaining funds are applied to principal. Prepayment penalty and residual cash flow are not extremely stable sources of funds. Since the NIM trust must pay interest to the NIM noteholders each month, the structure will typically include a cap or corridor to help stabilize the cash flow and ensure that timely interest will be paid to NIM noteholders.

COUNTERPARTY RISK

The use of derivative instruments introduces counterparty risk for the trust, and therefore the way counterparty risk is managed in securitizations should be understood.

The risk of counterparty default can be partially mitigated by entering into swaps with highly rated counterparties and using commonly developed methods in the derivatives market for doing so (e.g., margin, netting, and overcollateralization). The majority of the swaps in securitizations involving investment-grade-rated notes contain rating triggers specifying certain steps that must be taken by the counterparty if its debt rating migrates below a certain level. Typically, the counterparty must, at its own cost and within a specified time period, usually 30 days, either (1) find a replacement counterparty with a rating higher than the rating specified in the trigger; (2)

post a specified amount of collateral; or (3) obtain a guarantee from an entity with a rating higher than the rating specified in the trigger. The counterparty may also need to receive confirmation from the specified rating agencies that the rating of the notes will not move downward as a result of these actions. If the counterparty does not satisfy these requirements, then depending on the swap documents, either the swap is terminated automatically or the trust may have the option of terminating the swap. Upon a termination of the swap, it is probable that there would be a swap termination payment due by the trust to the swap counterparty or from the counterparty to the trust.

The rating trigger decreases but does not eliminate the trust's potential exposure to interest rate and counterparty risk. To illustrate, if the swap counterparty is downgraded below its rating trigger, it may decide to pursue (1), (2), or (3) described previously. Since there is a finite number of swap providers to the marketplace, a downgrade below a rating trigger could require a swap provider to pursue these remedies for a very large number of swaps. This would translate to a very high cost to the counterparty at a time when its credit situation is already deteriorating. Alternatively, the counterparty may not pursue the remedies described above, thereby either automatically terminating the swap or leaving the decision to the trustee (noteholders) whether or not to terminate the swap.

If the trustee does not terminate the swap, then the transaction is exposed to a counterparty in a deteriorating credit situation for the future payments due under the swap agreement. If the swap is terminated, the trust may owe a sizeable termination payment to the counterparty. The method for determining the swap termination payment is specified in the swap documents for each transaction but typically it is based on the mark-to-market value of the swap. At the time of termination, the swap has a value based on its specified fixed and floating rates, the current and anticipated future interest rate environment, and remaining term of the swap. Depending on how interest rates have moved since the swap was initially settled, one of the parties will be in the money and one will be out of the money. The party that is out of the money will owe the value of its position to the party that is in the money. Therefore, if the swap is terminated, the trust will be exposed to the interest rate risk that it was trying to hedge and it may owe the counterparty a termination payment. Depending on where it is specified in the distribution waterfall, the termination payment could be senior to interest or principal that is due to the transaction's noteholders. When evaluating a transaction, one should consider the interest rate risk to which the trust is exposed without the hedge, the counterparty risk of rating downgrade or default, and the possibility of a potential termination payment being paid senior to current interest and principal due noteholders.

KEY POINTS OF THE CHAPTER

➤ *The types of OTC interest rate derivatives commonly used in securitizations are interest rate swaps, interest rate caps, and interest rate corridors.*

➤ *OTC derivatives expose the SPV to counterparty risk.*

➤ *In an interest rate swap, the two counterparties agree to exchange periodic interest payments based on some notional amount and some reference rate (typically LIBOR).*

➤ *An interest rate swap allows an SPV to transform the nature of the SPV's cash flows and interest rate exposure.*

➤ *There are two economic interpretations of an interest rate swap: (1) a package of forward/futures contracts and (2) a package of cash flows from buying and selling cash market instruments.*

➤ *There are different types of swaps that are used in securitization transactions: (1) plain vanilla swap, (2) amortizing swap, and (3) basis swap.*

➤ *In a plain vanilla swap the notional principal remains unchanged during the life of the swap with one party paying a fixed rate and the other party a floating rate based on a reference rate.*

➤ *In an amortizing swap the notional amount declines over time based on either a predetermined amortization schedule, actual collateral balance, or the actual bond balance*

➤ *In a basis swap both parties pay a floating rate based on different reference rates.*

➤ *An interest rate swap is used in securitization transactions to alter the cash flow characteristics of the assets (liabilities) to match the characteristics of the liabilities (assets).*

➤ *In a securitization involving collateral that is amortizing, an amortizing swap is employed to reduce the risk of overhedging.*

➤ *A basis swap is utilized in securitization transactions to hedge against basis risk: interest rate scenarios where the benchmark index for the liabilities may rise more rapidly than the asset benchmark index.*

➤ *The proceeds from interest rate derivatives are utilized in the waterfall for one or more of the following purposes: (1) cover losses on the collateral, (2) build overcollateralization by paying off bond principal, and (3) cover basis risk shortfall.*

➤ *Caps and floors are agreements between two parties, whereby one party for an up-front fee agrees to compensate the other if the reference rate is different from the strike rate.*

➤ *The buyer of a cap (floor) benefits if the reference rate exceeds (is below) the strike rate; the seller of a cap (floor) receives a premium but must make payments to the buyer if the reference rate exceeds (is below) the strike rate.*

➤ *The terms of a cap and a floor include: (1) the reference rate, (2) the strike rate, (3) the length of the agreement, (4) the frequency of reset, and (5) the notional amount.*

➤ *A collar is a combination of a cap and a floor, which is a corridor that fixes interest payments or receipt levels.*

➤ *In a securitization transaction, an interest rate cap can be used to hedge against a rise in interest rates and an interest rate corridor can be used as an interest rate cap where the liability of the seller is limited to a specified maximum rate (ceiling) with the cost to the buyer reduced accordingly.*

➤ *Another use for an interest rate cap or corridor in a securitization transaction is for yield maintenance.*

➤ *Because of counterparty risk, the majority of the swaps in securitizations involving investment-grade-rated notes contain rating triggers specifying certain steps that must be taken by the counterparty if its debt rating migrates below a certain level such as (1) find a replacement counterparty with a rating higher than the rating specified in the trigger, (2) post a specified amount of collateral, or (3) obtain a guarantee from an entity with a rating higher than the rating specified in the trigger.*

CHAPTER 7

Operational Issues in Securitization

Operational risk in securitization transactions has been the highlight of attention in recent years, and clearly operational risks are more significant than the risks of legal structure. Challenges to legal structure of the transaction happen only in remote contingencies such as bankruptcy. However, if there is an operational hiccup, it may affect the cash flows immediately.

Operational risks refer to the risk that any of the agents responsible for the various operations or processes that lead to transformation of the securitized assets into investors' cash inflows may not do what they are supposed to do, or there might be failure of systems, equipments, or processes that may lead to leakages, costs, delays, and the like. The Basel II document defines operational risk as "the risk of loss resulting from inadequate or failed internal processes, people and systems or from external events. This definition includes legal risk, but excludes strategic and reputational risk." In the context of securitization, the term *operational risk* may or may not include legal risks, depending on context.

Operational issues in securitization have attracted quite some attention in recent past. The increased attention to operational issues stems from at least two reasons. First is a realization that the ultimate test of sustainability of a transaction on its own is not so much a true sale, but a true independence from the originator, in absence of which true sale loses its very meaning. The second reason is that operational issues that affect the originator's business almost equally affect the performance of the securitization transaction as well.

A survey by Standard & Poor's (2005a) confirms that the structured finance market regards operational risks as a major area of concern. More than two-thirds of participants identified operational risk as a major area of concern, and 78% regarded servicer quality as a major area of focus. The main area of operations in securitization is handled by servicers, and some administrative functions are handled by the trustees. In this chapter, we discuss the role of servicers and trustees and the risks inherent therein.

THE SERVICING FUNCTION

The term *servicing function*, or the *collection and servicing function*, is an industry term that includes the array of functions whereby an interface is provided to the obligors as well as the investors. All the various activities that the originator would have, in normal course of business, performed in relation to the obligors—sending invoices, monitoring collections, sending reminders, taking recovery action, and so on—and all the activities in relation to distribution of the cash so collected to investors are covered by the catchall word *servicing*.

The U.S. Securities and Exchange Commission (SEC) Regulation AB seeks to define servicing function as follows: "We propose to define 'servicer' as any person responsible for the management or collection of the pool assets or making allocations or distributions to holders of the asset-backed securities."

TYPES OF SERVICERS

As the origination, servicing, and resolution of assets becomes increasingly fragmented, the usual hold-all function approach to retail assets is giving way to specialized services. Broadly speaking, for residential and commercial mortgages, three types of servicing functions have emerged, the fourth type below is the contingency that any of the first three may have to be replaced in exceptional cases:

- *Primary servicer*. The primary servicer is the entity who originated the loan and maintains the franchise with the obligors. Usually, it is the originator who has regular dealings with the borrower.
- *Master servicer*. At the transaction pool level, the master servicer is responsible for ensuring the smooth functioning of the entire

transaction, including adherence by each servicer of the servicing functions.

- *Specialized servicer.* Normally, the specialized servicer is brought in when an asset becomes nonperforming. Essentially, this is the servicer having expertise in the resolution of such problem loans. The loan might end up in foreclosure, may be restructured, or may otherwise be corrected.
- *Backup servicer.* Generally a standby servicer who would step in if there are any events of default with the primary or master servicer. We take up backup servicers later in this chapter.

For *commercial mortgage-backed securities* (CMBS) transactions, there might be more than one master servicer, particularly in conduit or fusion conduit deals.

The allocation of functions between the primary and the subservicers may not be very clear. For CMBS transactions, the Commercial Mortgage Securities Association (2005) has developed a recommended splitting of functions between the primary servicer, subservicers, and special servicer.

SERVICER STRENGTHS

Servicing is essentially a process-oriented job and requires organizational strengths to accomplish the processing within defined time and up to standards expected in the market.

Staff Strengths

Servicing demands both knowledge and experience—knowledge of the business processes inherent for the asset type involved and experience in handling the same. Experience in the relevant industry for a fair length of time shows the ability of the servicer to provide value addition.

Organizational Structure

The servicing entity should be organizationally designed to support servicing requirements. At the same time, the organizational structure should keep space for growth and continual updates of the required functionalities. The organizational structure should provide for systems of supervision and review to monitor performance and compliances at various levels.

What type of organizational structure is best suited for efficient servicing organizations? While the question certainly cannot have absolute answers, rating agency S&P feels centralized platforms usually represent a potential for greater economies of scale. Depending on the servicing activity, a combination of transactional and functional departments—e.g., payment processing versus asset/portfolio analysis—usually results in lower per-loan servicing costs. The rating agency feels outsourcing and/or offshoring transactional-based activities (such as bank lockbox and tax/insurance third-party service providers) and certain functional-based activities (such as call centers, customer service, property inspections, and financial statement analysis) also may result in lower costs, and may provide a level of experience not available within the organization.

Training

As organizations continuously need to hone skills, prepare for succession management and have resource development, they need to spend on training. Training has become an essential part of every learning organization, but it is considered very significant in the servicing industry. Training is also seen as a motivator as the employees feel motivated by the fact that their employer is spending on their personal development. Depending on the job being performed by the employee concerned, training is required for both soft skills as also the technical skills required for the job.

Staff Turnover

The servicer's organization should be stable and resilient to periodical jerks. Employee turnover is an indicative measure of the stability and general management of a company. High turnover is detrimental to efficiency and profitability. Rating agency S&P says that it observes a higher turnover rate in residential mortgage and other consumer product servicing industry, of close to 15% to 20%, while for commercial products, it is low at about 5% to 10%.

Systems

Servicing being process-oriented, investment in systems and technology is a significant strength in servicing business. A proper servicing system should exist, and wherever possible, the servicer should make use of external technology support such as for automated dialing and/or document imaging systems. A review of how effectively and efficiently the various systems are integrated to avoid manual rehandling of data is addressed. Along with system controls and administration of security functions within each system.

Business continuity planning and disaster recovery can be critical issues. Most servicing organizations maintain data back-up, protection against fire, piracy and breakdown. As continuity in servicing is significant, most servicing organizations also maintain alternate sites to shift the servicing location, should it be required. Ideally, the alternative system hot site and the business recovery site should be at least 25 miles from a company's main servicing location to ensure adequate power and minimize inaccessibility or transportation disruptions. Both the system recovery and business continuity plans must be tested at least annually to ensure workability. The servicer should target ability to recover functionality within 48 hours of the disaster event.

Internal Controls

Existence of robust internal controls is key to any process-oriented business. Critical in ensuring adequate internal controls are procedure manuals and internal audit. Procedure manuals are important for standardization of responses as also for continuity of operations. Adherence to systems and procedures is the key focus of internal audits.

Loan/Asset Administration

As the servicer's main function is to process the assets and payments, the servicer must demonstrate functional proficiency in processing the asset. The various components of asset administration include:

■ *Establishing new loan records.* This includes testing the correctness of data, intimation to the borrower and apprising the borrower of his responsibilities.

- *Document tracking.* This will be relative to the nature of the transaction, and may include ensuring the collection of physical documents, for example mortgages, and also relevant filings such as security interest perfection.
- *Payment processing.* The duties for payment processing should be well laid, and there must be reporting and reconciliation systems to eliminate errors. Where appropriate, lockbox services should be used.
- *Insurance.* Once again, this would be relative to the type of asset, but in most cases there would be some insurance taken to insure against the risks relating to the asset.
- *Taxes and other compliances.* Monitoring necessary tax and other compliances is important.
- *Investor reporting.* Appropriate investor reporting formats and well-differentiated allocation of duties on investor reporting is critical to servicing function.
- *Obligor service.* Servicers are responsible not only for interface with the investors but also with the obligors. One of the most common obligor service jobs is to intimate the obligor on his outstanding amount and answer queries about any charges in the invoices.
- *Servicer advances.* Servicers are commonly required to support the transaction with advances for any delinquent interest and principal, and sometimes for tax and insurance payments. Where such advances are required, the reconciliation of the amounts advanced and netted out on a regular basis is necessary.
- *Asset-aging analysis.* One of the critical servicing jobs is to be able to manage the collections effectively, for which aging analysis of the receivables is most important.
- *Delinquency minimization.* Servicers are supposed to have well-established systems for handling delinquencies. The follow up sequence—automated diallers, letters—are well laid down. If there is a manual follow up, the response should be documented at all times.

SERVICER QUALITIES

Standard & Poor's (2004) has identified expected qualities for servicers for asset classes. Because they are important, we briefly describe them next.

Consumer Finance

This includes credit card and other forms of consumer credits. Here, the servicer should demonstrate the following abilities:

- Effective credit card utilization monitoring and portfolio retention initiatives.
- Demonstrate effective fraud detection procedures.
- Customer service environment that provides satisfactory degree of customer care, including an automated call distribution system, voice response unit, and Internet site for customer inquiries, transactions and overall productivity management.
- Management of delinquent portfolios including monitoring roll rate migration, FICO scoring and behavior modeling, loss mitigation counseling, and effective skip tracing.
- Demonstrate sound collection procedures with appropriate staff allocations and product-specific experience levels.
- Collection staff training including extensive Fair Debt Collection Practices Act (FDCPA) requirements and testing, soft skills instruction and negotiation techniques.
- Satisfactory oversight of collection staff, including continuous call monitoring, scoring, and feedback as well as periodic refresher training and certification courses.
- Effective procedures for payment plans, and matrix of approval levels for staff, middle and senior management. Satisfactory history of cure rates, promise-to-pay success rates versus recidivism rates.
- Demonstrate procedures for timely charge-off of delinquent accounts between 120 to 180 days and review by senior management.
- Maintain effective procedures for recovery of postcharge-off assets including internal and external initiatives.

If the servicer is a special servicer, that is, for delinquent consumer finance transactions, the servicer should demonstrate the following:

- Demonstrate effective portfolio due diligence of acquired portfolios to ascertain effectiveness of prior collection effort and likelihood of recovery based on primary, secondary, or tertiary nature of portfolio.

- Postpurchased review of pricing model and technology to determine efficacy of purchasing decisions.
- Demonstrate development and implementation of recovery models. Review recovery assumptions and case histories of purchased portfolios.
- New loan setup should be executed from electronic file downloads due to the higher volumes.
- Extensive data scrubbing of all new portfolios, including effective identification of skip-tracing needs.
- Procedures for borrower contact, repayment and/or restructuring plans, settlement authorizations, including automated promise-to-pay monitoring, and required daily monitoring of collections.
- Extensive FDCPA training and compliance monitoring.
- Daily portfolio-specific recovery modeling and goal planning for each collector and team.
- Technology and degree of system interface between call center(s), servicing systems, and alternative payment vehicles (speed pay, quick collect, Western Union).
- Accepting additional collateral, short payoffs or liquidations, and appropriate analysis templates for decision making.
- Rigorous monitoring of restructured assets.

Commercial Finance Servicers

Commercial finance servicers include equipment leases, commercial loans, and SME loans. Here, the critical abilities include:

- Demonstrate controls for tracking sales tax, personal property tax, and UCC filings. Maintain sufficient staff, systems, and expertise to proactively monitor lessee compliance and credit positions, administer lease modifications, perform lease-end remarketing and dispositions of used equipment, and engage in reasonable inventory valuation practices.
- Demonstrate sound collection procedures with experienced staff allocated to higher delinquency levels.
- Demonstrate an adequate recovery performance history through channels such as equipment resales, deficiency collections, and

lease modifications. Realized residual values should be tracked and reasonable.

- Maintain an appropriate charge-off policy, typically between 120 and 180 days, and monitoring of charge-off recoveries, which should have a neutral effect on earnings and reserves.
- Demonstrate sufficient procedures and documentation controls regarding resolution approvals.

Franchise Loan Servicers

As franchise lenders' security interests extend over a variety of business assets, it is necessary for the franchise loan servicer to be able to monitor a variegated set of security interests. The demonstrable abilities include:

- To the extent applicable, based on the loan's collateral, monitor the status of real estate taxes and other levies against the loan collateral/borrower that could negatively affect lien position, and take appropriate measures.
- Maintain sound procedures to track the status of all applicable security interest filings and take appropriate action to ensure that security interest filing renewals are completed before their expiration dates.
- Collect and analyze franchisee's operating statements at least semiannually (preferably quarterly) and identify negative trends. The financial review process should include a fixed charge coverage ratio analysis calculated at the unit and corporate borrower level.
- Maintain watchlist functions so that loans experiencing negative trends or potential default issues are monitored more intensively.
- Follow proactive collection procedures for borrowers with past due payments.
- Monitor borrowers' loan covenant compliance and take prudent action regarding any such nonmonetary defaults.
- Perform collateral site inspections no later than after a loan enters the watchlist stage.

- Possess acceptable credit analysis skills among staff for identifying and evaluating key elements of franchise concept, unit, and borrower performance.
- Proactively identify and implement the optimal strategy and tactics for recovering troubled franchise assets.
- Have sufficient staffing levels and asset manager industry experience for executing franchise loan workout plans.
- Management staff experience demonstrates success in resolving troubled franchise credits, including credits in bankruptcy.
- Acceptably track all key activities covering the special servicing process.
- Demonstrate expertise in evaluating the correct course of action relating to each asset, and with adequate documentation substantiate asset recovery recommendations and decisions.
- Asset business plans are prepared within the first 90 days or less of delinquency.
- Show acceptable controls regarding decision-making and approval processes.
- Control third-party vendor engagements through standardized agreements, competitive bidding, management approvals, and centralized tracking.

Commercial Mortgage-Backed Finance Servicers

Primary Servicers

- As applicable, perform all duties according to Commercial Mortgage Securities Association industry standards, and regulatory requirements (i.e. REMIC rules) for CMBS portfolios.
- Maintain adequate procedures for monitoring and disbursing real estate taxes. Penalties for late payments should be tracked separately on a dollar-per-loan count basis.
- Have acceptable procedures for tracking security interest filing expirations and obtaining continuations with adequate lead-time, usually six months.
- Have sound procedures for obtaining, spreading, normalizing and analyzing property financial data. Including *net operating income* (NOI) adjustments and *debt service coverage ratio* (DSCR) calculations.

- Maintain sound procedures for obtaining periodic inspection reports and monitoring related follow up actions.
- Maintain tracking of borrower requests, and act promptly and expeditiously in responding to those requests.
- Have formalized loan watchlist procedures.
- Have adequate early delinquency/default collection efforts. This includes sufficiently proactive time lines for telephone and written borrower contact.

Master Servicers

- Properly track individual pooling and servicing agreement's requirements on specific deals and closely track subservicer compliance.
- Have procedures for wire remittance from subservicers, and their reconciliation, including procedures for tracking and balancing reports received from subservicers having more than one securitization issue.
- Have good procedures in place for tracking and monitoring *principal and interest* (P&I) advances.
- Monitor special servicer performance in handling its assets, updating valuations/appraisal reductions, and recoverability testing of advances.
- Monitor material fluctuations in collateral value, taking such fluctuations into account as part of the decision-making process regarding advances and determination of nonrecoverability.
- Demonstrate understanding of the impact of nonrecoverability determination, and take reasonable steps to prevent, cash flow interruptions to investment-grade certificate-holders.
- Monitor late reporting/remitting and tax disbursement penalties incurred by subservicers.
- Routinely monitor subservicer tracking and disbursement reports relating to taxes, insurance, reserves, and Uniform Commercial Code (UCC) refilings to identify exceptions.
- Routinely monitor and require subservicers have adequate D&O, E&O, and force-placed insurance coverage in place on all loans as a matter of policy.
- Maintain sound procedures for tracking insurance loss drafts and claims disbursements.

- Track subservicer delinquency reporting and collection activity.
- Have adequate procedures for overseeing subservicer handling of borrower/property financial statements and property inspections.
- Maintain an integrated watchlist for all master serviced loans (i.e., primary plus subserviced loans).
- Have adequate procedures for authorizing advances and tracking reimbursements.
- Maintain appropriate staffing and procedures for approving borrower requests such as modifications and assumptions.
- Have an adequate subservicer onsite audit program conducted with a frequency commensurate with each subservicer's volume.
- Routinely ensure that all compliance certificates, financial statements, and reports required by the pooling and servicing agreement are forwarded and reviewed on a timely basis.

Special Servicers

- The company should have a demonstrated track record of resolving problem assets. If the company's track record is of short duration, the achievements may be based on the prior experience of key managers for overseeing and disposing of troubled loans or *real estate owned* (REO).
- Possess expertise in handling a variety of assets types, although company may have a concentration of experience with one particular property type.
- Demonstrate an ability to evaluate the correct course of action relating to each asset. Policies are in place to maximize the recovery proceeds of each asset, taking into account the interests of all certificate-holders and outlined within the framework of the resolution business (loan or REO) plans.
- Exercise judicious management of all trust assets and expenses during the workout process.
- Require the creation of individual asset (loan) business plans within 90 days of transfer to the special servicer (usually a 150-day delinquency benchmark). Plans are approved through proper delegations of authority.
- Properly document all specific asset management recommendations, including foreclosures, restructures, note sales, and borrower settlements, with proper delegation of authority for approvals.

- Have procedures in place for transferring assets from loan to REO status with timely notifications to all internal and external parties.
- Have procedures in place for REO management. REO business plans and budgets should be prepared within 60 to 90 days of acquisition of title.
- Maintain procedures for selecting, engaging, and overseeing third-party property managers.
- Require formalized procedures for property management company financial reporting.
- Review monthly property manager financial reporting, which is done by in-house staff having accounting and audit backgrounds.
- Maintain procedures for monitoring property manager reporting compliance and bank account activity and reconciliations.
- Follow formalized and sound procedures for REO dispositions.
- Follow recovery actions that are consistent with REMIC rules and time constraints.
- Select, engage, and monitor brokers with adequate controls. Listing agreements should not be longer than six months, and can be canceled by notice from the property owner. Sales offers are substantiated and approved by senior management.
- Control third-party vendor engagements through standardized agreements, competitive bidding, management approvals, approved vendor lists, and system tracking.
- Maintain an acceptable process for review of appraisal and environmental reports. No foreclosure actions are completed without an environmental review from a qualified expert.
- Manage the legal function through an approved counsel list. Billings are closely monitored.

Residential Mortgage Servicers

Primary Servicers

- As applicable, perform all loan servicing-related duties in accordance with investor guidelines and prudent industry practice.
- Demonstrate acceptable and efficient loan boarding procedures that maximize automation and ensure acceptable data integrity controls.

- Demonstrate satisfactory controls in payment processing environment with proper handling of live checks and research items as well as solid oversight of vendor relationships.
- Maintain an investor accounting, reporting, and remitting structure that is functionally driven providing for the requisite segregation of duties among reporting, remitting, and reconciling functions.
- Maintain satisfactory investor accounting and default management ratings from the respective *government-sponsored entities* (GSEs).
- Maintain satisfactory Uniform Single Attestation Program (a Mortgage Bankers Association standard) rating and compliance.
- Perform rate adjustments on ARM loans in accordance with investor and regulatory guidelines.
- Maintain satisfactory compliance with Real Estate Settlement Procedures Act (RESPA) guidelines in all escrow administration functions.
- Demonstrate solid oversight of vendor relationships for escrow administration functions (i.e., hazard and flood insurance, real estate tax bill procurement).
- Maintain provisions for force placed hazard and flood insurance coverage via an insurance carrier with an acceptable claims paying ability rating.
- Demonstrate satisfactory compliance with lien release statutes in all 50 states.
- Maintain effective customer service, and depending on volumes, provide an automated call distribution system, voice response unit, and Internet site for customer inquiries, transactions, and overall productivity management.
- Demonstrate sound collection procedures and timelines in accordance with minimum standards specified by investors and agencies.
- Have satisfactory training in FDCPA and other applicable regulations.
- Maintain acceptable collection technology including an autodialer or powerdialer for calling campaigns and call center productivity management.
- Maintain additional technology as needed, including credit scoring and behavior modeling, workflow automation, advanced telephony, and call scripting.

- Perform periodic property inspections on delinquent loans to ensure that all collateral is sufficiently monitored and protected against loss.
- Demonstrate sound collection procedures and timelines in accordance with minimum standards specified by investors and GSEs.
- Maintain acceptable collection technology including an autodialer or powerdialer for calling campaigns and call center productivity management.
- Have appropriately aggressive and proactive focus on loss mitigation via mailing and calling campaigns.
- Maintain demonstrated ability to perform net present value analysis to determine best exit strategy.
- Demonstrate acceptable foreclosure and bankruptcy timeline management pursuant to investor guidelines.
- Maintain proactive case management and attorney oversight.
- Maintain effective REO property management marketing and disposition procedures including asset management guidelines, marketing plan, vendor organization and oversight, eviction and marketing timeline management, and sale results.

Subprime Services

- Develop and implement aggressive collection timelines that address the credit profile of various nonconforming borrowers.
- Hire and retain experienced nonconforming collectors.
- Implement and encourage employee career-pathing to retain experienced collectors and minimize turnover.
- Provide in-depth collection training, including extensive FDCPA instruction, soft skills training and negotiation techniques, as well as role-playing in a simulated call center environment.
- Nonconforming servicers should perform welcome calls within five to 10 days of a new loan closing to reinforce terms of the repayment obligation and to encourage positive pay habits.
- The nonconforming servicer should track the contact rate on welcome calls.
- Bilingual collectors should be on staff in accordance with specific portfolio demographics.

- Expanded collection calling hours, including evenings and weekends, should be in place to optimize contact with recalcitrant borrowers.
- Credit scoring and behavior modeling technology should be in place to strategically align calling campaigns with the latest borrower profiles.
- Advanced telephony should be utilized for optimum contact opportunities including inbound call volume.
- Consistent and frequent call monitoring to ensure that collectors remain effective and are following regulatory guidelines.
- Monthly property inspections to ensure that collateral is not compromised.
- Demonstrate advanced analytical environment capable of measuring and tracking roll rate migrations and promise-to-pay.
- Success rates, short-term repayment plan cure rates, prime-time calling percentage, and best time-to-call criteria.
- Effective skip tracing environment, including skip-tracing-locate-rate percentage.
- Demonstrate early loss mitigation initiative in advance of foreclosure referral. Advanced loss mitigation analytics should include fully automated net-present-value analysis, including updated borrower financial statement and property valuation, resulting in best-exit-strategy-workout plan.
- Full and complete file review prior to foreclosure to ensure that the collection effort has been exhaustive and that all regulatory guidelines have been met.
- Automated (electronic) file referral to approved counsel.
- Maintain corporate-approved list of external counsel for representation in foreclosure and bankruptcy cases.
- Maintain dual track of loss mitigation and foreclosure to ensure that foreclosure sale is the last resort.
- Closely manage foreclosure and bankruptcy timelines with external counsel. Issue monthly report cards on attorney performance.

Special Servicers

- Highly experienced default management team to perform due diligence on distressed asset portfolios.

- Demonstrate proficiency at portfolio triage, including rapid assessment of incoming distressed portfolios, identification of assets requiring immediate attention, development of action plans, and assignment of resources for new assets.
- Effectively manage flow of new assets into servicing stream.
- Identify reasons for default and make loan cash positive if possible.
- Demonstrated advanced portfolio analytics and attorney oversight methodologies.
- Demonstrated skip-tracing abilities, including advanced technology tools, and skip-tracing-locate rate.
- Highly experienced collection staff averaging more than five years industry experience.
- Implementation of early and proactive loss mitigation approach.
- Fully automated net-present-value analysis based on current borrower financial statement and property valuation, best exit strategy developed.
- Highly experienced foreclosure and bankruptcy team that can track problem assets, court delays, chronic filers, and maximize timeline compliance. Expeditiously move for lift of stay in all cases.
- Aggressive dual-path strategy combining loss mitigation efforts with proactive foreclosure timeline management.
- Provide adequate documentation to substantiate asset recovery strategies and decisions.
- Exhibit acceptable controls over decision-making and approval processes.
- Demonstrate strong vendor management methodologies, including standardized agreements, competitive bidding process, management approval matrix, and independent monitoring and tracking.
- Exhibit formalized and prudent procedures for REO management and disposition.
- Asset managers should have extensive REO management experience.
- Utilize cash for keys to expedite property vacancy where cost-effective.
- Select, engage, and monitor brokers with adequate controls. Sales offers are substantiated and approved by senior management.

Master Servicers

- Demonstrated ability to track individual pooling and servicing agreements on specific deals and closely monitor subservicer compliance.
- Master servicing guide published on the Intranet.
- Exhibit adequate procedures for establishing wire remittance arrangements with new subservicers as well as reconciling incoming wires from subservicers.
- Exhibit satisfactory segregation of duties among the investor accounting and reporting functions.
- Satisfactory procedures and system security for reconciling unpaid principal balances to scheduled balances.
- Sound procedures for tracking and balancing reports received from subservicers administering multiple issues.
- Sound procedures for tracking and monitoring principal and interest advances.
- Monitor late reporting and remitting penalties incurred by subservicers.
- No unreconciled items aged more than 90 days.
- Routinely monitor subservicer tracking and disbursement reports for escrow items.
- Master servicers routinely monitor requirements that subservicers have adequate insurance coverage in force on all loans.
- Maintain sound procedures for tracking insurance loss drafts and claims disbursements.
- Routinely review subservicer delinquency reporting and collection activity.
- Exhibit sound procedures for authorizing advances and tracking reimbursements.
- Ensure adequate staffing, expertise, and procedures for administering special requests such as modifications and assumptions.
- Adequate subservicer review program mandating periodic on-site audits based on loan volume and criteria watchlist as well as routine desk reviews.
- Annual compliance process for all subservicers pursuant to master servicing participation program. Ensure that all compliance certificates, financial statements, and required reports are received on a timely basis.

- Maintain exception-based tracking system for trailing documents.
- Maintain web site for investor downloads and access to pool level transaction data.

SERVICING TRANSITION

Securitization transactions are presumably independent of the originator due to the legal isolation the transaction achieves due to "true sale." However, the truth of the sale might turn out to be a glib illusion if the servicing platform is so intimately originator-dependent that it is difficult to perceive its transfer. Transferability of servicing has been a key issue in several securitization transactions, either because the servicing fees were impractically fixed or because the servicing was intrinsically dependent on the originator's organization.

Conseco Finance's securitization transactions showed that impractical fixation of servicing fees can disrupt the performance of a transaction. As one would presumably do when the originator is the servicer, the servicing fees were subordinated, and were meager. When Conseco filed for bankruptcy, the servicing had to be transferred. The servicing fee was 50 basis points and it was subordinated, which means the servicer would get nothing unless there was an excess spread. This is a kind of "onerous asset" that can be avoided in bankruptcy proceedings, which is what the company pleaded before the court. The court increased the servicing fee to 125 basis points and made it senior to the noteholders, thereby reducing the excess spread of the transaction.

There have been some cases where successful transfer of servicing function has been possible, such as when Guardian Savings and Loan failed, wherein Financial Security Assurance as the guarantor was able to have the servicing transferred. In the case of Spiegel and NextCard as well, the servicing fee was too low to attract a backup servicer.

The portability of the servicing function is quite dependent on the nature of the collateral. For a further discussion, see Standard & Poor's (2005b).

BACKUP SERVICER

As is evident from difficulties faced in several transactions, the portability of the servicing is itself a problem, and more significantly, the willingness of the backup servicer to pick up servicing as per terms assumed in the transaction cannot be assumed. Adequate backup servicing arrangements is key to the transaction.

Backup servicers may be classified into *hot, warm,* and *cold.* The jargon comes from information technology business where these terms are used for backup servers. A hot backup servicer is a sort of an alternate that keeps itself in absolute readiness to take over the servicing anytime. Generally, a hot backup will upload collateral data from the primary servicer more frequently, often weekly, and in many cases will shadow service the assets in question to assure the most seamless transfer possible should the need for the same arise. Obviously, hot backup servicers are quite expensive to retain.

Warm backup servicers update data from the primary servicer less frequently, usually monthly, and therefore are less expensive to keep on standby.

Cold backups perform the least frequent monitoring of the primary servicing data, providing updates possibly quarterly or even semiannually.

As every backup arrangement implies a cost, one must take a practical view to organize the backup arrangement. However, a mere right to appoint a backup servicer, or a commitment on the part of a backup servicer to take over servicing, is meaningless unless accompanied by the readiness to do so.

REPORTING BY THE SERVICER

Pursuant to Regulation AB, the role of the servicer and the reporting by servicer has been a topic for intensive discussion in the industry. Among other things, Regulation AB requires a certification along with a 10-K report to be filed by each servicer servicing 10% or more of the pool.[1]

Apart from regulatory intervention on servicer reporting, industry bodies have over time tried to evolve minimum servicer report-

---

[1] For details, see Chapter 28 in Kothari (2006).

ing standards. The Commercial Mortgage Securities Association (CMSA), for example, has investor reporting package in operation for several years. The Australian Securitization Forum and the European Securitization Forum have all come out with investor reporting standards.

Regulation or industry standards apart, the servicer reporting requirements are laid down in the pooling and servicing agreement. (See Chapter 24 in Kothari (2006) for some model clauses.)

ROLE OF TRUSTEES IN OPERATION OF THE TRANSACTION

The role of trustees in securitization transactions is far from standardized. The institution of trustees comes up for purely logistical reasons or to comply with legal requirements, but investors seem to place increasing reliance on the trustees.

The legal role of trustees is to act as a single window conduit for the investors. Trustees hold the legal title over the assets or the securities in trust for the investors. They enforce all covenants on the part of the contracting parties, and ensure that the servicer is performing his duties as per contract. The trustees would seek a noteholders' vote in exceptional circumstances.

In addition, the traditional role of the trustees includes acting as authenticating agent, registrar, transfer agent, asset and account custodian and analytics provider, in addition to holding legal or security interest on the assets. These responsibilities can be expanded or reduced by a trust deed. Sometimes, trustees may get involved in actual operations and provide services as backup servicers. But trustees taking over the role of servicers may raise issues of conflict of interest.

Like most other spheres of activity, technology is fast entering to make trustees' discharge of duties more efficient. Tadie (2005) mentions how technology is assisting trustees in better discharge of trustee functions:

- *Covenant maintenance.* An automated electronic ticker system enables periodic reviews of an asset-backed security's covenant to be conducted on an ongoing basis for the life of a transaction.

- *Funds collection and investment.* Electronic collection and tracking technologies facilitate the flow of incoming cash from servicers and its eventual investment according to the bondholder's wishes.
- *Bond analytics.* Proprietary programs calculate cash flow waterfalls and allocate bond payments for multiclass structures; historical data-capture systems help generate customized reports for issuers, projecting valuations for residuals under varying economic assumptions.
- *Investor communications.* The Internet, proprietary electronic bulletin boards, and automated voice response systems enable communication with investors through multiple channels in addition to telephone and face-to-face interactions with relationship managers.

As for servicers, there have been attempts to standardize trustees' reports too. For instance, in 2005 the Bond Market Association (now the Securities Industry and Financial Markets Association) in 2005 finalized a format of trustee report for collateralized debt obligations.

FRAUD RISK

Among the operational risks in an asset-backed transaction, the risk of fraud should not be underrated. Fraud risk remains present in every sphere of activity, but there is reliance on several independent agencies each handling a fragment of the transaction in securitizations. This is the perfect setting for a fraudster, who takes advantage of the fact that there is no one with overall responsibility for the transaction; each party has a split segment of responsibility. The servicer is concerned only with what he is paid for, the originator is presumably hands-off, and the trustees are legal watchdogs who step into action only when they are made to smell something wrong.

While instances of systematic Ponzi-type devices exist in the past, such as Towers Healthcare, one of the recent instances of fraud in asset-backed securities was National Century. National Century Financial Enterprises (NCFE) filed for bankruptcy in November 2002 and brought to the fore some unique risks of mishandling securitization funds. NCFE specialized in health-care funding and used to buy health-care receivables from several health-care centers in the United States. These receivables were securitized. Shortly before the bankruptcy filing, it was revealed that the company was misusing the funds collected on behalf of its securitization clients. Investigations revealed frauds by the company's top executives, resulting in a filing of the bankruptcy petition. Approximately $3.5 billion of asset-backed securities defaulted. Some of the classes were rated triple-A by more than one rating agency.

Investors have sued the trustees as well as the placement agents, for example *City of Chandler, et al., v. Bank One, N.A., et al.* (D. Az.); *Metropolitan Life Ins. Co. v. Bank One, N.A.* (D.N.J.); *Bank One, N.A. v. Poulsen, et al.* (S.D. Ohio); and *State of Arizona et al. v. Credit Suisse First Boston Corporation, et al.* (Superior Court of Arizona). The SEC has sued the former principal executives of the NCFE.[2] Later, seven of the former executives of the company were indicted for fraud.

KEY POINTS OF THE CHAPTER

➤ *While a good deal of emphasis has been placed on true sale or legal robustness of a securitization transaction, which examines whether securitized assets will remain unaffected by the bankruptcy of the originator, today there is concern in a securitization with operational risk.*

➤ *The has been increased attention to operational issues in securitization because of (1) a realization that the ultimate test of sustainability of a transaction on its own is not so much a true sale, but a true independence from the originator and (2) operational issues that affect the originator's business are equally likely to affect the performance of the securitization transaction.*

➤ *Operational risk is the risk that a party (originator/servicer, third-party servicers, and trustees) involved in the various operations or processes that lead to the transformation of the securitized assets into investors' cash flows may not do what they are supposed*

---

[2] The full text of the SEC complaint is at www.sec.gov/litigation/complaints/comp19509.pdf.

to do or that there might be a failure of systems, equipments, or processes that may lead to leakages, costs, delays, and the like.

➤ Because, in most securitizations, the originator is the servicer as well. If the originator goes into bankruptcy, it is crucial to examine whether it would be possible to shift the servicing to a replacement servicer.

➤ For residential and commercial mortgages, the three types of servicers are the primary servicer, master servicer, and specialized servicer.

➤ Generally, there is a standby servicer who would step in if there are any events of default with the primary or master servicer.

➤ In evaluating the ability of a servicer to perform its duties, the following attributes are examined: strength of the staff, organizational structure, training, staff turnover, systems, internal controls, and loan/asset administration.

➤ The portability of the servicing function, fixation of proper service fees, and proper place of the service fee in the waterfall of the transaction are all important.

➤ In addition, whether the transaction is being serviced by the originator or independent servicers, there are significant servicer qualities which are almost as important to the health of the securitization transaction as the quality of the borrowers.

➤ Even after all checks have been put in place for servicing quality, fraud is still a risk that may affect securitization transactions with equal severity as any other type of transaction.

Review of ABS Collateral

Collateral Classes in ABS: Retail Loans

In the previous chapters, we described the process of securitization, specifically with reference to mortgage-backed securities. Where the assets are not mortgage-backed, the securities that result out of securitization are referred to as *asset-backed securities*. Since securitization is essentially a device of integration and differentiation of assets, the asset that goes into the securitization process is of utmost significance. In this chapter, we study several prevailing asset classes, all belonging under the general label of asset-backed securities.

COLLATERAL CLASSES: BASIS OF CLASSIFICATION

Existing Assets and Future Flows

From the viewpoint of whether the asset pool will comprise of existing cash flows, or expected cash flows, we make a broad distinction between existing assets and future assets.

In an existing asset securitization, the cash flow from the asset exists and there is an existing claim to value. In a future flow securitization, there is no existing claim or contractual right to a cash flow; such contractual rights will be created in the future. For example, an airline company securitizing its future ticket receivables is a case of a future flow securitization, since it is based on expected cash flows. On the other hand, in case of securitization of loan receivables, we have an existing contractual claim on the cash flows—so, it is an existing asset.

The distinction between existing assets and future flows is relevant from several viewpoints:

1. In future flows, as the cash flows are to be originated in future, there is a performance risk on the originator. Sometimes, this performance risk may be mitigated by guarantee by a third party. For instance, in the case of construction of infrastructure facilities, it is quite common for some state agency to provide a guaranteed return. In either case, if the originator fails to perform, or the guarantor fails to pay the guaranteed sum, there would be no cash flows to pay the investors. Hence, future flows transactions cannot be independent of the originator. This is in direct contrast to an essential securitization principle wherein the securities are liquidated from out of assets without piggy backing on the originator. Hence, the structuring as well as rating of future flows securitizations has to bear in mind originator dependence. We return to this issue later as we discuss future flows.

2. It is also obvious that the potential users of future flows securitization are corporates, whereas the principal originators in case of existing asset transactions are financial intermediaries.

3. Given the nature of cash flows, the key risks that affect existing asset transactions such as default risk, prepayment risk, and the like are not applicable to future flows. There are other significant volatilities, mostly having to do with the business and the source of revenue, that enter the picture.

4. Off-balance-sheet treatment of securitized assets is a common feature of most securitizations. However, in the case of future flows, there is no off-balance-sheet treatment usually. This is understandable, since there is no on-balance sheet asset such as receivables, as in case of existing asset transactions, that would go off the balance sheet.

5. Motivations such as capital relief do not apply to future flows.

6. From a legal and taxation viewpoint as well, future flows are treated as closer to debt than sale of assets.

Cash and Synthetic Structures

A securitization transaction may either aim at transferring assets for cash or may simply aim at stripping the risk inherent in credit assets and transferring the commensurate risk. While the former are known as *cash securitizations*, the latter are called *synthetic securitizations*.

In the case of synthetic transactions, the focus is on risk transfer. Here, assets are not actually transferred, but the risk/returns from assets are transferred using a derivatives contract. Truly speaking, risk transfer-based transactions are not an asset class but a type of transfer technology. A synthetic transaction may relate to a pool of mortgage loans, auto loans, or, for that matter, even future flows. Hence, Figure 8.1 shows a combined picture of existing assets, future flows and risk transfers.

Retail versus Whole Sale Assets

Yet another basis for making a distinction between asset classes is by the nature of the obligors in the pool—retail versus whole obligations. The distinction between retail and wholesale loans is not merely having to do with the size of the funding but also the purpose of the loan. Normally, in case of business loans, the purpose of the loan is to acquire an asset which is a source of cash flows or cash savings. Retail loans are typically personal loans.

Securitization of corporate or business loans are termed as *collateralized debt obligations* (CDOs). We will discuss the special features of a wholesale loan portfolio from the viewpoint of securitization in Chapter 11.

FIGURE 8.1   Classification of Assets on Basis of Existence of Assets

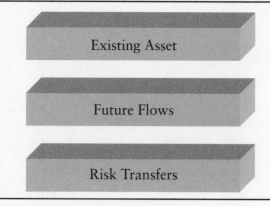

COLLATERAL CLASSES: MAIN TYPES

The main types of existing asset securitizations (the same collateral classes may, arguably, be securitized synthetically as well) are mortgage-backed and asset-backed pools. In general, mortgage-backed loan pools consist of mortgage loans and asset-backed securities comprise all other existing asset transactions. The resulting securities are referred to as mortgage-backed securities and asset-backed securities, respectively. Mortgage-backed securities make a distinct class since the loans have the backing of real property.

There are some products that are classified as asset-backed securities even though they contain residential mortgage loans. Specifically, home equity loans, more specified, closed-end home equity loans, are loans to individuals with impaired credit and/or high loan-to-value ratios to purchase a home. These individuals are referred to as subprime borrowers. Despite the fact that closed-end home equity loans are mortgage loans, they are referred to as *mortgage-related asset-backed securities* and treated as part of the asset-backed securities market.

In Figure 8.2, we have taken a third type of transactions—those backed by operating revenues. This is a unique type, mostly used for financing acquisitions. Here, the collateral is the residual profits or operating surplus of an entity, hence the name operating revenues securitization. An operating revenues securitization, for obvious reasons, cannot use a true sale structure because an operating entity cannot conceivably make a true sale of its operating assets. The structure used is a secured loan, that is, a loan secured by an all-pervading security interest on the operating assets. The use of this device has been more common in the United Kingdom, due to special features of UK bankruptcy law.

Mortgage-backed securities are typically classified into residential mortgage-backed and commercial-backed, depending on the type of loan involved in either case. Commercial mortgage-backed loans are typically wholesale loans. The structure of commercial mortgage-backed securitizations differs substantially from that of *residential MBS* (RMBS) transactions.

In case of asset-backed securities, we have already commented on the distinction between retail and wholesale loan pools. Included in the retail variety are asset classes, the major ones being auto loans, credit cards, home equity loans, student loans, and the like, the first

FIGURE 8.2 Main Classes of Existing Assets

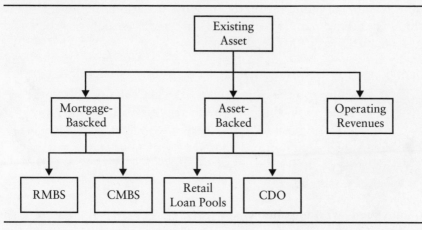

being discussed in the remainder of this chapter. In the wholesale loan category, we include primarily CDOs, which are discussed in Part Four of this book.

CREDIT CARD RECEIVABLES

At first look, credit card receivables seem to be too short term an asset to be amenable to securitization; but not surprisingly credit card issuers have made good use of securitization markets almost everywhere in the world. Credit card receivables are short term, but they are revolved into creation of fresh receivables on a fairly steady basis. If a card user swipes the card, the amount that he or she utilizes is payable within a certain time. However, a credit card is a revolving line of credit. Therefore, they represent a steady stream of cash flows, and are a good candidate for securitization.

Though unsecured, credit card companies make high interest income due to the finance charges, fees, late fees and periodic membership fees. They have put in place systems whereby the card company has a constant watch on the account, and can immediately block a card or reduce its credit for delinquencies. The maximum amount that can be lost on a card is thus controlled. Consequently, over time, card companies have positioned themselves very well to make profit from a very well-diversified base of plastic money users.

For credit card issuers, securitization is one of the very important avenues of sourcing funds, as most traditional financiers have shunned taking funding exposure on credit card receivables. As Mason and Biggs (2002, p. 1) point out:

> Credit card companies rely on securitization for funding and, if the window to the asset-backed market were to close over an extended period, their growth models would fail. However, the securitization market has proved resilient even in the face of the disruptions caused by Russia's default and the demise of Long-Term Capital Management in 1998 and the events of September 11 2001.

As a component of the ABS market, credit cards, along with auto loans, are supposed to form the two pillars of the ABS market. From the viewpoint of resilience, the credit card market has been tested for quite some time; practices have largely been standardized and the default and downgrade history so far, barring some cases of fraud, has been quite satisfactory.

Credit card securitizations use a revolving structure where the amount of principal collected during a certain period is rotated back to the originator to acquire fresh receivables. The amortization starts after a fixed period. The revolving method used to securitize credit card receivables is also used for several other short-term receivables such as consumer finance and home equity lines of credit.

The first case of credit card securitization dates back to 1986 when Salomon Brothers applied the fast emerging securitization device to buy credit card receivables from Banc One and sell them in the form of "Certificates for Amortizing Revolving Debts" (nicknamed CARDs) in a structured, credit-enhanced transaction. Since then, the market has never looked back. Credit card ABS has been the largest component of the U.S. ABS market for several years, but has lately given the first position to home equity loans, primarily due to the massive growth of the latter collateral class. For example, according to the Securities Industry Financial Markets Association (SIFMA), in 1995, the amount of credit card ABS outstanding was $153.1 billion and represented 48% of the U.S. ABS market. While by the third quarter of 2007 there was $335.1 billion credit ABS outstanding, it represented only 14% of the U.S. ABS market.

Credit card securitizations have been relatively less significant asset class in Europe. In 2006, for instance, the share of credit card receivables securitization to the total issuance for the year was less than 1%.

Transaction Structure

A credit card debt is a retail asset. The credit card account is an ongoing service between the credit card company and the customer. When a card is used, the card company generates receivables from the customer; it is this receivable that is securitized. Therefore, the legal relation between the card company and the cardholder remains intact, and the card receivables are transferred to the trust.

The accounts, the receivables from which are to be transferred to the trust are selected based on selection criteria. The criteria are mostly standard and would rule out only such accounts as have been treated as delinquent.

Revolving Asset Structure

The use of the revolving device, whereby over a certain reinvestment period, principal collections are not used to pay down the securities but instead are used to buy new receivables and *replenish* the principal balance of the asset pool, is not limited to credit cards. Apart from several other short-term assets, the revolving feature is increasingly used in several other cases, including CDOs.

A revolving asset structure is not really a future flow securitization. In a future flow transaction, the receivables transferred to the SPV at the inception is much less than the funding raised from the investors, as the transaction relies on receivables to be generated and sold in the future. For revolving transactions, however, at the inception the value of the asset transferred to the special purpose vehicle (SPV) equals (or, taking into account overcollateralization and seller's share, exceeds) the funding raised from the investors. However, there are assets acquired by the SPV on an ongoing basis until the amortization period starts.

A revolving asset securitization is, therefore, akin to a revolving credit arranged by the originator. On an ongoing basis, the originator will be able to avail of funding until the amortization period starts.

The portfolio of assets represents a revolving credit to consumers in which the outstanding principal may fall, so the trust deed contains provisions that the cash collected from the consumers will be trapped in the SPV unless the total amount of receivables in the trust is at least equal to or greater than the total outstanding funding.

Seller's Interest

In addition, to cover the contingency of the assets suffering a decline, a buffer is kept in the form of a *seller's interest*. The seller's interest is the excess of receivables sold by the seller into the trust over the total amount of funding outstanding. This excess is not by way of overcollateralization (which, if required for credit enhancement purposes, may be in addition to the seller's share), as the seller's interest is not subordinated to the investors. The seller's interest also levels off temporary fluctuations in the card balances, such as more card purchases during a holiday or festive season. The seller's interest also absorbs dilutions in the transferred accounts due to noncash reasons, such as a reversal of debit to the card due to return of goods and processing errors.

Discrete and Master Trust Structure

Credit card securitizations could either use a discrete trust or a master trust structure. Recently, the master trust structure has been the most widely used structure.

Where it is a *discrete trust*, the receivables transferred are to the extent required for the resulting securities, beneficially owned by the investors. A *master trust* is like an envelope entity that pools together assets that service several securitization transactions. Hence, it is like a fungible pool of assets backing several issuances made at different points of time.

In master trust mechanics, the master trust is an umbrella body covering various issuances under the trust. It may be likened to the assets sitting on the originator's own balance sheet. Think of the assets on the balance sheet—there are various liabilities that are paid off from a common asset pool. Similarly, a master trust exports a sizeable portion of the originator's assets into the so-called master trust. There is no demarcation of the assets attributable to a particular issuance, represented by an *issuer trust* or *series trust*. The assets are held under a common pot of the master trust from where pro-rated allocation is done to the issuer trusts. The excess of total assets in the master trusts over all the issuance amounts outstanding at the given time is the seller's interest. The allocation of cash flow by the master trust to the various issuances or series is very similar to a corporation equitably allocating its cash flow to its various liabilities.

Allocation of Interest

The allocation of the collections by the master trust to the various issuer trusts is done based on the outstanding amount of the relevant trusts, and the outstanding seller's interest. The finance charges and the fee income, net of the servicing fee and the charge-offs, is distributed to each series. From this allocated amount, each series takes care of its own coupon, and the excess spread in the series is dealt with (retained or returned as the seller's interest), as per the terms of the scheme. Most master trusts also provide for utilization of the surplus excess spread; that is, over what is required as a condition to the rating need, to support the other series under the master trust. This is a sort of a "loan" from one series to another, as the amount so lent by the lending series is recoverable whenever the recipient series has enough excess spread of its own. Thus, there is a cross-collateralization of the excess spread from one series to the other, implying an additional support granted by the seller to the series in need of support, as the excess spread was returnable to the seller. In addition, as a levelling provision, the master trust documents may also provide for the pro-rated allocation of the excess spread of each of the schemes should the allocated interest in a particular month fall short of the coupon required to service investors.

Thus, the master trust method provides an interseries credit enhancement to the investors.

Allocation of Principal and Prepayments

The various series under the master trust might have differing requirements of principal for amortization. Those that are still under a reinvestment period will not need any principal at all; thus, the principal is first allocated proportional to the outstanding investment of the series that are under an amortization period, either scheduled or early amortization. Notably, the proportions of outstanding investment here would mean proportions obtained as at the time when amortization started: otherwise, the schemes which have already partly amortized their outstanding investment will see a reduced allocation. Once again, the surplus principal so allocated to the various schemes may be distributed to the schemes in deficit—the schemes that have hit early amortization triggers. (Early amortization triggers are discussed later.) The remaining surplus principal is the principal available for replenishment, and is therefore released for purchasing assets from the originator.

Delinked Structure

A fully ramped structure, the traditional picture of a securitization transaction, envisages simultaneous issuance of senior and subordinated securities. For master trusts, the single trust allows creation of various securities at different times, so the next stage of development is perfectly logical—the issue of senior and subordinated securities is delinked. In other words, subject to satisfaction of certain conditions, the senior securities may be issued without issue of subordinated securities that may be issued at an opportune time.

The *delinked structure* creates a common funding pot, which may continue issuing various series of Class A notes at different points of time, as long as there is a required extent of *collateralized interest*, the value of assets exceeding the total amount of Class A funding.

One of the important differences between the traditional master trust structure and the delinked structure is that, in the latter case, as the various Class A series are issued from the same vehicle, the amount of excess spread for each series is the same. Also, there is an automatic sharing of the excess spread of the entire asset pool by each of the issued classes.

Components of a Credit Card Structure

Below we discuss the various components of cash inflows and outflows/losses that impact the credit of a credit card portfolio. Notably, apart from the uniqueness of these components, the underwriting of credit card debt itself is different from regular loans, as it is a revolving credit.

Portfolio Yield

The portfolio yield is the rate of return on the credit card portfolio, and in the context of securitization, those parts of income transferred to the trust. Typically, in almost every transaction, the credit card issuer transfers the finance charges, fees collected from the cardholders including late fees, overlimit fees, charges for bounced cheques, interchange or merchant discount (the discount deducted on payments to the merchants), and recoveries on previous charge-offs. Understandably, this yield changes from period to period and there is no fixed rate of return for credit card debt. The portfolio yield is quite an important parameter in credit card securitizations, as it determines the level of excess spread in the transaction.

Charge-Offs

By the very nature of the credit card debt, there is a high amount of charge-offs; that is, debt written off as bad by the industry. There are periodical fluctuations in the loss rate reflecting the prevailing economic situations—unemployment and economic insecurity in general. The charge-off rate also differs greatly as between prime and subprime issuances. In addition, industry analysts say the charge-off rate is related to the vintage of the card—how long the cardholder has been enrolled. It is believed that the charge-off rate starts from nil at origination and peaks to something like 9% in the 18th–24th month, and thereafter, settles at about 6% or the industry average.

Credit Scores and the Charge-Off Rate

Credit card origination is done partly by the data in possession of the card originators, and partly relying on a personal credit rating bureau. A personal credit rating bureau supplies credit score information on individuals, which, in most cases, is based on credit scoring models provided by Fair Isaac and Company. Hence, the scores provided by the said scoring agency are referred to as *FICO scores*—an individual with 650 to 800 points of score is considered to be quite good.

Payment Rate

The *payment rate* is defined as the monthly payment of interest and principal, divided by the total outstanding on the card in the prior month. Card issuers typically require a certain minimum payment to be paid; in addition, cardholders are entitled to either clear off the full balance or any part thereof. The payment rate is relevant to a securitization transaction as it determines the period it will take for a transaction to amortize once the amortization period starts.

Servicing Fee and Base Rate

It is typical of credit card securitizers to fix a servicing fee of 2%. A base rate implies the total of the servicing fee and the coupon payable to the investors, such that the portfolio yield, minus the charge-off rate, minus the base rate, is the excess spread.

The coupon itself may be a fixed or floating rate. Credit enhancement levels required for floating rate issuances are slightly higher than those for a fixed rate, as rating agencies stress the index rate also.

The analysis of all the factors affecting the excess spread—yield, charge off, and coupon—is important in a transaction, as the early amortization events are generally linked with the excess spread.

Early Amortization Triggers

Because a revolving transaction permits the issuer to keep the funding in the transaction and keep supplying further assets in lieu of those that pay off, the transaction maintains the funding level during the revolving period. However, this raises several questions: What if the quality of the asset pool deteriorates? What if the excess spread levels decline? What if there are other contingencies that require the leverage of the transaction to be reduced by paying down the funding?

As a result, all transactions with a revolving feature are coupled with an *early amortization trigger* (EAT). The EAT is akin to acceleration call in traditional bank finance—if the borrower's financials suffer an adverse material change, the bank recalls the loan.

Hitting an early amortization trigger obviously spells a liquidity crisis for the originator, as the line of funding dries up as the trigger is hit. Hence, it is very important for the originator to avoid hitting the trigger. Early amortization is also obviously a prepayment risk for the investors.

One common trigger is based on the excess spread, computed based on a three-month rolling average. If this average spread falls to zero, the transaction enters an early payout. If the excess spread levels fall but do not hit the EAT, the transaction may commonly provide for trapping of the excess spread in a cash reserve.

The other EAT is the *purchase rate*; that is, the rate at which new receivables are originated by the originator for purchase by the trust. Decline in the seller's interest is also commonly a trigger. Following is an example of the EATs in a typical credit card securitization deal:

Seller/Servicer Events
- Failure or inability to make required deposits or payments.
- Failure or inability to transfer receivables to the trust when necessary.
- False representations or warranties that are not remedied.
- Certain events of default, bankruptcy, insolvency, or receivership of the seller or servicer.

Legal Events
- Trust becomes classified as an *investment company* under the Investment Company Act of 1940 (relevant for U.S. transactions—in other cases, refer to other regulatory statements).

Performance Events
- Three-month average of excess spread falls below zero.
- Seller's participation falls below the required level.
- Portfolio principal balance falls below the invested amount.

AUTO LOAN SECURITIZATION

Auto loan securitization is essentially retail collateral, as auto finance is essentially a variant of consumer finance. Other consumer finance receivables include the receivables arising out of typical consumer finance and installment credit transactions.

Forms of installment credit have been prime movers of auto sales in recent years. At certain phases in the economic cycle, auto finance becomes the most important way of selling vehicles. In most markets, a larger part of vehicles sales are installment-funded than are bought with consumer equity.

If auto financing is the key to auto sales, auto loan securitization is the key to refinancing of auto loan transactions. In various countries, there prevail different modes of funding of vehicles such as

- Secured loans
- Conditional sales
- Hire purchase
- Financial leases
- Operating leases

In a broad sense, auto loan securitization covers each of these methods of funding, except for the last one. Operating leases and rentals are a different product in view of the nature of the cash flow and the inherent risks.

Outside the mortgage-backed market, auto loan securitization was the second application of securitization, the first being computer lease securitization. Captive finance companies of the Big 3—Ford Motor Credit Co., General Motors Corp., and DaimlerChrysler—are the leading issuers of auto-loan-backed securities.

Ever since, auto loans have formed an important segment in the ABS market not only in the United States but all markets. The appealing features of auto loan markets are high asset quality and ease in liquidation of delinquent receivables. Auto ABS has traditionally been the number one component in the U.S. ABS market, but was relegated to second in 2001 with its share going from about 19% in 1995 ($59.5 billion) to 9.5% in 2006 ($202.4 billion) according to the SIFMA.

In terms of the quality of the collateral, the market mostly consists of prime auto ABS—about 70% of the total issuance falls in this category. Relatively, the share of subprime auto ABS has been increasing over time.

In Europe, out of ABS excluding MBS and CDOs, auto ABS constitutes an important asset class. In the United Kingdom, the first auto ABS transaction took place in 1997 by Ford Credit. In Asian markets, finance companies have been particularly active in securitization of auto loan receivables.

Collateral Quality

The quality of the auto loan pool depends upon the quality of the underlying collateral, lending terms (loan-to-value ratio, LTV ratio), and tenure. Recent years have seen tremendous competition in the auto loan financing segment with concomitant deterioration in the quality of the loans; there are an increasing proportion of used car loans versus new car loans, while the LTV ratio has worsened and financings are for a longer period now. There is a big push to car sales given by zero annualized percentage rate schemes.

The most important factor that affects the quality of the auto loan pool is the quality of the underwriting systems followed by the financier. Vehicle financings proposals are generally originated at the dealer's floor. The finance company generally outsources the field investigation and then underwrites the loan based on documents and inspection reports. For prime loan pools, there are strict norms that the proposal must comply with in terms of LTV and debt-to-income ratios. Another way of distinguishing between prime and nonprime portfolios is based on the age of the vehicle; new vehicle financings are considered prime and used vehicles are taken as subprime.

One of the most critical factors in all asset-based financings is the movement of the LTV ratio over time. The initial LTV ratio is a reciprocal of the down payment. If the value of the vehicle and the down payment are both expressed as percentage of the same number, the initial LTV is (1 minus the down payment). However, over a period of time, the rate of depreciation of the vehicle and the amortization of the loan would continue to affect the LTV ratio. The loan amortization of an *equal monthly installment* (EMI) structure will see an increasing principal recovery over time and, therefore, a slightly negatively convex outstanding balance.[1]

---

[1] For more details on the nature of capital recovery, see Kothari (1996).

Typical Structures

The payment structure of auto loans normally ranges from three to six years, ideal for direct pass-throughs as well as collateralized bonds. In the U.S. market, most auto loan transactions have traditionally been structured as principal pass-throughs, but there is a visible trend towards an increasing use of the revolving feature to extend the maturity of the investment and soft bullet structures.

Credit Enhancements

The most common forms of credit enhancement in auto loan securitizations are excess spread, cash reserve, and subordination.

Auto loans are usually extended at *annualized percentage rates* (APRs), equivalent of a periodic internal rate of return multiplied by the number of periods in a year. The weighted average of the APRs in a pool is significantly higher than the weighted average cost of funding the securitization transaction. This leads to the excess spread, and if the credit pricing was right, the excess spread levels must be enough to absorb the expected losses of the pool, leaving for other forms of credit enhancement to take care of the unexpected losses. Therefore, trapping the excess spread is an easy yet powerful credit enhancement in auto loan transactions. The extent of excess spread to support a pool will be affected by the prepayment rate. Prepayments lead to unscheduled termination of the contract, whereby the excess spread ceases. Excess spread also comes down due to involuntary preclosure, that is, repossession, which is affected by the delinquency rate.

A common practice in auto loan deals by the captive finance companies is to give subvention funding; that is, a low APR or zero APR financing to promote vehicle sales. This would lead to cases of negative excess spread. That is, the weighted average cost of the bonds being higher than the weighted average APR of the pool. This would necessitate the creation of a yield supplement in the pool, either by cash reserve or overcollateralization.

Specific Issues in Auto Loan Securitization

An important legal issue for auto loan securitization is whether the assignment of receivables achieves a *true sale* recognized by law. This would be particularly important in the case of auto lease transactions where the ownership of the physical property may be registered in the name of the originator. In many countries, transfer of physical ownership of assets in lease and hire purchase transactions poses logistical problems. Therefore, a sale of receivables is done, but not backed by a sale of the underlying physical assets.

This is where legal examination is required as to whether the ownership of the asset retained by the originator will create either any disabilities on the part of the transferee or any concerns on the part of the originator.

Another significant legal issue is whether there are any obligations arising out of the physical asset, such as any qualitative obligations, or those arising out of insurance contracts, environmental or third party liabilities. As a general rule, for financial leases, such liabilities do not affect the financier, but the law is evolving in this regard and legal precedents differ in various countries.

KEY POINTS OF THE CHAPTER

➢ *Asset securitizations are classified as existing asset securitizations and future flow securitizations.*

➢ *In an existing asset securitization, the cash flow from the asset exists and there is an existing claim to value.*

➢ *In a future flow securitization, there is no existing claim or contractual right to a cash flow; such contractual rights will be created in the future.*

➢ *The goal of a securitization transaction may be either to transfer assets for cash or simply strip the risk inherent in credit assets and transfer the commensurate risk.*

➢ *In a cash securitization, the goal is to transfer the risk for cash.*

➢ *In a synthetic securitization the focus is on risk transfer.*

➢ *A basis for making a distinction between asset classes in a securitization is according to the nature of the obligors in the pool: retail versus whole obligations.*

> *The distinction between retail and wholesale loans is not merely having to do with the size of the funding but also the purpose of the loan.*

> *In the case of business loans, oftentimes the purpose of the loan is to acquire an asset which is a source of cash flows or cash savings.*

> *Retail loans are typically personal loans.*

> *Securitization of corporate or business loans are referred to as collateralized debt obligations.*

> *The main types of existing asset securitizations are mortgage-backed and asset-backed pools.*

> *In general, mortgage-backed loan pools consist of mortgage loans and asset-backed securities comprise all other existing asset transactions.*

> *There are some products that are classified as asset-backed securities, even though they contain residential mortgage loans. They are referred to as* mortgage-related asset-backed securities *and treated as part of the asset-backed securities market.*

> *Mortgage-backed securities are typically classified into residential mortgage-backed and commercial mortgage-backed, depending on the type of loan involved.*

> *Another type of transaction involves those backed by operating revenues and this is a unique type mostly used for financing acquisitions.*

> *Credit card securitizations involve the securitization of a retail asset, credit card debt.*

> *Credit card securitizations utilize a revolving structure where the amount of principal collected during a certain period is rotated back to the originator to acquire fresh receivables.*

> *In a credit card securitization there is a revolving period wherein new receivables are acquired with principal repayments and when the revolving period ends, the amortization period begins.*

> *In a credit card securitization, to cover the contingency of the assets suffering a decline, a buffer is kept in the form of a seller's interest.*

➤ While credit card securitizations could either use a discrete trust or a master trust structure, the master trust structure is the most widely employed structure.

➤ The allocation of the collections by the master trust to the various issuer trusts in a credit card securitization is done based on the outstanding amount of the relevant trusts and the outstanding seller's interest.

➤ In a credit card securitization, the portfolio yield is the rate of return on the credit card portfolio, and in the context of securitization, those parts of income transferred to the trust.

➤ In a credit card securitization, the payment rate for the portfolio is the monthly payment of interest and principal, divided by the total outstanding in the prior month.

➤ Since a revolving transaction permits the issuer to keep the funding in the transaction by reinvesting the principal received during the revolving period, these transactions include an early amortization trigger.

➤ Examples of early amortization triggers in a typical credit card securitization are seller servicer events, legal events, and performance events.

➤ Auto loan securitization uses retail collateral because auto finance is essentially a variant of consumer finance.

➤ The appealing features of auto loan markets are high asset quality and ease in liquidation of delinquent receivables.

➤ The quality of the auto loan pool depends upon the quality of the underlying collateral, lending terms (loan-to-value ratio), and tenure, with the most important factor being the quality of the underwriting criteria established by the originator.

➤ While in the U.S. market most auto loan transactions have traditionally been structured as principal pass-throughs, there has been increasing use of the revolving feature to extend the maturity of the investment and create soft bullet structures.

➤ The most common forms of credit enhancement in auto loan securitizations are excess spread, cash reserve, and subordination.

CHAPTER 9

Asset-Backed Commercial Paper Conduits and Other Structured Vehicles

Technically speaking, the distinction between an *asset-backed security* (ABS) and *asset-backed commercial paper* (ABCP) is primarily one of the tenure of the paper. *Commercial paper* (CP) by definition is short-term funding,[1] and is therefore mostly used for short-term assets such as trade receivables. ABS is medium term to long term in nature; the same instrument, if issued in the form of CP, will be ABCP. However, in many cases ABCP tries to be exactly the opposite of other asset classes such as credit card securitization. A credit card securitization finances a short-term asset with longer-term securities, while ABCP conduits raise short-term funding and make at least partial investments in longer-term paper, thereby trying to capture the the so-called arbitrage possibilities.

The term *commercial paper* is related to the liabilities of ABCP vehicles. As for their assets, they were initially envisaged to acquire trade paper. Over time, howerver, these vehicles have gone about investing in all forms of securities, including, as the subprime mortgage crisis would reveal, a huge amount of subprime mortgage-backed securities.

---

[1] *Commercial paper* might have different meanings in different countries. It is typically taken to mean funding for a term up to 270 days, in some cases, going up to 365 days. The definition of the word *security* is in the U.S. Securities Act and excludes securities with maturities up to nine months. Hence, CP of 270 days' maturity is exempt from securities regulation. Commercial paper is issued mostly in the form of promissory notes.

The word "conduit" implies that unlike discrete closed-end securitization issuances, these transactions are evergreen. They continue to raise funding over time, and continue to add assets. Most conduits have linkages with banks—the banks provide them liquidity support discussed later in this chapter.

ABCP is a device used by banks to see operating assets such as trade receivables funded by issuance of securities. Traditionally, banks devised ABCP conduits as a device to put their short-term credit assets off their balance sheets, have the same funded by ongoing issuance of short-term paper, and back up the paper issuance by the conduit by some form of liquidity support.

The genesis of ABCP dates back to 1983 when Citibank (Citrioco LP, later known as Ciesco) used it to wean back corporates that migrated to capital markets for cheaper funding. In Europe, the first conduit was set up by Barclays (Sceptre) in late 1992. Today, ABCP conduits exist in all global financial centers, in some cases with local names such as BdT in France.

TYPES OF ABCP CONDUITS

The issuance of ABCP is a standard and ongoing feature, so banks mostly run ongoing programs for ABCP issuance. These are run on the balance sheet as a specific entity, called a *conduit*. The conduit is a thinly capitalized *special purpose vehicle* (SPV), satisfying the general criteria for bankruptcy remoteness. On a continuing basis, the conduit continues to acquire assets and funds by issuing CP. However, there is almost necessarily an asset-liability mismatch, requiring the bank to provide liquidity support to the conduit.

It is not difficult to understand why liquidity support is needed. As noted earlier, originally, ABCP conduits were planned as devices for buying trade paper originated by major clients of banks. However, over time, they have bought all kinds of securities, including ABS. Hence, on the liability side, most of the liabilities of the conduits are short term, and on the asset side, we have a mix of short-term and medium-term paper. There is, obviously, an asset-liability mismatch. The conduits hope to be able to manage the mismatch by continuously rolling or revolving their liabilities, but then, to be able to repay the liabilities as they mature, the conduits tie up a liquidity support, mostly with the sponsoring banks.

Next we discuss the different types of conduits based on different criteria.

Conduits Based on Liquidity Support

Depending upon whether the bank provides full or partial liquidity support to the conduit, ABCP can be either *fully supported* or *partly supported*.

ABCP conduits are virtual subsets of the parent bank. If the bank provides full liquidity support to the conduit, for regulatory purposes, the liquidity support given by the bank may be treated as a *direct credit substitute* in which case the assets held by the conduit are aggregated with those of the bank. Though the early ABCP conduits were directly and fully supported by the banks, subsequent regulation, essentially capital rules, have made fully supported conduits unpopular.

There also emerged a variant of fully supported conduits, which were supported, but not visibly or directly. For example, a support provider would either agree to purchase the outstanding paper, or would agree to provide a loan to redeem the paper. Such a support has a structural similarity to the fully supported type discussed above and therefore has the potential of being treated for regulatory purposes the same as fully supported conduits.

Conduits Based on Number of Sellers

Not only are ABCP conduits set up by banks, there are also large issuers who set up their own conduits. Hence, from the viewpoint of the number of originators throwing their receivables into the program, ABCP conduits are known as *single-seller* and *multiple-seller* conduits. In the latter case, the credit enhancements (and/or liquidity enhancements) are found both at the level of transfer by each originator (originator-level enhancement) and at the program level. The growth of multiseller conduits has far outpaced that of single-seller conduits. As of mid-2007, about 32% of all conduits were multiple-seller conduits. Figure 9.1 shows the structure of a multiseller conduit.

FIGURE 9.1   Structure of a Multiseller Conduit

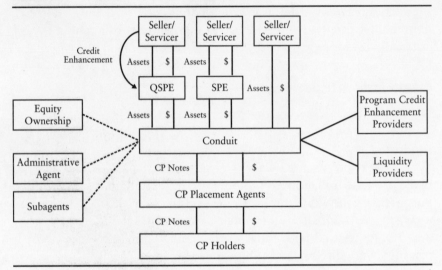

Conduits Based on Asset Type

While ABCP conduits were basically intended to hold trade receivables, eventually they invested in such financial assets such as trade receivables, securities, repos, and total return swaps. Hence, based on their asset focus, there may exist the following specialized types of conduits.

There are *arbitrage conduits*, which hold either high-quality credit assets (hence *credit arbitrage*) or securities (hence, *securities arbitrage*), where the idea is to essentially gain regulatory or economic capital arbitrage by holding these assets in conduit balance sheets. Standard & Poor's defines an arbitrage conduit as one where 95% or more of the assets are securities. *Hybrid* conduits hold both securities and credit assets. As of mid-2007, arbitrage, credit arbitrage and hybrid conduits made up about half of all conduits with an equal percentage for each.

A *repo/TRS* conduit finances highly rated financial institutions mostly by repo transactions, or by entering into total return swaps. Only about 3% of the conduit universe is made up of repo/TRS conduits as a of mid-2007.

Yet another type of vehicle has emerged over time, *structured investment vehicle* (SIV). Unlike traditional conduits where capital is minimal, in the case of a SIV, there will be significant capital. In traditional conduits, capital is replaced by credit enhancements—pool level and program-wide enhancements (discussed later in this chapter). In the case of SIVs, capital is used for enhancement purposes. The SIV typically finances itself by issuing *capital notes*, which are contingent notes that would count as economic capital. The credit risk of a conduit is monitored closely, and the conduit is required to bring more capital based on the assets. The typical leverage permitted on capital is 10 to 15 times. SIVs are tightly monitored by the trustees as well as the rating agencies. During the 2007 subprime crisis, the net asset value of most SIVs fell below the required tests of minimum collateral forcing many of them to liquidate. SIVs represent about 13% of the conduit universe.

TRADITIONAL SECURITIZATION AND ABCP

ABCP has emerged over time as an independent class of short-term ABS by itself. Though the basic legal structure and principles of structured finance used are similar, there are some very basic differences between ABS (also, to distinguish from CP, called *term securitization*) and ABCP:

- Conduit investments are revolving and fluctuating, whereas ABS mostly has a fixed pool size.
- ABS collateral type is mostly homogenous with ABCP conduits buying a variety of assets.
- In ABS, it is common to see maturity matching, or to see short-term assets such as card receivables funded by issuing long-term paper. Conduits do the contrary—they might fund long-term assets by issuing short-term paper, which they do on a continuous basis. The liquidity support of the sponsoring bank allows them to play with the mismatches.
- There is no scheduled amortization of the assets held by conduits.
- Unlike term securitizations, ABCP conduits are going concerns with no fixed winding up date.

ABCP COLLATERAL

As noted earlier, ABCP was primarily designed to acquire and fund trade receivables of larger corporations. However, as the product evolved over time, the collateral composition shifted heavily into investing in financial instruments. Today, ABCP conduits invest in all possible financial instruments such as *collateralized debt obligations* (CDOs)[2] lease receivables, and corporate loans.

To see this, consider that in 1993 the assets of conduits according to a Moody's report authored by Rutan and Berthelon (2007) consisted of the following:

Trade and term receivables: 60%
Credit card receivables: 12%
Corporate loans: 12%

and the balance in other assets.

Fast forward 13 years to June 2006. U.S. multiseller conduits held the following assets according to Moody's:

Trade receivables: 13%
Credit cards: 15%
Commercial loans: 11%
Auto loans: 10%
Securities: 9%
Mortgage warehousing lines and other mortgage investments: 9%
Highly rated CDOs: 3%

and the balance in other assets.

CREDIT ENHANCEMENT STRUCTURE

As explained above, a conduit is the issuer of CP because the program provides an issuance window to several seller-level trusts, each of which are SPVs. Typically, for multiseller conduits the assets are pooled at the level of the seller and are transferred into individual SPVs. The sellers are, for a trade receivables conduit, the custom-

---

[2] We discuss CDOs in Part Four.

ers of the sponsor bank who want to have their trade receivables financed. At this level, enhancement is done to an extent sufficient to ensure that the interest being sold from this SPV to the conduit will allow the conduit to seek the desired rating. This means that unless the conduit itself is credit-enhanced, the rating of the interest sold by the SPVs to the conduit should match up with the desired rating of the CP to be issued by the conduit, say AAA.

The enhancement granted at the seller level is called *seller level enhancement* or *pool level enhancement*. When all these pool interests, duly credit enhanced, are sold to the conduit, there might be a credit or liquidity enhancement at that level too, which is called *program level enhancement*. See Figure 9.2.

The program level enhancements may include both a credit enhancement and a liquidity enhancement. At the program level, the

FIGURE 9.2   Partially Supported, Multiseller ABCP Program Structure

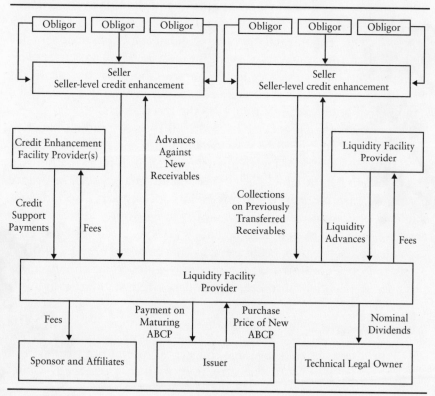

basic objective is to obtain a liquidity enhancement (as the interest sold to the conduit has already been credit enhanced), and the credit enhancement at this level is primarily required to be able to tie up liquidity facilities with independent banks. Liquidity support is discussed later.

It is important to understand that the credit-enhancement hierarchy is mostly relevant for partially supported conduits; for fully supported conduits, what matters is the quality of the supporting bank.

Pool Level and Program Level Enhancement

The pool level enhancements provide support to the value of assets in the particular pool. The program-wide enhancement supports all outstanding paper at the given time, and therefore provides a fungible enhancement.

The pool level enhancement should primarily cover the credit risk of the assets. In addition, where appropriate it should cover exchange rate risk, interest rate risk, and for noninterest-bearing assets, the carrying costs. The normal methods of enhancement here are similar to those used for typical securitizations discussed in Chapter 5: over-collateralization, excess spread, recourse, subordination, or swaps with the originator. The pool level enhancement may typically be done with a pool level SPV that buys the receivables.

Program-wide enhancement covers all the outstanding paper in the pool and is designed to provide support when the losses out of a pool exceed the pool-level enhancement. The typical methods of enhancement here will include letters of credit, guarantee or insurance cover and cash collateral. The program-wide support also indicates the level of commitment of the sponsor to ensure the quality of the assets. According to Standard & Poor's (2005c, p. 20), the presence "of at least 5% program-wide credit enhancement of unrated pools of assets provides comfort that the program-wide, credit-enhancement provider is incentivized to keep the underwriting standards high."

Deleverage Triggers

ABCP programs have deleverage triggers, a mechanism that we will see is also used by CDOs. These are in form of *stop-issuance* or *wind down* triggers, which stop the conduit from issuing any further CP or acquiring further assets, if and as long as the triggers are in place. In view of the two-tier nature of the conduit, the triggers may be set at both the pool level and the program level.

Pool level triggers may include the following:

- Insolvency or bankruptcy of a seller/servicer.
- Downgrade of a seller's long- or short-term credit rating below a specified level.
- Cross-default of a seller under other debt obligations.
- Material adverse change in a seller/servicer's ability to perform its duties as servicer.
- Deterioration of portfolio assets below specified levels of write offs, delinquencies or dilution.
- Depletion of credit enhancement below a required minimum amount.
- Default or breach of any covenant, representation, or warranty by a seller or servicer.

Typical program-wide triggers are:

- Failure of the conduit to repay a maturing CP or an outstanding liquidity advance when due.
- Any program documents cease to be in full force and effect.
- Default or breach of any covenant, representation, or warranty by the conduit.
- The net worth of the conduit falls below a certain level.
- Draws on program-wide credit enhancement exceed a certain amount.

When the triggers are in place, the money collected from the assets will not be used for further asset creation, but will be used to pay down the paper as it comes due.

LIQUIDITY SUPPORT

Liquidity support basically comes in the form of facilities to draw from a line of credit. The line of credit provider, quite often, is the administrative agent himself. For single-seller conduits, liquidity support is usually 100%.

The liquidity provider also needs to have a certain rating, and in the event of rating downgrade, the liquidity provider is required to collateralize the liquidity commitment with cash.

Depending on the way the liquidity facility is drawn up, it may go beyond mere liquidity support and provide credit support to the transaction as well. For example, sometimes the liquidity provider enters into an asset purchase agreement, which provides additional protection to the investors. According to Standard & Poor's (2005c, p. 22):

> The liquidity provider also may be willing to provide an asset purchase agreement that provides added protection to investors. The liquidity facility provider's willingness to agree to such an arrangement will be based on the provider's independent document review and evaluation of the underlying pool of receivables. Though liquidity banks typically fund for nondefaulted receivables, the banks may be more willing to provide more than just protection against timing mismatches when the originator of the receivables has other banking arrangements with the provider and is an investment-grade client.

PARTIES TO AN ABCP PROGRAM

The parties to an ABCP program include:

- A program sponsor
- An administrative agent
- A manager
- A placement agent
- An issuing and paying agent

Program Sponsor

The *program sponsor* is the one who originates the whole idea and refers assets to the conduit. Program sponsors are usually banks and financial intermediaries who use the conduits as extensions of the bank's credit book to house specific assets with capital market funding.

It is not necessary for the conduit sponsor to own equity in the conduit. As SPVs are typically structured, the legal equity of the conduit is usually small and is owned by unaffiliated parties such as charitable trusts. However, the sponsor does have material interest in the conduit, mostly by way of credit enhancements. These credit enhancements allow the bank to reap much of the excess spreads earned by the conduit, so the prime beneficiary of the conduit is mostly the sponsor. This practice led the Financial Accounting Standard Board (FASB) to put in place a different method for recognizing the economic equity of the conduit (FIN 46R).

Administrative Agent

Just as most securitization transactions have servicers, there is an administrative agent to handle the regular administration of the conduit. The administrative agent may be the program sponsor or one of his affiliated entities because the control of day-to-day affairs of the conduits vests in the agent. The functions of the administrative agent extend to issuing, managing, and repaying the CP, advising on purchase of assets, and handling the interface with the sellers.

The administrative agent's duties in connection with the day-to-day operations of the program include:

- Arranging for the execution and safekeeping of the program documents.
- Maintaining operating accounts.
- Investing excess funds in permitted investments.
- Maintaining general accounting records.
- Preparing financial statements and arranging audits.
- Preserving books and records.
- Giving notices to other key parties.
- Preparing monthly portfolio reports.

The administrative agent's duties in connection with the issuance and repayment of CP include:

- Instructing the issuing and paying agent and the depositary.
- Purchasing and selling assets.
- Extending loans to borrowers.

- Determining when draws on liquidity and credit enhancement facilities are necessary.

The administrative agent's role may also include credit advisory services such as:

- Identifying and referring new sellers to the conduit.
- Conducting due diligence reviews of prospective sellers.
- Structuring the acquisition of asset interests and any necessary hedging arrangements.
- Monitoring the ongoing performance of each transaction.

In short, the administrative agent does everything for the conduit that the bank would have done if the assets were housed on the bank's balance sheet.

Manager

The manager essentially is a legal functionary to ensure that the conduit is not treated as controlled by the sponsor. If such control is established, the conduit may lose its legal independence from the sponsor. Hence, the manager may be assigned the role of appointing the board of directors. In addition, the manager is responsible for items such as calling meetings of the executive committee.

Placement Agent

The role of the placement agent is just as the name suggests: place CP in the market. The placements are typically done through investment banks and money market brokers.

Issuing and Paying Agent

The settlement and recordkeeping function common to all fixed income issuance is done by the issuing and paying agent.

RATING OF ABCP CONDUITS

As opposed to ABS where the rating is done based on a particular pool, for ABCP a rating is given for the program. For obvious reasons, the quality of the management of the conduit and the fungible program-wide enhancement are relevant factors in rating the program. The distinction between traditional ABS rating and program rating is that the conduit rating is similar to the rating of corporates.

The significant aspects of rating of the conduit are considered by rating agencies are:

- Quality of management
- Credit quality of assets
- Receivables eligibility criteria

We describe each next.

Quality of Management

Unlike ABS where the inanimate pool of assets drives the ratings, the rating of ABCP conduits stress more the entity, that is, the quality of the management of the conduit. The administrator is the management of the program. Adding assets to the book of a conduit is similar to underwriting a credit asset in a bank, so the credit asset policy of the conduit becomes extremely significant here. It is necessary to ensure that the conduit is not being saddled with assets rejected by the regular credit assessment of the bank. As Standard & Poor's (2005c, p. 8) states:

> In reviewing a conduit's underwriting criteria, assurances will be sought that the conduit's credit and investment policy is at least as conservative as that of the program administrator where the administrator is a financial institution.

Sound transaction underwriting would involve a thorough analysis of seller risks, including evaluation of overall creditworthiness, risk of fraud, product and performance risk, and the capacity of the seller to meet its representation and warranties.

Credit Quality of Assets

For multiseller conduits, the asset quality will be driven by the underwriting standards used by each originator who sells receivables into pools. For each pool, an assessment of the experience of the originator and the underwriting standards for the assets become important. The sizing of the enhancement for each pool is done based on traditional ABS rating principles—historical delinquency rates and loss severity. In assessing the quality of the pool, obligor concentration is one of the factors to specifically examine. Obligor concentration to a pool does what correlation does to CDOs as we will explain in Chapter 13. Transactions typically establish obligor concentration limits and industry concentration limits.

Receivables Eligibility Criteria

There is expected to be an ongoing acquisition of receivables in the pool, so it is significant to define the eligibility and, in particular, the ineligibility criteria. In view of the heterogenous nature of receivables, it is not possible to standardize the criteria, but some of the common criteria according to Standard & Poor's relate to delinquent and defaulted accounts, excess concentration, unperformed contracts, bill and hold receivables, tenor, and obligor characteristics.[3]

KEY POINTS OF THE CHAPTER

➤ *Technically speaking, the distinction between* asset-backed commercial paper *(ABCP) and asset-backed security (referred to as* term securitization *to distinguish it from commercial paper) is primarily one of the tenure of the paper.*

➤ *ABCP was primarily designed to acquire and fund trade receivables of larger corporations but the collateral composition shifted heavily into investing in financial instruments. Today, ABCP conduits invest in a wide range of financial instruments.*

➤ *The issuance of ABCP is a standard and ongoing feature, so banks mostly run ongoing programs for ABCP issuance on their balance sheet as a specific entity called a* conduit.

➤ *A conduit is a thinly-capitalized special purpose vehicle satisfying the general criteria for bankruptcy remoteness.*

---

[3] For a further discussion of each of these, see Standard & Poor's (2005c).

➤ *There are different conduits based on different criteria: (1) liquidity support, (2) number of sellers, and (3) asset type,*

➤ *Depending upon whether the bank provides full or partial liquidity support to the conduit, ABCP can be either fully supported or partly supported.*

➤ *ABCP conduits can be either single-seller or multiple-seller conduits with the latter being the most common form.*

➤ *In a multiple-seller conduit, the credit enhancement (and/or liquidity enhancements) are found both at the level of transfer by each originator (originator-level enhancement) and at the program level.*

➤ *Conduits are classified based on their asset focus and include (1) arbitrage conduits, (2) hybrid conduits, (3) repo/total return swap conduits, and (4) structured investment vehicles (SIVs).*

➤ *Arbitrage conduits are those which hold either high-quality credit assets (hence credit arbitrage) or securities (hence, securities arbitrage), where the idea is to essentially gain regulatory or economic capital arbitrage by holding these assets in conduit balance sheets.*

➤ *Hybrid conduits hold both securities and credit assets.*

➤ *Repo/total return swap conduits finance highly rated financial institutions mostly by repurchase agreement (repo) transactions, or by entering into total return swaps.*

➤ *In comparison to traditional conduits where capital is replaced by credit enhancements, in SIVs there is significant capital (i.e., capital is used for credit enhancement purposes).*

➤ *SIVs (1) typically finance themselves by issuing capital notes (contingent notes that would count as economic capital), (2) are monitored closely for credit risk by trustees and rating agencies, and (3) required to bring more capital based on the assets.*

➤ *While the basic legal structure and principles of structured finance used are similar, the basic differences between ABS (i.e. term securitization) and ABCP are (1) conduit investments are revolving and fluctuating whereas ABS typically has a fixed pool* size; (2) ABS collateral type is mostly homogenous while ABCP conduits buy a variety of assets; (3) in ABS it is common to find maturity matching or to see short-term assets funded by issuing long-term paper while ABCP conduits do the opposite by funding long-term assets by issuing short-term paper on a continuous basis; (4) there is no scheduled amortization of the assets held by conduits; and (5) unlike term securitizations, ABCP conduits are going concerns with no termination date.

➤ For multiseller conduits, there is seller level enhancement (or pool level enhancement) and there might be program level enhancement.

➤ Program level enhancements may include both a credit enhancement and a liquidity enhancement.

➤ Pool level enhancements provide support to the value of assets in the particular pool and primarily cover credit risk and where appropriate currency risk, interest rate risk, and the risks associated with the cost of carry.

➤ Program-wide enhancement, which covers all the outstanding paper in the pool, is designed to provide support (via letters of credit, guarantee or insurance cover and cash collateral) when the losses out of a pool exceed the pool-level enhancement.

➤ Program-wide support also indicates the level of commitment of the sponsor to ensure the quality of the assets.

➤ Deleverage triggers are included in ABCP programs, providing a mechanism in the form of stop-issuance or wind down triggers which stop the conduit from issuing any further CP or acquiring further assets, if and as long as the triggers are in reached.

➤ Deleverage triggers may be set at both the pool level and the program level.

➤ In an ABCP program, liquidity support basically comes in the form of facilities to draw from a line of credit with the liquidity provider being required to have a certain rating.

➤ The parties to an ABCP program include (1) a program sponsor (the entity originating the whole idea and referring assets to the

*conduit), (2) an administrative agent, (3) a manager, (4) a place-
ment agent, and (5) an issuing and paying agent.*

➤ *In contrast to a term securitization (i.e., ABS) which is rated
based on a particular pool, for ABCP a rating is given for the
program.*

➤ *The distinction between traditional an ABS rating and a program
rating is that the conduit rating is similar to the rating of a corporation.*

➤ *The significant aspects of rating a conduit that are considered by
rating agencies are (1) quality of management, (2) credit quality
of assets, and (3) receivables eligibility criteria.*

CHAPTER 10

Securitization of Future Cash Flows: Future Revenues, Operating Revenues, and Insurance Profits

In this chapter, we discuss some unique examples of securitization—securitization of future cash flows, whole business or operating revenues securitization, and securitization of embedded profits in insurance businesses. All of these have a common thread: they all relate to profits or cash flows out of future operations. These applications illustrate how the securitization methodology has been used to raise capital market funding for something which has always been the traditional domain of the banker—financing business operations. The idea is to understand and quantify the volatilities and build risk mitigating factors for each.

FUTURE REVENUES SECURITIZATION

While traditional asset-backed transactions relate to assets that exist, future flows transactions relate to assets expected to exist. There is a source, a business or an infrastructure, from which the asset will arise. The business or infrastructure in question will have to be worked upon to generate the income; in other words, the income has not been originated and set apart such that repayment of the securities is a self-liquidating exercise. On the other hand, future flows is close to corporate funding in that there needs to be a performance on the assets or infrastructure to see the cash flow with which the securities will be paid.

What Future Flows Are Securitizable

The essential premise in a future flow securitization is if a framework exists that will give rise to cash flows in the future, the cash flow from such framework is a candidate for securitization. If the framework itself does not exist, the investors would be taking exposure in a dream; their rights would probably be worse than for secured lending. For example, if the cow exists, but not the milk, the milk can be securitized, as whoever owns the cow would be able to milk it. If both the milk and cow do not exist, it is not a proper candidate for securitization.

Thus, revenues from air ticket sales, electricity sale, telephone rentals, and export receivables from natural resources have been the subject of future flows securitization. However, in an apparent overdrive, sometimes, even something as integrally performance-based as the sales of goods or services are considered out of businesses that require continued performance.

Some Key Features of Future Flows Deals

Uncertain Receivables

By its very nature, future flows receivables are uncertain and largely unpredictable. Therefore, the originator transfers a certain portion of the receivables, and retains the excess over the transferred portion as the seller's interest. The transferred portion is the core receivable, which based on a past track record and after applying stress levels can be predictably certain. The transferred portion is used for investors' service—hence, the transferred portion may also be visualized as the required amount of investor service. Thus, over a period the extent of the seller's interest varies based on its origination.

Cash Flow Trapping

A future flows deal, in its essence, is a cash flow trapping device. There is purportedly a mechanism of the sale of receivables—often backed by true sale opinions—but evidently, as what is being sold is yet to be generated, the whole concept will have no meaning unless the trustees could have physical trapping of the cash flows generated by the subject receivables before they are routed to the originator.

Prioritization of the Transferee

In a traditional asset-backed transaction, the transferee is concerned with only the cash flows that have been transferred. In a future flows transaction, the transferee is entitled, at least in the first stage, to the entire cash flow from the subject receivables, though the transferred interest is substantially lesser. After retaining the portion relating to the transferred interest, the trustees relay the balance of the cash to the transferor on account of the transferor's interest. It is from this amount that the transferor meets its regular operating expenses. In other words, by virtue of the cash flow trapping, the transferee gets a priority over even the operating expenses of the transferor.

High Extent of Overcollateralization

In most future flow transactions, the extent of overcollateralization is substantially higher than for asset-backed transactions. This is to safeguard against the fact that the investors are likely to be affected by the performance risk of the originator. Investors may have a cushion against the credit risks, but the fact that the airline does not fly at all or the electricity company does not generate power at all, is not guarded against, except by substantial overcollateralization or cash reserves.

Restrictions on the Borrower's Business

Being a quasi-lending type exposure, a future flow deal typically places restrictions on the borrower's ability to borrow and create encumbrances or liens, and similar covenants.

No Originator Independence

While asset-backed transactions are structured so as to be independent of the originator (except to the extent of servicing), future flows deals are substantially, if not completely, dependent on the originator. Therefore, seldom have future flow deals been able to traverse the rating of the originator; their motive is not to arbitrage the originator rating but the sovereign rating, as discussed in the next section. Or, alternatively, the motive is to achieve a higher extent of funding than permitted by traditional methods.

Not Off-Balance Sheet

As future flows securitizations are not off-balance sheet, many of the typical merits of off-balance-sheet financing such as gain on sale and capital relief do not apply.

Why Future Flows Securitization?

Following are essential questions to ask in a future flows securitization:

- What is the temptation of the originator in assigning future incomes?
- Would the originator not be better off in securing a traditional secured funding?

It is important to completely understand the answer to these questions, as it also highlights the proper application of future flows transactions. Conceptually, future flows transactions would make sense for the originator if it helps the originator to reduce its overall cost of funding. This would be possible only if (1) the transaction helps the originator to borrow more; and/or (2) the transaction helps the originator to borrow at less costs.

The extent of borrowing possible in future flows deals is determined by the cash flows and the level of overcollateralization required. A traditional lender, in contrast, is mostly concerned with values of assets on the balance sheet. For example, a typical working capital financing bank looks at the current assets on the balance sheet. If the balance sheet assets are four months of cash flow, a bank might provide 75% thereof, or three months of working capital. A securitization investor looks at cash flows for a regular servicing: with a collateralization of two times, a securitization transaction might result in funding of even 20 months of cash flow. Therefore, it is quite possible for a future flow deal to result in an increased extent of borrowing.

On the cost of borrowing, the essential question is: Does future flow securitization remove any of the risks of traditional lending? All traditional lending is subject to the performance risk of the originator. If the originator does not perform or function at all, a lender would face default. The same is true for securitization. However, future flows transactions remove two significant risks—credit risk and sovereign risk.

Credit risk, divested from the performance risk of the originator, implies a situation where the originator has cash flow, but does not pay up investors. This problem would be resolved in securitization if the transaction gives the *special purpose vehicle* (SPV) a legal right over the cash flow that is trapped at the source.

Another important objective of future flow transactions has been to remove sovereign risk. This applies for cross-border lending, as several of the future flows transactions in the past have been targeted at cross-border investments. If an external lender gives a loan to a borrower, say, from an emerging market country, the risk the investor faces is that in the event of an exchange crisis the sovereign may either impose a moratorium on payments to external lenders or may redirect foreign exchange earnings. A future flow deal tries to eliminate this risk by giving investors a legal right over cash flow arising from countries other than the originator's, thereby trapping cash flow before it comes under the control of the sovereign.

As such, one of the motives in future flow securitization is to allow the originator, individually a strong company but based in a country with a poor sovereign rating, to pierce the sovereign rating.

Types of Future Flow Deals

One of the most common examples of a future flows securitization is securitization of cross-border cash flows.

Take the instance of a typical transaction by, say, a Mexican originator. The Mexican company has an option of borrowing from international markets, but the lenders would be concerned with currency risk and sovereign risks. This originator, say, exports crude oil to the United States. The cash flow emanating out of the United States will be securitized and transferred to the SPV set up in the United States. The importers buying the crude oil from this originator would sign a notice and acknowledgement of assignment so as to subject them to U.S. law and force them to make payments to the SPV.

Now, the investors are secured against exchange risk, as the export receivables are in U.S. dollars. The investors are secured against sovereign risk as the cash flows are payable by U.S. companies which are not subject to the sovereign's controls. The only risk the investors face is if the company is not producing and exporting at all, or the company redirects its exports to some other countries not covered by the legal rights of the investors.

While the above is a typical future flows deal based on sales of goods or services, the future flows transactions may be classified into the following broad categories:

- *Based on exports of goods or services.* This is the most common type of future flow deals. Examples include the sale of pulp, oil, or metals from Latin American countries.
- *Based on sales of goods or services.* Several transactions taken place all over the world such as airline and train ticket receivables fall under this category.
- *Financial futures flows.* Financial futures flows refer to flows to a financial intermediary such as inward remittances to a bank. Here, there is no asset but merely a cash flow. The remittance money that is flowing through a bank is not the receivable or asset of the bank. The bank receives money from a remitter and repays the same to the remittee. In case of foreign inward remittances, the bank receives this flow in foreign currency, and repays the money in domestic currency. It is the foreign exchange inflow part that is securitized.
- *Other futures flows.* In addition, there are numerous examples such as the net settlement of telephone revenues and toll road receivables. Each of these receivables is a class by itself—the extent of dependence on the servicer may range from vital and essential to merely peripheral.

Structural Features

As future flows transactions are confronted with several risks relating to the originator as well as the obligors, most future flows transactions rely on structural features in addition to credit enhancements. These features include those described below.

Subordination Structures Generally Do Not Work

Based on the level of dependence the transaction has on the servicer, future flows transactions may either be completely originator-dependent or may have a peripheral dependence, although not essential. A toll revenue securitization is a good example. Here the infrastructure giving rise to the income in the future already exists and all one has to do is to collect it to pay off investors. On the other hand, take the case of airline ticket receivables. There is a substantial performance risk on the entity. In the latter type cases, the rating of the transaction is generally capped at the entity rating of the originator.

If the originator's rating were to serve as a cap, subordination, which is basically intended to provide a rating upliftment, does not work for future flows.

Overcollateralization and Cash Reserve

One of the most significant forms of credit support to future flows transactions is the creation and maintenance of overcollateralization and a reserve. Overcollateralization implies the degree of *debt service coverage ratio* (DSCR) of the transaction. In view of the fluctuating nature of income, after taking a base level of income,[1] a degree of overcollateralization is reiteratively worked out to find the amount of funding. The debt service required should sufficiently be covered by expected income.

In addition, the excess of the inflows over the required debt service is typically pooled into a few months' cash reserve. The cash reserve helps smooth the temporary periods of volatility in the cash flow.

---

[1] An easy approach may be to know some standard deviations from the average of the inflows.

Early Amortization Triggers

The range and the scope of *early amortization triggers* (EATs) for future flow is often very wide. As for credit cards, as explained in a previous chapter early amortization is done by using the cash flow representing overcollateralization and trapping the cash representing the seller's interest. The triggers may include:

- Cash flow-related early amortization triggers:
  - If debt service coverage drops below the periodic required amount (e.g., 5.0×) for a payment period or below a monthly required amount (e.g. 3.0×).
  - If any portion of interest and principal payments is not made in a timely manner.

- Third-party-related early amortization triggers:
  - If a correspondent bank does not meet minimum credit rating requirements and that bank is not replaced in accordance with the terms of the transaction.

- Company-related early amortization triggers:
  - If litigation is instituted against the company that is likely to have a material adverse effect on the transaction.
  - If the company becomes insolvent.
  - Failure of the servicer to comply with terms of the transaction.

- Sovereign-related early amortization triggers:
  - If the sovereign interferes in any material way with the company's ability to direct cash flow to the transaction.
  - If the sovereign takes over a substantial part of the business of the company.

What Early Amortization Means to the Originator

While the relevance of putting early amortization features in a transaction is understandable, it is necessary to realize that early amortization amounts to drying up the resources of the originator (by inherently calling back a loan or accelerating the repayment of the loan) when things start turning bad for the originator. The EATs are comparable to acceleration clauses in bank loans.

Representations and Warranties of the Seller

Compared with a traditional asset-backed deal, the representations ("reps") and warranties of the seller in a futures flow deal are far more comprehensive. This enables the transferee to relate a delinquency to a breach of the same and remit the delinquent receivables back to the seller.

Third-Party Guarantees a Common Feature

In several emerging market future flows, after a credit enhancement of the receivables to a volume for a AAA rating and making the transaction acceptable to international investors, obtaining an insurance wrap or a bond guarantee is quite a common feature.

WHOLE BUSINESS OR OPERATING REVENUES SECURITIZATION

The idea of whole business securitization developed in the United Kingdom during the mid-1990s when the cash flow of a nursing home were securitized. This led to a spate of transactions in various spheres such as pubs, hospitals, entertainment and amusement sites, airports, theaters and ferry services. The market for whole business securitization is still largely limited to Europe, and there too, with a concentration in the United Kingdom.

The devise of whole business securitization (also known as *corporate securitization*, *corporate entity securitization*, *operating revenues securitization*, or *hybrid finance*) sprang basically from the *leveraged buyout* (LBO) market and the crux of a whole business securitization is the securitization of an LBO. Whole business securitization captures the residual value of a business (i.e., the valuation of the business) and creates securities that represent this residual value.

Given the ability to apply this device to the cash flow of almost any business, the concept virtually breaks down all limitations of securitization and extends it to almost any business that satisfies certain features.

Objectively, there is not much difference between a plain secured borrowing and whole business securitization. In a plain borrowing, the borrower obliges itself to pay to the lender, and the obvious source of payment is the cash flow of the borrower. The lender might have security interest in all or some of the assets of the borrower to secure the loan so granted. In a securitization, on the other hand, the investor is given a legal right over some of the assets of the originator which are legally isolated from the originator. In whole business securitization, because the idea is to make the whole of the cash flow of the business available for liquidating the securities, there is no question of isolating the assets of the originator. In other words, the investors are given a claim over all the cash flow of the originator, which remain within the legal and contractual control of the originator, and so the assets from which the cash flow arises. The only difference between secured lending and a whole business securitization is that in the latter case, investors acting through the SPV will have greater legal control over the originator, so that they can effectively assume the control of the originator's business in the event of default.

In our discussion of whole loan securitizations that follows, we point out the major differences of this type of securitization and a traditional securitization. Table 10.1 summarizes the major differences.

Methodology

Secured Loan Structure

The common methodology in most whole business securitizations is for the issuer SPV to issue bonds in the market and with the funds so collected, provide a loan to the operator (originator). Whole business transactions are based on a loan structure rather than a true sale structure. While in a traditional securitization the SPV purchases the assets of the originator, in a whole business transaction the SPV gives a loan to the operating company against which it obtains a charge or security interest over substantially the whole of the assets of the operating company. The loan is based on certain capitalization of the

TABLE 10.1 Major Differences between Traditional Securitization and Whole Business Securitization

	Traditional Securitization	Whole Business Securitization
Basic nature	Isolation of specific and identifiable assets and dedicating these assets for payment to investors.	Raising of funding for an operating company as an alternative to a traditional loan, with greater control over the assets of the operating company and hence higher rating.
Legal feature	Based on a true sale of the identifiable assets.	Based on a secured loan secured by a fixed and floating charge over substantially all the assets of the operating company.
Cash flow securitized	Predictable cash flow from the identifiable assets.	All the identifiable cash flow of the operating business.
Motivations	Off-balance sheet; lower cost; additional source of funding.	Alternative source of funding with probably higher leverage and cheaper cost.
Countries where used	All over the world.	United Kingdom and countries with similar corporate law and bankruptcy laws.
Investor comfort	Investors look at the identifiable assets; and investors do not have a general recourse against the originator.	Investors have a general recourse against the operating company; however, investors are subordinated to preferential claims and other fixed charge holders.
Accounting	Off-balance sheet.	On-balance sheet.
Typical maturities	Usually not very long; coterminous with that of the receivables.	Usually long, going up to 25–30 years.
Servicer responsibilities	Usually passive servicing; collection and repayment.	Usually active handling of the receivables and the assets.
Impact of operator bankruptcy	Designed so that the transaction is bankruptcy remote.	Designed so that the receiver can preempt the bankruptcy of the operator and take control of the assets prior to actual bankruptcy; reduces risk of bankruptcy but does not avoid such risk altogether.

operating profits or *earnings before interest, taxes, depreciation, and amortization* (EBITDA) of the operating entity.

The originator agrees to repay the loan in fixed installments of interest and principal; these installments are used by the SPV to pay off the bonds. The central legal document in the transaction is the loan agreement whereby the SPV gives a loan to the operator. This loan agreement is backed by a fixed and floating charge over the entire estate of the operating company, which creates a special protection in bankruptcy.

An interesting question is why is the whole business securitization founded on secured loan and not a true sale? One needs to go to the root of the true sale issue before coming to an answer. As an essential feature of securitization, true sales have been used to isolate identified assets of an originator and put them into a separate vehicle that solely subserves for the benefit of investors. In a whole business securitization, first of all, the isolation of assets is impracticable as the assets in question are the operating assets of the originator from which the cash flow will emanate over time. These assets are virtually the entire estate of the originator. So if you are thinking of isolating the whole from the whole, you are either isolating nothing or leaving behind nothing.

Bankruptcy Protection

More significantly, the key purpose of isolation by true sale is bankruptcy protection; the specific assets should be available for payment to the investors without being subject to any other claims. In the United Kingdom and such other jurisdictions, there is not exactly the same comfort as you would see in a true sale, but largely similar comfort can be obtained by a receivership device whereby, before the declaration of bankruptcy by the originator, a receiver would take possession of the whole or substantially the whole of the assets of the company and leave behind nominal assets, thereby leaving no motive on the part of the other creditors to take the operating company to bankruptcy.

Whole business securitizations are not designed to be bankruptcy remote as far as the originator is concerned; they cannot be, as there is no sale, and hence, no true sale, of the assets to the lending SPV.

However, the security interest that the SPV holds gives it a specific power—to appoint an administrative receiver. This power is a typicality of the U.K. insolvency laws and is found in insolvency laws of certain other countries as well.

Structural and Credit Enhancements

Whole business securitizations are characterized more by structural protection, that is, a strong collateralized lending transaction, than by usual hierarchy of credit enhancements in traditional securitizations.

The relevance of subordination as a credit enhancement is highly limited, as the risk is not a pool of assets but in a single business; the probability "distribution" of risk of a single business has two extremes only—the business succeeds or fails. Several U.K. whole business transactions have been structured with subordinated notes, but for difficult business scenarios, the subordinated as well as the senior notes might have suffered downgrades,[2] a vindication of the principle stated above.

The stress is more on operational constraints, cash flow control, and waterfall stipulations. Once again, these controls are common in project finance—securitization of whole business transactions uses a combination of structured finance and secured lending methodology to result in a more effective investor service.

The common structural enhancements used are as follows:

- *Breach of covenants/Administrative receivership.* As noted below, the ability of the trustees to appoint an administrative receiver is key to the presumable *bankruptcy remoteness* of whole business structures. The right to appoint an administrative receiver is given to a floating charge holder (trustee), and therefore, the legal structure should clearly empower the charge-holder to step in and appoint an administrative receiver. Detailed trigger events when this right will be available need to be specified. The security interest of the trustees is wide and comprehensive—apart from all

---

[2] See FitchRatings: Note Acceleration in Whole Business Securitization, April 2, 2004, graphic giving scenarios where different senior securities will suffer downgrade.

hard and operating assets of the entity, it generally also includes, by an agreement with the holding company, a controlling block of equity of the operating company and dividends.

- *Financial covenants.* The transaction should constantly ensure maintenance of a minimum debt service coverage. The whole business investors are paid out of residual profits, so the amount of cash flow, say *free cash flow*, available for investor service are the operational profits, after interest, depreciation (for capital assets replacement), and taxes. This cash flow should generally cover the debt service to investors at least 1.1 times or so. Failure of the covenant, remaining unrectified for a certain amount of time, would amount to a default event, allowing the trustee to crystallize the security interest and appoint an administrative receiver. Of course, the issuer is always allowed ways of curing such breach, such as the posting of cash collateral.
- *Liquidity facilities.* Almost all whole business transactions are backed by liquidity support to save the transaction from failing on payments during periods of temporary stress such as strikes and lock outs. Generally speaking, a liquidity facility of at least 12 to 18 months' service is insisted upon. Usual requirements for a rating of the liquidity provider will also be applicable.
- *Working capital facilities.* The operating business, based on its needs, should have adequate provision for working capital. It is notable that as the investors in whole business transactions are entitled to residual cash flow, in terms of waterfall, investors are relegated behind working capital lenders. However, in terms of powers, the investors in whole business transactions have substantial powers conferred by the all pervasive security interest.
- *Restrictive covenants.* To ensure that the business character of the operating company does not significantly change, covenants are placed restricting acquisition of unrelated businesses or assets, disposal of assets, payment of dividends unless certain DSCR norms are complied with.

Cash Flow Waterfall

The cash flow waterfall is, by itself, an effective structural protection in a whole business transaction and should be put together very carefully. The cash flow waterfall should not be so restrictive that it hinders management's effective operations. Generally speaking, the cash flow waterfall has three alternative scenarios:

- Preenforcement, meaning until the trustees' security interest has been enforced.
- Postenforcement, meaning after the trustees have decided to invoke the security interest.
- Postacceleration, meaning if decided to take the business down the winding up route.

The preenforcement waterfall typically provides for the following priority ("issuer" below refers to the SPV issuing notes to investors, and the cash flow to which the waterfall applies are those after regular operating expenses):

1. Security trustee fees, note trustee fees, fees and expenses of the paying agents and agent bank.
2. Other third-party obligations of the issuer and obligors.
3. Amounts due to working capital facility provider.
4. Interest and principal due under the issuer's liquidity facility.
5. Amounts due towards satisfaction of minimum capital expenditure spend.
6. Amounts due to swap counterparties.
7. Third-party liabilities of the issuer.
8. Scheduled interest on senior-term advance.
9. Scheduled principal due on senior-term advance.
10. Scheduled interest due on junior-term advance.
11. Scheduled principal due on junior-term advance.
12. Issuer tax liabilities.
13. Payments to maintenance capital expenditure other than minimum capital expenditure spend.
14. Amounts due to swap counterparties in respect of termination payments as a result of a downgrade of a counterparty.
15. Any surplus to the borrower for general corporate purposes if the restricted payment condition is satisfied, including the payment of a dividend.

If the enforcement event has occurred, the trustees may remove any capital expenditure and the residual cash flow flowing back to the operating company from the waterfall. Instead, a cash collateral account may be created to trap the cash flow and retain it in the operating company.

If an acceleration event has occurred, the trustees may decide to direct all cash flow to the repayment of secured loans in priority to all unsecured claims.

Businesses Where Whole Business Securitization Is Possible

In the U.K. market, there have been several whole business transactions rated by rating agencies, and the businesses involved spanned a wide range: pubs, service stations, hotels, theme parks, ferry service, London City Airport, care homes, theaters, food, water, ports and shipping, health care, telecom equipment, real estate, and timber.

It is difficult to define any central theme that connects these various businesses. However, Pfister (2000) in a special report by Moody's identified some significant features that make a business a more likely candidate for whole business securitization:

- Predictable asset base and ease of replacing the borrower.
- Ability to place financial covenants, such as DSCR, in the loan document and restrict the rights of the borrower to be able to take preemptive action.
- Ability to place restrictions on operation of the business, such as permitted disposals, permitted indebtedness, permitted business activities, permitted merger and acquisitions, minimum maintenance capital expenditures, negative pledge, change of control, and amendments to main contracts.
- Sufficient amount of equity component in business.
- Alternative use value of the properties—for instance, the fungibility of a nursing home into a house or office.

The concept of whole business securitization draws upon the long-term residual value of a business, so the business attributes of the entity to be a suitable whole business candidate should be such that the entity itself is a good value. It is a good business even in different hands. On the contrary, if the business solely rests on managerial efficiency or personal talent, it is no different from the issuance of secured bonds. The underlying concepts of a whole business securitization are essentially the same as valuation of a business for takeover or LBO. Some significant attributes for whole business securitization are:

- *Entry barriers.* To be value in itself, the business should be a sort of an oligopoly. The best examples are public utilities, established amusement properties, and infrastructural assets. In any event, the business should be one that does not have appreciable risk of obsolescence or substitution.
- *Demonstration of successful presence.* The entity should have been in business successfully for several years to establish a track record of residual profits. As stated by Fitch (2004): "The business must be able to demonstrate a minimum of three years' stable trading, but 10 to 15 years is ideal. Preferably, this trading record will include periods of macroeconomic growth and decline to demonstrate business trends during different stages of an economic cycle."
- *Maintainability of future profits.* Whole business transactions are essentially concerned with future sustaintable profits, so it should be possible to project future profits with reasonable certainty. Transactions typically look at long maturities; therefore, the business should have a long-term future and should not be a long-term risk. Ideally, for a whole business securitization candidate, according to Fitch (2004) it "is necessary for a low-risk strategy to be in place; to run a business as is, and not pursue risky options such as operational diversification, major acquisition trails or extensive development activity within the security group."
- *Realizable asset value.* Clearly, a whole business transaction cannot substantially depend on the soft assets of the business, such as manpower and skill sets. It has to be backed by substantive hard assets. Two types of assets generally back whole business transactions—properties and operational assets. In the Madame Tussaud's transaction, for example, apart from the properties at prime locations, the museum also has its operating assets—the wax models.
- *Brand value.* The entity must have a strong brand presence to sustain the profitability of the enterprise over long run.

■ *Management.* Stable management and efficient internal controls account for the long-term success of any business.

SECURITIZATION OF INSURANCE PROFITS

We conclude this chapter with a discussion of an interesting development in the securitization arena: securitization of the embedded value of insurance contracts. While risk securitization has been around for a while and securitization of future annuities or endowment contributions is also near routine, a new asset class of the securitization market has recently been introduced: securitization of value of in-force life insurance policies, or the embedded value of life insurance.

Unlike other alternative risk transfer devices, this securitization is not essentially a risk transfer device; it is predominantly a device to monetize the profits inherent in already contracted life insurance policies. It is comparable to the securitization of the servicing fees of a servicer, the residual profits of a business, or the fees of asset managers.

In life insurance business, the key cash flows of the insurer consist of:

■ Inflows
  • Premiums
  • Annuities
  • Investment income and capital receipts
  • Fee income (for specific insurance contracts only)

■ Outflows
  • Policy benefits
  • Annuity payments
  • Investments
  • Surrenders
  • Expenses, both origination and continuing
  • Capital expenditure and investments
  • Taxes

The value of in-force life insurance policies tries to capitalize the net surplus out of these cash flows. Sometimes also known as *block of business securitization* (as the early usage of such funding was to refinance the initial expenses incurred in acquiring new blocks of policies), this funding method is based on structured finance principles whereby the residual income of the securitized block is monetized up front.

One of the early examples of this method is American Skandia Life Assurance Company (ASLAC). From 1996 to 2000, ASLAC issued 13 securitization transactions designed to capitalize the embedded values in blocks of variable annuity contracts issued by ASLAC. The trusts issuing the notes are collateralized by a portion of future fees, expense charges, and *contingent deferred sales charges* (CDSC) expected to be realized on the annuity policies.

Motivations for Insurance Securitization

One of the basic motivators for insurance securitization has been capital, as indicated by the declining *free asset ratio*. The free asset ratio measures the market value of the insurer's assets, minus its policy liabilities, essentially the economic capital or solvency of the insurer. The free asset ratio includes the implicit *value of in-force policies* (VIF). The implicit value is actuarially assessed net present value of future profits inherent in the current book of business. The *embedded value* of the insurer is said to be the total of the existing capital plus VIF.

The essential motive behind securitization of embedded value is to monetize the VIF. Under emerging insurance accounting rules, the VIF will not be considered as a part of the insurance capital in the future.[3]

On the other hand, the monetization of the surplus of in-force policies may be considered a part of capital if the repayment of the funding, raised by way of the transaction, is unambiguously linked to the surplus on the defined pool of policies. While the clean implicit item, unmonetized, requires regulatory clearance to be counted as capital, the funding way of the securitiztion of a surplus is a more definitive part of capital. Hence, the quality of regulatory capital improves as a result of the securitization.

---

[3] For example, see the Integrated Prudential Sourcebook of the FSA, U.K., Annex 2G.

Transaction Structure

The crux of structuring the transaction is to look at residual profits from a pool of insurance policies; hence, the transaction is fairly similar to the whole business transactions discussed earlier in this chapter. However, there is understandably no need to put the kind of financial covenants required in whole business transactions.

In addition, to have clean impact on regulatory capital, these transactions may use either a reinsurance vehicle or a contingent loan.

KEY POINTS OF THE CHAPTER

➤ *The common element of securitization of future flows, whole business or operating revenues securitization, and securitization of embedded profits in insurance businesses is that they all relate to profits or cash flows out of future operations.*

➤ *While traditional asset-backed transactions relate to assets that exist, future flows transactions relate to assets expected to exist, examples being air ticket sales, electricity sale, telephone rentals, and export receivables from natural resource.*

➤ *The essential premise in a future flows securitization is if a framework exists that will give rise to cash flows in the future, the cash flows from such framework is a candidate for securitization; if the framework itself does not exist, the investors would be taking exposure in a dream because their rights would probably be worse than for secured lending.*

➤ *The key features of future flows deals are (1) the transferring of only a certain portion of the receivables to the trust with the originator retaining the excess over the transferred portion; (2) the use of a cash flow trapping device; (3) the prioritization of the transferee since that entity is concerned with only the cash flows transferred; (4) greater overcollateralization than traditional asset types that have been securitized; (5) restrictions on the borrower's business; (6) unlike traditional securitizations that are structured to be independent of the originator, future flows* deals are highly dependent on the originator's performance; and (7) not off-balance sheet.

➤ The extent of borrowing possible in future flows deals is determined by the cash flows and the level of overcollateralization required.

➤ Future flows transactions are classified depending on whether the securitization is based on: (1) exports of goods or services; (2) sales of goods and services; (3) financial futures flows; or (4) other futures flows.

➤ Unlike traditional securitizations, future flows transactions are confronted with several risks relating to the originator as well as the obligors and, therefore, these transactions rely on both structural features and credit enhancements to deal with risks.

➤ The structural features in future flows transactions include (1) either complete originator-dependence or peripheral originator dependence; (2) creation and maintenance of overcollateralization and a reserve; (3) early amortization triggers; (4) more comprehensive representations and warranties of the originator/seller than in a traditional securitization; and (5) an insurance guarantee in the case of emerging market future flows deals.

➤ A whole business securitization (also known as corporate securitization, corporate entity securitization, operating revenues securitization, or hybrid finance) captures the residual value of a business (i.e., the valuation of the business) and creates securities that represent this residual value.

➤ In most whole business securitizations the SPV issues bonds in the market and with the funds so collected provides a loan to the operator (originator).

➤ Whole business transactions are based on a loan structure which is in contrast to a traditional securitization wherein the SPV purchases the assets of the originator (a true sale structure) rather than making a loan (based on the capitalization of operating profits) to the operating company.

➤ In a whole business securitization, the originator agrees to repay the loan in fixed installments of interest and principal and the

SPV using these installment payments to pay off the obligations on the bonds it issued.

➤ *Whole business securitizations are not designed to be bankruptcy remote as far as the originator is concerned because there is no sale, and hence, no true sale, of the assets to the lending SPV.*

➤ *Unlike traditional securitizations, whole business securitizations are characterized more by structural protection (i.e., a strong collateralized lending transaction) than by the typical hierarchy of credit enhancements.*

➤ *The common structural enhancements in whole business securitizations are (1) breach of covenants/administrative receivership, (2) financial covenants, (3) liquidity facilities, (4) working capital facilities, and (5) restrictive covenants.*

➤ *The cash flow waterfall for whole business securitizations generally cover the following scenarios: (1) preenforcement (i.e., until the trustees' security interest has been enforced); (2) postenforcement (i.e., after the trustees have decided to invoke the security interest); and (3) postacceleration (i.e., if decided to take the business down the winding up route).*

➤ *Some significant attributes of the operating entity in a whole securitization are (1) entry barriers, (2) demonstration of successful presence, (3) maintainability of future profits, (4) realizable asset value, (5) brand name, and (6) stable management and efficient internal controls.*

➤ *A relatively new asset class in the securitization market is the securitization of the value of in-force life insurance policies, or the embedded value of life insurance.*

➤ *Unlike other risk transfer devices, securitization of life insurance profits is not essentially a risk transfer device but predominantly a device to monetize the profits inherent in already contracted life insurance policies.*

Collateralized Debt Obligations

Introduction to
Collateralized Debt Obligations

At one time, *collateralized debt obligations* (CDOs) were considered part of the asset-backed securities market. The reason was that like *asset-backed securities* (ABS), CDOs employed the securitization technology to pool assets and finance the purchase of that pool of assets by issuing securities (the CDOs). However, there are several elements that distinguish CDOs from the ABS we reviewed in earlier chapters. In this chapter, we explain CDOs. We begin the chapter with a discussion of why they require a separate study than ABS.

WHY STUDY CDOs?

CDOs have three distinctive features that warrant an independent study of this structured product. We describe these features in this section.

Arbitrage Motive

As explained in Chapter 2, ABS are created to lower funding costs and for risk management purposes. The first CDO transactions were primarily motivated by transferring assets off the balance sheet of a bank and are referred to as *balance sheet CDOs*. Today, the dominant motivation for the creation of a CDO is arbitrage opportunities. The term *arbitrage* here is used in a very loose way because there is, in fact, risk to the sponsor of a CDO and, therefore, investors. What the sponsor of a CDO does is create of pool of assets and funds those assets by selling securities (the CDOs). So far, this is not different from a typical ABS transaction. However, the purpose is to earn a return on the pool of assets that exceeds the funding costs to acquire those assets. The difference between the return earned on the assets and the funding costs is shared by the CDO sponsor, CDO manager, and CDO equity investor. Just how it is shared by these three entities is a part of the CDO waterfall, which we describe in more detail in this and the next two chapters.

Pool of Corporate Exposures

While a *residential mortgage-backed security* (RMBS) or auto-loan securitization transaction is backed by a pool of retail loans, a CDO is a pool of wholesale or corporate loans or exposures. This, by itself, has a significant impact on the credit risks and, therefore, the required enhancement levels in the case of CDOs. We discuss some of the significant differences between retail and wholesale loan pools later in this chapter.

Use of Synthetic Technology

If the idea of a CDO is to create a pool of corporate exposures, those exposures need not be funded debt such as loans or bonds issued by the respective corporate. Selling protection or insurance-like coverage, usually via a credit derivatives transaction, with reference to the same corporate also creates an exposure which is, in substance, similar to a holding a loan or a bond issued by the corporate. Lots of CDOs have assimilated synthetic asset pools rather than acquiring loans or bonds for cash. The synthetic CDO technology later grew into index trades in credit derivatives, which grew into trillions of dollars of volume. We discuss index trades later in this chapter.

TERMINOLOGY: CDO, CBO, CLO

The term CDO owes its origin to the *collateralized mortgage obligation*[1] (CMO) market where RMBS transactions migrated from a pure pass-through form to use the bond or obligations form, backed or collateralized by a pool of mortgages. When banks used the same

---

[1] See Chapter 3.

device to securitize pools of corporate loans, the natural term to use was collateralized loan obligations or CLOs.

The term CLO is restricted to a pool of straight loans. However, quite often, corporate exposures are held in the form of bonds. Hence, *collateralized bond obligations* (CBOs) would refer to securitization of a pool of corporate bonds. More likely than not, a securitization of corporate exposures would include both loans and bonds—hence, the term CDO was more appropriate. A CDO is a generic name for collateralized loan obligations and collateralized bond obligations.

Over a period of time, the CDO technology has continued to proliferate, and lots of collateral types have come up using the same essential structuring principles: Hence, in the marketplace, one may hear many similar sounding terms referring to the collateral type that has gone into making a CDO or CDO-like structure:

- *Collateralized synthetic obligations* (CSOs). A CDO that consists of a synthetic asset pool.
- *Collateralized fund obligations* (CFOs). A CDO-like structure that acquires investments in hedge funds or private equity funds
- *Collateralized commodity obligations* (CCOs). A structure that acquires exposures in commodity derivatives
- *Collateralized exchange obligations* (CXOs). A structure that acquires exposures in exchange rate derivatives, and so on.

TYPES OF CDOs

CDOs may be classified into various types from different perspectives as shown in Table 11.1. In this section, we describe each type briefly. A detailed discussion of CDO types, along with the structure of each, is provided in the next chapter.

Cash and Synthetic CDOs

CDOs may acquire assets in cash or synthetically. The cash asset CDO acquires assets in a traditional manner—raising the funding required equal to the size of the CDO and investing the same in acquiring the assets. The assets are acquired either from one originator (as for balance sheet CDOs) or from the market (as for arbitrage CDOs).

TABLE 11.1   Classification of CDOs

Based on mode of assets acquisition
- Cash CDO
- Synthetic CDO:
  - Fully tranched
  - Single tranche
- Hybrid CDO

Based on what it holds:
- High-yield CDO
- Investment grade CDO
- Emerging market CDO
- Structured finance CDO or CDO^2 (i.e., squared)
- Primary market CDO

Based on purpose:
- Balance sheet CDO
- Arbitrage CDO

Based on leverage structure
- Cash flow structure
- Market value structure

Based on asset ramping
- Fully ramped up
- Partly ramped up
- To be ramped up

For synthetic CDOs, the assets are acquired synthetically, that is, by signing up credit derivative deals selling protection against the assets. The process of creating synthetic assets can be described briefly as follows: In a credit derivative, a protection seller agrees to make a certain payment, called a *protection payment*, when a particular entity, called a *reference entity*, undergoes a specific *credit event*. As compensation for selling this protection, the protection seller receives a periodic payment, called a *premium*, which is comparable to the spread earned in actual funding transactions. Since the protection seller thus acquires credit risk on the reference entity, and earns a premium representative of credit spreads, the protection seller is said to have synthetically created a credit asset. This credit asset is an unfunded asset, implying that the protection seller has not extended any funding.[2]

A synthetic mode of acquisition of assets is now well accepted as a mode of reaping credit spreads on assets without having to acquire them as such.

The basic difference between cash and synthetic CDOs is the amount of funding raised and the manner of its investment. A synthetic CDO does not have to pay for the assets it acquires unless the protection payments are triggered, so the amount of funding required for synthetic CDOs is much lower. Typically, the CDO's sponsor goes for a cash funding from investors only to the extent required to have a triple A rating on the seniormost of its securities, as this funding is essentially a credit enhancement to absorb the risks of the portfolio of synthetic obligations of the CDO. The difference between the total of synthetic assets and the cash funding of the CDO is covered by an unfunded protection bought on a credit default swap, called a *super-senior swap*, a sort of a synthetic liability or synthetic funding of the CDO. Thus, the cash funding or cash liabilities of the CDO are invested in cash assets (typically highly rated collateral), and the total of synthetic assets is equal to the sum of funded liability as well as unfunded liability.

Of course, a CDO may not be purely cash or purely synthetic CDO—it may be a hybrid CDO. While no synthetic CDO would be purely devoid of cash assets—it would raise a fraction of its total synthetic assets in the form of cash funded securities. But it would invest this cash in high-grade assets, mostly in nondefaultable securities. In other words, the reinvestment of cash raised by the CDO is not to create credit risk. Where a synthetic CDO invests the cash it raises in defaultable assets such as corporate bonds or asset-backed securities, the CDO is creating both cash assets as well as synthetic assets—that is when we refer to it as a *hybrid* CDO.

Balance Sheet and Arbitrage CDOs

CDOs may be aimed at transferring the assets of a particular originator and thereby reducing the balance sheet size of the originator, or at earning arbitrage profits for the equity holders. The assets of a

---

[2] See Appendix A for a discussion on credit derivatives.

balance sheet CDO come from the balance sheet of a particular originator, typically a bank. The assets of an arbitrage CDO are bought from the market. The purpose of a balance sheet CDO might be to provide liquidity to the originating bank—so, it may be a funding device like any other asset-backed security. The purpose of an arbitrage CDO is simply to create and encash the difference between the rate of return on the assets that the CDO acquires, and the funding cost of the liabilities that the CDO issues. This differential is shared among the investors and the asset managers—the senior investors get their relatively higher spread, the juniormost investors (often called equity investors) get paid very high residual returns, and the collateral manager is paid management fees.

Balance sheet CDOs are also aimed at regulatory and/or economic capital relief, which cannot be a motive in arbitrage transactions.

Both balance sheet and arbitrage transactions can be cash or synthetic. If it is a balance sheet cash transaction, the purpose is most likely liquidity. If it is a balance sheet synthetic transaction, the purpose is most likely regulatory or economic capital relief or balance sheet management. In the case of arbitrage transactions, both in cash and synthetic form, the purpose is the same—making profits.

CDO Types Based on Collateral

The collateral-based classification is, understandably, mostly related to arbitrage CDOs. Based on its investment objectives, CDOs may acquire investment-grade assets or high-yield bonds. CDOs may be specifically aimed at emerging market debt. A CDO may be focused on high-grade assets such as assets with double-A or triple-A rating. Unless a CDO has such focus, it will typically invest in a mix of assets, with the focus being more on mezzanine to lower-mezzanine assets, as that is where the potential for making "arbitrage" profits lies.

Structured finance CDOs—CDOs buying securitized instruments—have been very popular in recent years. These CDOs resecuritize exposure in assets that have been securitized already, so these are also called *resecuritizations* or CDO^2 (*CDO squared*). Several CDOs also make investments in *real estate investment trusts* (REITs) or particular tranches of RMBS.

Sometimes CDOs make investments in trust-preferred securities, a hybrid between preferred stock and subordinated debt. These types of CDOs are, accordingly, called *trust-preferred CDOs*.

Primary market CDOs create loans—that is, they do not buy loans that have been given already but originate a specific pool of loans.

Par Value and Market-Value-Based Structures

The crux of CDOs lies in counterbalancing diversification and leverage. The diversification is on the asset side and the leverage is on the liability side. The leverage implies risk, which may go up during the life of the CDO if the quality of the assets on the asset side suffers. CDOs try to take corrective action to keep the leverage under check and, if required, to reduce it by putting limits on leverage such as on overcollateralization tests and interest coverage tests (discussed later in Chapter 13). These tests may be based on the par value of the assets or on the market value of the assets; accordingly, CDOs may be referred to as market value CDOs or par value CDOs.

Fully Ramped-Up and To-Be-Ramped Up Structures

The process of ramping up assets in CDOs is discussed in Chapter 13. A fully ramped CDO is one where the assets are ready for acquisition as soon as the funding takes place. Typically, a balance sheet transaction is fully ramped up. On the other hand, in the case of arbitrage transactions, the manager needs some time to build up the assets. During this time, the funds of the CDO are kept invested in some safe mode. Some CDOs, particularly synthetic CDOs, are intended to result into an exposure from a future date and is referred to as *forward-starting CDO*.

TYPICAL STRUCTURE OF A CDO

In comparing the typical structure of a CDO with a retail ABS transaction, the three key features of CDOs that we discussed earlier become important.

Since a CDO is a pool of corporate exposures, it typically would consist of 20 to 500 loans or bonds to make the pool, as against traditional ABS, which have anything between 500 to 100,000 loans comprising the pool. The number of obligors making up the pool is a reflection of the *granularity* of the pool—obviously, CDO pools have much less granularity. Distinctive features that result from this nature of the collateral are as follows:

- In analyzing the credit risk and other features of the pool, in retail ABS, the common approach is to use a *top-down approach*; that is, to treat the pool as homogenous and apply characteristic features such as default rate, delinquency rate, prepayment rates, and so on to the entire pool. In other words, the pool-level characteristics are applied to the individual loans in the pool. In the case of corporate loan pools, the pool cannot be taken to be homogenous—so, the analyst studies the distinctive features of each loan in the pool, and aggregating the information about each loan, the pool-level characteristics are derived. We will call this a *bottom-up approach*.
- In statistical analysis of the probability of default of the pool, retail pools tend to exhibit the behavior as suggested by a normal distribution, given the large number of loans in the pool. The probability distribution of wholesale loan pools is more left-heavy, and has a longer and thicker tail—the probability distribution is similar to a binomial distribution.
- In the case of retail pools, it is valid to assume, given the nature of the loans, that the loans do not have an intra-obligor correlation. Even if the loans are correlated, they are all correlated with an external factor, such as property prices in the case of home equity loans or unemployment levels in the case of credit card transactions. The assumption that there is *internal correlation* in the pool is warranted. On the other hand, in the case of CDOs, there might be obligors belonging to industries or industry clusters which are correlated. Correlation is a very significant risk in the analysis of CDOs, and there are several CDOs that are structured to allow investors to trade in correlation.[3]

---

[3] The underlying argument is that presence of correlation in a pool makes lower tranches safer and senior tranches riskier. Thus, equity or junior investors are happier with correlation. Correlation trading is very common in the case of index trades.

Besides the above, there are other features of CDOs, some of which are particularly relevant to arbitrage CDOs:

- The objective of the transaction might be to generate profits being the difference between the rate of return on assets and the funding cost of the transaction. For obvious reasons, it would be in everyone's interest to prolong this source of profits for some-time—hence, most arbitrage CDOs are reinvesting type transactions. That is, as part of the assets in the pool repay or prepay, the proceeds are reinvested in acquiring more assets.
- Such reinvesting type transactions typically run for 7 to 8 years, and then they are repaid, normally by way of a bullet repayment.[4]
- If there is a reinvesting type CDO, there must be a CDO manager, who would decide what assets to add into the pool. CDOs may be actively *managed* or *static* CDOs. If it is static, it would not need any management of the pool as such, as the selection is done at the inception. However, if the CDO manager is free to add and sell assets at his or her discretion, the composition of the pool might change not merely because of amortization or prepayment, but because of a discretionary sale of assets by the manager.
- The selection of the assets is done so as to lead to a desired level of diversification.
- The credit enhancements typically used in CDOs would be subordination. There may be a level of excess spread that may be trapped in extraordinary situations. Structural protection is mostly in the form of control on the leverage of the transaction. This is discussed in Chapter 13.
- While the CDO manager has the right to reinvest the principal proceeds of the assets, the right to reinvest is controlled by two important tests: the *overcollateralization* (OC) and *interest coverage* (IC) triggers. These triggers are discussed later in Chapter 13, but broadly, if these triggers are in place, they require the manager to reduce the level of leverage in the transaction by using the principal proceeds to pay off senior liabilities.

---

[4] If, on the intended bullet maturity, the assets have not fully amortized, the manager has the option to auction the assets of the CDO—this is called an *auction call*, similar to a *cleanup call* in the case of traditional ABS.

■ In view of the reinvesting-type nature of the transaction, the pay-down structure of the liabilities is mostly sequential.

Some CDO structures, picked up from recent transactions, are listed in Table 11.2.

BASIC ECONOMIC DRIVERS OF CDOs

Why do CDOs exist? Why might it be possible for the manager of a CDO to provide higher returns to its noteholders than a mutual fund manager investing in debt instruments? Why would a CDO be able to attain higher leverage and still have some securities rated AAA, as compared to a mutual fund? Were CDOs simply the product of a benign credit market cycle, or have they become a permanent part of the financial landscape?

These are hard questions, and it might be too early to answer at least some of these questions, as CDOs have only recently been tempered with a downturn in the credit cycle—the subprime crisis in the summer of 2007 is the first major jolt to the CDO business. However, the apparent economic fundamentals of CDOs appear like this. CDO managers select a pool of relatively risky assets on their asset side. The asset risk is accentuated by a high leverage on the liability side with a junior class of 4% to 5% bearing the first-loss risk of the entire asset pool. The risk of assets, thus magnified, is mitigated by the diversification of the assets. Asset diversity and financial leverage are the two economic drivers of CDOs—leverage creates risk and returns, and diversity is what makes the leverage tolerable.

The leverage and diversity also explain some of the key questions that we just raised—the relatively higher returns of CDOs are explained by the leverage, and the leverage, in turn, is explained by the diversity.

Thus, the diversity in the pool becomes a mainstay of CDOs. Diversity is the opposite of correlation: If a CDO pool has a high level of correlation, the risk, along with the magnifying impact of the leverage, would soon hit the senior classes. Correlation causes the right-hand tail of the probability distribution of losses to become long and fat, exposing the senior classes to losses.

TABLE 11.2 Some Recent CDO Structures

	1	2	3
Date of the presale report	August 07, 2006	November 09, 2007	November 15, 2007
Name of the CDO	Hamilton Gardens CDO Corp.	Jubilee CDO VIII B.V.	One George CDO Pte. Ltd.
Originator/sponsor	Rabobank International	Bank of New York, NY	Standard Chartered Bank
Transaction type—balance sheet/arbitrage	Arbitrage	Arbitrage	Balance sheet
Transaction type—cash/synthetic/ hybrid	Hybrid	Cash	Cash
Collateral type	RMBS, CMBS, ABS, and long and short synthetics	Senior, mezzanine, and second-lien leveraged loans and high-yield bonds	Investment-grade corporate bonds (87.1%) and subinvestment-grade corporate bonds (12.9%)
Issue size	US$ 478.25 million	€400 million	SGDm 500
Pool size	US$ 500 million+ notional amount of synthetics	€388 million	SGDm 500
Collateral manager	Rabobank International	Alcentra Ltd	
Tenure	7.15	7.9 years	4 years

TABLE 11.2 (Continued)

Sizes of Liabilities	1		2 (In € million)		3 Class	3 (In SGD million)	3 Ratings
		Ratings		Ratings			
A1	315.0	AAA	240.0	AAA	A-1A	150.0	AAA
					A-1B	75.0	AAA
A2	54.25	AAA	24.0	AAA	A-2A	200.0	AAA
					A-2B	30.0	AAA
B	56.50	AA	42.0	AA	A-3	5.0	AA
C	25.00	A	20.0	A	B	5.0	A
D	27.50	BBB–	18.0	BBB	C	10.0	BBB
E			16.0	BB	D	5.0	BB
Equity	21.75[a]	NR	40.0	NR	E	20.0	NR
Cash reserve, if any	—		—				
Excess spread, if any	—		2.5%				
Any structural trigger	—		Interest diversion test (Note 2)		Interest diversion 101% (equal to Class D par value OC)		
Any OC/IC trigger	Yes (Note 1)		Yes (Note 3)		-		

[a] Subordinated notes.

222

TABLE 11.2 (Continued)
Note 1: IC/OC Triggers

Class	Overcollateralization Required at Effective Date	Interest-Coverage Required at Effective Date
Sequential test		
A/B	128.89	N/A
C	112.44	115.0
D	107.23	108.0
	101.85	105.0

Note 2: Interest Diversion Test

Class	Overcollateralization Required on the Effective Date	Expected Overcollateralization on the Effective Date
A/B	116.0	112.0

Note 3: IC/OC Triggers

Class	Overcollateralization Test	Interest-Coverage Test
A/B	116.0	112.0
C	112.0	107.0
D	108.0	105.0
E	106.0	101.0

Why do CDOs attain the levels of leverage that are typically not available to mutual funds? CDOs are stylized pools created with a specific target of asset quality, returns, and diversity. The pool is made to match the required asset quality.

CDO MARKET AND THE HEALTH OF BANKING

CDOs and their impact on the global financial system have been an intensively debated topic of late. U.K. regulator Howard Davies is credited with a statement wherein he equated CDOs with the toxic waste of investment banking. Alan Greenspan, former Chairman of the Board of Governors of the U.S. Federal Reserve Bank during his term in office reiterated on several occasions his unwavering acclaim for CDOs as responsible for maintaining the health of the global banking system. In a speech to the Federal Reserve Bank of Chicago's 41st Annual Conference on Bank Structure, Chicago, Illinois on May 5, 2005, he stated:

> As is generally acknowledged, the development of credit derivatives has contributed to the stability of the banking system by allowing banks, especially the largest, systemically important banks, to measure and manage their credit risks more effectively. In particular, the largest banks have found single-name credit default swaps a highly attractive mechanism for reducing exposure concentrations in their loan books while allowing them to meet the needs of their largest corporate customers. But some observers argue that what is good for the banking system may not be good for the financial system as a whole. They are concerned that banks' efforts to lay off risk using credit derivatives may be creating concentrations of risk outside the banking system that could prove a threat to financial stability. A particular concern has been that, as credit spreads widen appreciably at some point from the extraordinarily low levels that have prevailed in recent years, losses to nonbank risk-takers could force them to liquidate their positions in credit markets and thereby magnify and accelerate the widening of credit spreads.[5]

[5] The entire text is available at https://www.federalreserve.gov/boarddocs/speeches/2005/20050505/default.htm.

During the aftermath of the subprime crisis, lots of people spat venom on CDOs and structured products. There was an extent of over-enthused activity in the CDO space, and in a benign market, it is argued by some that it is quite possible that rating agencies went easy, buoyed by their models that looked at historical defaults. CDO structurers went to heights of optimism, ignoring the correlation risk that might exacerbate in a credit downturn. In principle, however, a CDO as a collective structured investment vehicle is based on a sound footing.

GROWTH OF THE CDO MARKET

The CDO market originated in the late 1980s. However, during the early years, the total issuance hardly ever exceeded a few billion dollars. The real impetus came around 1996 when the risk-return profile of the high-yield debt market and the pricing of a triple-A rated floater created excellent arbitrage conditions. In 1998, the collapse of Long-Term Capital Management created a premium for liquidity in the market. Around the same time, rating agencies became more comfortable with rating of CDOs including those for arbitrage purposes.

The growth in the market was phenomenal from 1998 to 2007. According to data from the website of *Asset-Backed Alert* (www.abalert.com), worldwide CDO issuance was $65 billion in 2000 and by 2006 it increased to $431 billion. In 2007, issuance was $412 billion, a decline from the prior year due to the difficulties in the subprime mortgage market. In 2008, those difficulties carried over and issuance is expected to decline dramatically.

The composition of the CDO market in terms of cash flow, synthetic, and market value CDOs as of the third quarter of 2007 was:

Cash flow and hybrid: $315 billion (76%)
Synthetic funded: $38 billion (9%)
Market value: $59 billion (15%)

It should be noted that the issuance size of synthetic CDOs does not correctly reflect the level of activity since the funding raised in synthetic CDOs is only a small proportion of the pool size.

The composition of the market in terms of purpose, that is, balance sheet and arbitrage transactions as of the third quarter of 2007 was $56 billion (13%) and $357 billion (87%), respectively. To an extent, these data may also have a bias as lots of balance sheet CDOs are in synthetic form, where the funding size is much smaller.

The composition of the market in terms of collateral type as of the third quarter of 2007 was dominated by structured finance, $215 billion (52% of the market). The balance was shared by high-yield and investment-grade securities. Structured finance CDOs were almost absent from the market prior to 2005.

The Spurt and Spike in CDO Activity in 2006 and 2007

The boom in CDO issuance that started in 2005 seems to have reached an anticlimax in the second half of 2007. The steep growth in CDO activity in 2005 and 2006 was essentially due to arbitrage activity. In markets where equities were relatively flat, investors were on the lookout for interesting yields. CDO structurers structured highly leveraged transactions. First, CDO squared, or CDO^2 (discussed in the next chapter) appeared to create double or triple layers of leverage, quite often with sub-CDOs having common obligors. Thereafter, structured finance CDOs (also discussed in the next chapter) became a rage in the market. These CDOs would buy typically mezzanine to lower pieces of ABS transactions, quite often subprime or home equity securitizations, and issue liabilities against the same. Not only were CDOs actual investors in subprime RMBS, many of them had also synthetic exposure in the form of trades on either the ABS index (i.e., the ABX.HE index) or otherwise by way of credit default swaps on subprime ABS.

The meltdown in the subprime RMBS market has caused a substantial number of downgrades on CDOs with subprime exposure. The second half of 2007 saw a substantial correction with new issuance declining, and existing CDOs going through downgrades and losses. Some CDOs have been prematurely terminated, forcing termination of assets or contracts at a bad patch of time, aggravating losses.

KEY POINTS OF THE CHAPTER

➤ A collateralized debt obligation *(CDO) employs securitization technology to pools assets and finance the purchase of those assets by the issuance of securities.*

➤ *A CDO is a generic name for collateralized loan obligations (the pool of assets consists of loans) and collateralized bond obligations (the pool of assets consists of bonds).*

➤ *A CDO may acquire assets in cash or synthetically.*

➤ *The cash asset CDO acquires assets in a traditional manner— raising the funding required equal to the size of the CDO and investing the same by acquiring the assets.*

➤ *The assets are acquired either from one originator (in the case of balance sheet CDOs) or from the market (in the case of arbitrage CDOs).*

➤ *For synthetic CDOs, the assets are acquired synthetically by using credit derivatives.*

➤ *The basic difference between cash and synthetic CDOs is the amount of funding raised and the manner of its investment: (1) a synthetic CDO does not have to pay for the assets it acquires unless it is required to do so as result of its position in a credit derivative; so funding is much less than in a cash CDO; and (2) in a cash CDO the assets are purchased while in a synthetic CDO the exposure to an asset is acquired by a position in a credit derivative.*

➤ *There are balance sheet and arbitrage CDOs and they may be of the cash or synthetic variety.*

➤ *The motivation for a balance sheet CDO is to transfer the risk of a particular pool of assets and thereby reduce the balance sheet size of the originator in order to obtain regulatory and/or economic capital relief.*

➤ *The motivation for an arbitrage CDO is to capture the spread between the return earned on the pool of assets that is the collateral for the CDO and the funding cost.*

➤ *Arbitrage CDOs are classified based on the type of collateral: investment-grade corporate bonds, noninvestment grade bonds, noninvestment grade loans, and structured finance products.*

➤ *The structured finance CDOs include the following types of securitized instruments: asset-backed securities, residential mortgage-backed securities, commercial mortgage-backed securities, and other CDOs, as well as REITs.*

➤ *CDOs may be actively managed or static CDOs.*

➤ *While a static CDO is one in which there is no need for any management of the pool because the selection of the assets is done at the CDO's inception, in a managed CDO, a CDO manager is free to add and sell assets at his or her discretion due to downgrades, amortization or prepayment.*

➤ *The selection of the assets by the CDO manager is done so as to lead to a desired level of diversification.*

➤ *The credit enhancements typically used in CDOs would be subordination but there may be a level of excess spread that may be trapped in extraordinary situations.*

➤ *Structural protection in a CDO is primarily in the form of control on the leverage of the transaction.*

➤ *There are tests that must be satisfied for CDOs with respect to asset quality (overcollateralization tests) and leverage (interest coverage tests) before the manager reinvests the principal proceeds of the assets.*

➤ *The liability structure of a typical CDO is mostly sequential.*

CHAPTER 12

Types of Collateralized Debt Obligations

In the preceding chapter, we briefly discussed the different types of CDOs. In this chapter, we describe in detail each type of CDO including their structure and special features.

BALANCE SHEET CDOs

Balance sheet CDOs are not a new type of securitization but rather an application of the securitization methodology. Balance sheet CDOs parcel out a portfolio of loans, usually low-rated loans or emerging market credits and below investment-grade bonds held by large banks. Balance sheet CDOs may be either cash CDOs or synthetic CDOs.

Traditional, Cash CDOs

The traditional, cash CDO structure was used for the first time by Nations Bank in 1997, and then by LTCB (PLATINUM), IBJ (PRIME), Sumitomo (WINGS) Bankboston (BANKBOSTON), Bank of Montreal (LAKESHORE), Sanwa (EXCELSIOR), and SG (POLARIS), and so on. The methodology in all of these was fairly simple—transfer of a near-homogenous portfolio of loans into a *special purpose vehicle* (SPV) and issue of liabilities that are easily sellable to investors.

The Creation of a Balance Sheet CDO

The way a balance sheet CDO is created is as follows:

- The originator identifies the portfolio that the originator intends to securitize (i.e., to pool). Let us say, the pool size is $1 billion.
- The probability distribution for the pool is worked out. Let us suppose the model comes up with a distribution suggesting that, with a credit enhancement of 2%, it may be possible to get a rating of BB, while a credit support of 3.5% may be enough to get a BBB rating. Similarly, the required enhancement levels for an A rating and AAA rating are worked out as 5% and 8%, respectively.[1]
- This would mean, we can have a Class A with AAA rating and a size of 92% of the pool.
- For liquidity support, we create a cash collateral of 1%—this is in addition to the credit enhancement of 8% in the transaction.
- An SPV is created for any securitization.
- The SPV raises cash worth $1 billion, partly contributed by the originator itself.
- With this cash, the SPV buys the pool worth $1 billion.
- Since at the time of purchase the loans in the pool will obviously carry a weighted average interest that exceeds the weighted average funding cost of the transaction, there will be an excess spread. The excess spread will also be available to absorb expected losses in the pool.

The transaction structure is shown in the Figure 12.1.

Legal Structure

In cash flow transactions, the structure used has been a true sale structure with a retained seller's interest; that is to say, the seller makes a legally perfected sale of the asset to the SPV but the size of the asset may not match with the funding of the CDO.[2] The funding raised by the CDO would be a capital market amount, say, in denominations of $100 million. Let us suppose the funding in a certain transaction is $500 million, and the total outstanding principal or par value of the loans being transferred adds up to $578 million. In such a case, the seller will sell loans worth $578 million, and the buyer SPV will

---

[1] For sizing up of the enhancements, relative to the target rating of a tranche, see Chapter 5.

[2] For more on true sale in securitization transactions, see Kothari (2006).

FIGURE 12.1 Balance Sheet Cash CDO

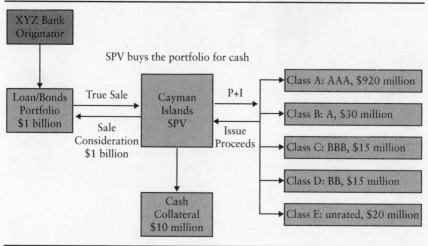

create two shares—a seller's share equal to $78 million, and investors' share equal to $500 million, which will be split into the various classes of liabilities being issued. Hence, there is no need to exactly match the amount of liabilities issued with the amount of loans transferred. Some transactions made use of the subparticipation structure, with a bunch of whole loans split between the seller and the investors by way of participation rights.

Underlying Assets

Usually portfolios of syndicated loans with ratings of BB to BBB are accumulated. Sometimes, better-rated loans are also pooled to help the balance sheet of the seller achieve better portfolio balance. In a typical balance sheet CDO, the number of exposures may be between 50 to 250 or so. The total pool size may be close to $400 to $500 million.

Diversity

Correlation risk can be fatal to a CDO. The whole concept of tranching, that is, creation of different classes of liabilities with varying probabilities of default, is based on the diversification of the asset pool. Hence, one of the important objectives of every CDO, be it balance sheet or arbitrage, is to achieve diversification.

While diversification is easier to attain in an arbitrage transaction as a collateral manager selects assets to suit the objective of the transaction, in balance sheet transactions, the assets are being parcelled out of the balance sheet of the bank. The bank's own portfolio may be lopsided, and it might be using the CDO to correct its balance sheet imbalance. Hence, the concerns about the bank's own portfolio inefficiencies infecting the CDO are more serious in balance sheet transactions.

Rating agencies and investors are more concerned about portfolio diversity measures in the case of balance sheet transactions. Moody's computes a pool's *diversity score,* discussed in the next chapter. It is also common to put concentration limits such as a limit of 2% per borrower, 8% per industry, and so on.

Reinvestment Period

CDOs may have a *static pool* as in case of RMBS or auto loan transactions, or they may have a *dynamic pool* as in case of credit card transactions. If the pool is static, assets in the pool may amortize over time or may prepay. These proceeds will be used to pay off investors, in the desirable order of paydown, which, in view of the amortizing nature of the pool, may most likely be a combination of sequential and proportional paydown.

However, it makes logical sense for a CDO to have a dynamic pool with a right with the originator to substitute new loans for loans that either prepay or amortize. This is because many of the loans may have sizeable principal repayments from the very first month. While commercial loans do not have the tendency to prepay as in case of residential mortgage loans, if at all they do, there might be a big chunk of principal inflow, as the ticket size per loan is quite big. In addition, unlike in the case of retail loans, commercial loans do not have a graduated monthly payment—many of them may have a balloon payment feature, or may pay a substantial part of the principal after a while, while not paying any principal for several months. Thus, if a CDO were to repatriate the principal that it receives from the assets to the investors, the investors will have a chaotic principal paydown.

Thus, reinvesting structure is quite common in the case of CDOs. During the reinvestment period, the originator may put in more loans into the CDO. Quite obviously, these loans are selected based on several *selection criteria* such as minimum rating, internal rating, seniority, collateralization, diversity, and so on. In addition, the OC/IC triggers, discussed in the next chapter, must also be in compliance.

The reinvestment period ends one year before the repayment starts. That is, one year before the scheduled repayment, the trustees start building up cash in the CDO for forthcoming repayment. Some transactions may provide for partial reinvestments and accumulate cash over time in preparation for the forthcoming maturity.

Credit Enhancement Structure

The actual enhancement structure will be based on the probability of default curve. Rating agencies normally run their proprietary models to work out the probability distribution and, thereby, to come up with the enhancement level. A typical credit enhancement structure of a balance sheet CDO may look as follows:

Senior AAA securities	92%
Mezzanine A securities	3%
Junior BBB tranche	1.5%
Junior BB tranche	1.5%
Subordinated, unrated tranche	1%
Cash collateral account (CCA)	1%
Originator's excess spread	NA

Thus the credit enhancement provided by the originator is 1% CCA, 1% junior unrated class, and the excess spread account. The excess spread is usually paid off by the trustees to the originator, but in case of deterioration in the quality of the portfolio as indicated by certain triggers, this amount may be trapped and used to pay off the investors. The structure may also provide for a lockout on coupon or principal payouts to subordinated classes in case of accumulated losses exceeding a particular level.

Structural Tests

If the tests relating to the *overcollateralization* (OC) and *interest coverage* (IC) are not satisfied, the CDO will use the cash flow waterfall to make a principal distribution to the senior classes until the breach of the structural tests is corrected. The working of these structural triggers is discussed in the next chapter.

Synthetic CDOs

When the credit derivatives device for shifting the credit risk associated with loans was developed in 1993, and became more common around 1997, balance sheet CDOs had already developed to an extent. Hence, it was easy to apply the synthetic technology to balance sheet transactions.

If the objective of the bank in creating a balance sheet CDO was not liquidity but risk management, capital relief, economic capital relief, and so on, the synthetic device would work very well.

The Creation of a Synthetic CDO

A synthetic CDO is created as follows:

- The originator identifies the portfolio that it intends to synthetically transfer (i.e., the loan pool). Let us say, the pool size is $1 billion.
- The probability distribution for the pool is worked out. Let us suppose the model comes up with a distribution suggesting that, to get a BBB rated tranche, an enhancement of 2% is required. We assume that the first level of loss support will come from the seller itself—in other words, the seller will retain a first-loss risk of 2%.
- In addition, suppose the model also suggests that there is a very nominal, say 0.001% probability of the losses in the pool exceeding 12%. In other words, if the originator had the right to seek compensation against losses in this pool (the *reference portfolio*) adding up to a total amount of 12% or $120 million (inclusive of the first-loss piece retained by the originator), that would provide the originator 99.999% (1 less the probability of losses exceeding 12%) confidence. Let us suppose we agree that it would be impractical to seek a higher confidence level.
- An SPV is created for any securitization.

- The SPV sells protection to the originator by way of a credit default swap, against the reference portfolio, for a total value of $100 million, over and above the first-loss piece of $20 million. That is to say, the notional value of the swap is $100 million on a portfolio size of $1 billion with a *threshold risk* of $20 million.

- The SPV issues *credit-linked notes* (CLNs) of a total value of $100 million. Let us suppose there are four classes (Classes A, B, C, D) of CLNs with a value of $25 million or 2.5% of the reference pool each. Let us also suppose the classes respectively have the following ratings: AAA, AA, A, and BBB. Since a CLN is a debt instrument with an embedded credit default swap, each investor in the CLNs is inherently a protection seller, selling protection with reference to the reference portfolio. The maximum amount of protection payment committed by each CLN investor is the amount invested. Thus, indirectly through the SPV, the originator buys protection equal to the sum total of CLNs issued by the SPV.

- The amount raised by CLNs is usually invested in a default-free investment, such as government securities or like collateral. The idea is that there must be no counterparty risk as far as the investors are concerned.

- The originator as the protection buyer pays the agreed premium to the SPV. In addition, the SPV also earns coupon from the default-free investment made by it. Usually, the premium paid by the originator is so set as to compensate the SPV for its *negative carry*, that is, the excess of weighted average coupon paid by it over the return from the default-free reinvestment.

- The originator is protected against losses exceeding 2%, but only up to a total level of 12%. If the losses exceed 12%, the originator suffers the loss. As we noted earlier, the probability of the losses exceeding 12% is nominal, but if the originator were to protect itself against that catastrophic risk as well, this can be accomplished by using a *super-senior swap*. It is referred to as a super senior because the position of this swap in the rating hierarchy is above a AAA tranche, which is the seniormost.

- If a credit risk event does not take place, the investors are paid coupons over time, and at maturity, the reinvestment in the collateral is liquidated to repay the principal to investors.

- Upon the occurrence of a credit event for which the originator has sought protection, the originator will continue to absorb losses up to the first-loss piece ($20 million). Once the cumulative losses exceed $20 million, the originator will make a claim for compensation from the SPV.
- The SPV will have to sell the collateral to the extent required and make payment to the protection buyer. Simultaneously, the SPV will write off the principal outstanding on Class D to the extent of losses paid by it.
- If Class D is fully wiped out, the losses move to Class C, and so on.

The transaction structure is shown in Figure 12.2.

Advantages of Synthetic CDOs over Cash CDOs

Cash CDOs and synthetic CDOs work in different spheres—cash CDOs are intended for raising liquidity, while synthetic CDOs are intended for risk transfers. Hence, the following discussion of advantages of synthetic over cash CDOs has to be related to the purpose of the originator. Briefly, synthetic CDOs will have the following advantages:

Minimizes Funding and Reinvestment Problems Synthetic CDOs minimize the funding relative to the pool size. As might have been noted in the example above, with a funding of only $100 million, we were able to achieve a risk transfer on a pool of $1 billion. In a cash CDO, the seller raises up-front cash of $1 billion. Until gainfully reinvested, this cash may continue to give a negative carry.

Splits the Funding and the Risk Transfers Synthetic securitization splits the funding and risk transfer aspects of securitization. The risk is transferred by way of credit derivatives. The funding can be taken care of by on-balance-sheet sources, based on the capital relief obtained by the risk transfer. In fact, once the risks are removed by risk transfer, funding by regular balance sheet means should be only more convenient.

Alleviates Problems Related to True Sale Cash securitizations are built upon a *true sale* structure, implying that the originator must make a transfer of the portfolio to the SPV. The transfer must be legally perfected

FIGURE 12.2 Balance Sheet Synthetic CDO

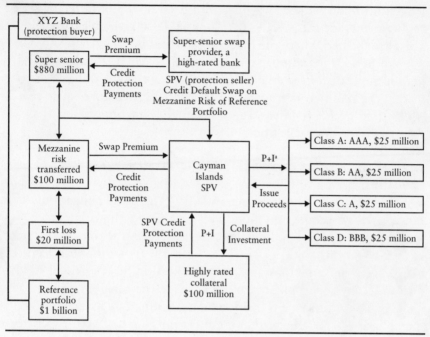

[a] P+I = Principal plus interest.

and done in a manner that will be respected in law and cannot be annulled by a bankruptcy court. True sales involve several legal difficulties, such as obligor notification, rule against transfer of assets in executory contracts, rule against transfer of fractional interests, and the like.[3]

All this having been done, there is no certainty that the transfer will still be regarded as a valid sale in law. This is because of a recharacterization risk that looms large in such transactions where significant credit enhancements are provided by the originator. The legal rationale is that if the originator truly transfers assets out, it must also cease to carry any risk on such assets. If the originator continues to support the assets with its own credit rather than the quality of the assets, the transfer may be treated as a funding taken by the originator rather than a true sale.

[3] For a detailed discussion on true sale issues, see Chapter 23 in Kothari (2006).

True sale concerns become all the more acute when the assets are located in multiple jurisdictions, with each having a different set of requirements for transfer. As per essential legal principles, the receivables are located where the place of payment is.

Synthetic transactions steer absolutely clear of this by not relying on the transfer of obligations at all. It is not the obligations but merely the risk that is transferred in synthetic structures. The risk is transferred by a derivative structure, which is unconnected with what the originator does with the obligor.

Does Not Require Artificial Separation of Origination and Servicing Functions   In cash structures, because of the true sale requirements, there is an artificial separation of the ownership and servicing of the obligations. The house-owner becomes the housekeeper; that is, the originator who was the owner of the credit assets before assumes the role of a servicer of the obligations. In other words, as far as the obligors are concerned, all the servicing functions and all the collection functions will still be discharged by the originator. In most cases, the obligors do not even come to know this role transition.[4] The originator's association with the obligor is so obtrusive that it almost puts a cloak on the transfer.

This artificial change of the originator role into a servicer role leads to an elaborate legal, logistical, and systems exercise. The originator has to keep collecting the receivables but not comingle them with its own; it must maintain a segregation of what it collects on its own account and that it collects as an agent of the SPV, a tremendous burden on the systems for retail portfolios. The originator must transfer the agency collections immediately to the SPV or dispose as per the instructions of the SPV. The originator can and should charge a service fee for what it does, which is mostly nothing but its profits in disguise. The originator can be replaced in certain circumstances by a backup servicer, who must be identified up front, although that contingency is remote. The potential transfer of the servicing function to a backup servicer is again a greatly burdensome task; if the backup servicer has to be identified right away, there may be costs attached to this commitment as well.

---

[4] Obligor notification is a requirement in many countries, but it is seldom ever done in practice. Such countries still recognize the transfer as an "equitable transfer."

The essence of all this is that the originator must, on the surface, keep on doing all that it was doing before the transfer, but agree behind the facade with the SPV that it is doing it as an agent.

The rigmarole of servicing/origination separation is completely ruled out in synthetic transactions. The originator's relation with the obligors is left untouched, both legally and on the surface.

Lesser Legal Costs Securitization requires massive legal documentation—for achieving the transfer of assets and the elaborate representations and warranties it gives, changing the role of the originator into a servicer and setting up the servicer responsibilities and transfer of collateral. All this has to be done in a manner that will not lead a court to question the truth of the transaction. This requires hefty payments by way of legal fees for documentation, setting up the structure and vehicles, and opinions.

Besides, another important part of the legal costs is the duties and taxes payable on the transfer of receivables itself—stamp duties are payable in many countries on transfer of receivables. Some countries impose value-added tax on transfer of receivables as well.

Credit derivatives have a much simpler documentation. A few-page ISDA can do what cash structures take 200 pages to write on. There is no transfer of receivables—therefore, there are no stamp duties whatsoever.

No Up-front Taxation Cash structure securitization typically incurs a problem of up-front taxation of the originator's profits. The originator's profit equals the weighted average return of the portfolio less the weighted average coupon payable to the investors. At the end of the day, the originator must capture that profit and extract it from the SPV. Originators use various devices, often in combinations, to extract their profit—up-front gain on sale by way of the difference between the transfer price and the carrying value, service fees, interest rate strip, cleanup call option, interest rate swap, and so on. While an up-front gain on sale is certainly taxable immediately, the other devices might defer the taxability of the profit. However, tax officials have an inherent right to question such deferment and accelerate the same to tax it immediately, particularly in cases where the gain on sale has been reported up-front in the originator's books of account.

For example, if an originator extracts its profit by way of an excess service fee, the tax officer might contend that this fee is nothing but a disguised deferred profit, which can be used to increase the fair value of the transfer and thus taxed immediately.

Any such contingency is ruled out for synthetic transactions where there is no transfer of the reference asset at all.

Avoids Double Taxation of Residual Profits Another common problem with cash structures is the double taxation of the originator's residual income. Residual income refers to the income on the most subordinate piece in the liability structure of the SPV,[5] which is mostly held by the originator. The yield on this piece is mostly set such that the remaining profit in the SPV after servicing all external investors is swept by the originator.

For tax purposes, this may be treated as residual economic interest in the SPV, and therefore, equity of the SPV. Any payment to service equity is not allowable as a deduction for tax purposes, leading to a tax on such distribution as the income of the SPV. This very income, when received by the originator, will be treated as income again and is liable for tax. Thus, the originator's residual tax may come to be taxed twice unless the SPV is a tax-transparent or tax-free entity.

In contrast, the originator's profits on the portfolio in a synthetic transaction are not disturbed at all. The originator merely pays the swap premium as the cost of buying protection and continues to pocket the entire credit spread on the pool. The credit default premium is paid to the SPV, which is an allowable expense, and the premium is an amount just enough to pay the weighted average cost of the SPV, leaving no such residual profit to come for double taxation.

No Accounting Volatility Cash structure securitizations are characterized by volatile accounting for income and assets by the originator. This is a result of the accounting standards on securitization accounting. The most important global accounting standards relating to securitization are the FAS 140 and the IAS 39.

---

[5] This juniormost piece seldom takes the form of legal equity, but is nevertheless an economic equity of the SPV. The legal form can be preference shares with participation rights, subordinated loan, or zero-coupon bond.

The standards permit and require off-balance-sheet treatment for securitizations that qualify for such treatment. The off-balance-sheet treatment is based on what is called *sale treatment*. Logically, if there is a sale and that sale is responsible for a profit, the profit must be booked at the time of sale, even if the profit is actually realized over or after a period of time. Thus, securitization accounting standards require that in computing this gain or loss on sale, it is not merely the apparent gain on sale (that is, the difference between the transfer price and the carrying value of the portfolio) that should be considered, but also the retained elements of profit such as excess service fees, excess interest on a subordinated bond, excess discounting rate for a cleanup call, interest rate strip, and value of interest rate swap. That is, if the originator has set up the transaction as to create a source of profit in the future, this must also be brought up front and treated as a part of the consideration for computing the gain or loss on the sale. This source of future profit will also be simultaneously treated as an asset. That is, the accounting standards will lead to a gain on sale that is in excess of the apparent gain, leading to creation of ephemeral assets.

These sources of future profits are mostly subordinated and therefore uncertain. The future profit is also sensitive to other volatilities affecting the pool such as prepayments, early amortization triggers, and the like. Over time, the originator is supposed to reevaluate the assumptions made at the time of initial recognition of the gain on sale and the asset representing retained interests. The values of both will change based on the change in assumptions, leading to an extremely volatile accounting of income and assets by securitizers.

Synthetic transactions remove the volatility in originator accounting as far as the gain on sale issue is concerned. As the assets are never sold in the first place, there is no question of any gain on their sale. The inherent gain on origination is captured over time as the assets pay off, and that is dealt with by normal revenue recognition principles. The only source of volatility on the originator's books is the value of the derivative, but if the derivative is a good hedge against the portfolio, the value of the derivative will only make good the losses on account of the impairment of the portfolio, thus removing or reducing volatility rather than creating or augmenting it.

Does Not Reduce Book Size   Quite often, banks and financial intermediaries see a source of pride in the growth of their balance sheet assets. Securitization results in assets going off the books and therefore reduces the book size. Credit derivatives, on the other hand, do not affect the asset-recognition on the books. The book size is not affected.

The best part is that while the financial books are not affected, the regulatory books are. For regulatory accounting purposes, credit derivatives mostly lead to a reduction in risk-weighted assets, and thus capital relief. With this relieved capital, a bank may create more leverage and therefore grow its book size.

Retains Flexibility in Customer Service   Having flexible business relations with the obligors is most necessary with any financial intermediary. Most credit assets are the result of an ongoing relation with the obligor. To retain this relationship, financial intermediaries serve the obligors, which often include prepayments, advance payments, waivers, rebates, rescheduling, further lending, change from one lending scheme to another, and collateral waivers. In traditional securitization of say a residential mortgage, the house-owner changes into a housekeeper; for every little odd thing as painting the house or replacing a heating unit, the originator will look to the trustees, now vested with security interests on the assets transferred to the SPV. This greatly reduces the business flexibility of the originator.[6]

On the other hand, credit derivatives do not, in any way, affect the business operations of the originator. If the portfolio is static and a particular obligor has to be prepaid, the only implication is that the notional value of the swap may have to be reduced. Most capital market transactions are done with dynamic portfolios with substitution rights reserved with the originator, so the originator may, subject to conditions, call back an obligor from the portfolio and reinstate another.

Bullet Repaying Notes   For synthetic transactions, the maturity profile of the notes is generally a bullet repayment. For a cash transaction,

---

[6] In practice, the flexibility to an extent is retained by the originator retaining a call or substitution option for such assets needed back for obligor service. But the call back option is constrained by both legal and accounting restrictions, and is generally as complicated as the initial transfer itself.

principal is usually paid down over time as the principal inherent in the assets in the pool is realized. For synthetic transactions, there is no principal repayment inherent in the assets (as the cash assets are actually the financial investments made by the SPV), and the swaps are normally for a fixed term. Fixed income investors prefer a bullet repaying investment than one that amortizes or pays an uncertain amount of principal over time.

ARBITRAGE CDOs

Making use of the technology provided by traditional asset-backed securitizations, but with the motivation to generate arbitrage opportunities provided by perceived inefficient pricing of securities, particularly high-yield securities, there emerged in the market a new class of securitization product—arbitrage CDOs. Early examples of arbitrage CDOs are JPMorgan's BISTRO and Citibank's C*Star.

As noted earlier, the term "arbitrage" is loosely used. It does not have the same meaning in finance. *Arbitrage* in the sense used here means trying to capture via active management the spread between the return on assets and funding costs. In the early stages of the arbitrage CDO market, the collateral used was high-yield corporate debt. This asset class was selected because of what was thought to be significant arbitrage opportunities provided by the difference between implied default rates and expected default rates on high-yield corporate debt. The implied default rate is inherent in the pricing of the debt, whereas the expected default rate is based on the probability distribution of the downgrade of a particular rating. If the implied default rate is higher, there is an opportunity to make a profit.

Besides, the pooling process creates the source of profit—arbitrage CDOs are based on the underlying principle of modern portfolio theory as formulated by Markowitz: If there are n risks that are less than positively perfectly correlated and those risks are aggregated in a portfolio, the portfolio risk is less than the sum of the individual risks.

The purpose of an arbitrage CDO is not to liquidate the assets held on the balance sheet of the originator, but to accumulate assets from proceeds of the CDO to make an arbitrage profit. Arbitrage CDOs can be issued by anyone, but most typically are issued by investment banks, investment management boutiques, asset managers, and the like. Some arbitrage transactions are sector-specific such as real estate investments, and are obviously issued by managers having special expertise in the particular sector.

Arbitrage CDOs may be either in cash form or synthetic form, discussed below.

Arbitrage Cash CDOs

The steps in creating an arbitrage cash CDOs are as follows:

- The sponsor who puts the whole show together first starts to line up investors who are likely to invest in the CDO. Of crucial importance is the equity investor, as the entire structure is a kind of inverted pyramid with the equity tranche at the bottom. The typical equity investors are hedge funds, private equity funds or high-net-worth individuals looking for a yield kicker.
- Based on the investors' returns/risk requirements and investible funds, a possible portfolio size and composition is outlined. The entire portfolio does not have to be ramped up at the time of taking the deal to the market—typically, CDOs do allow a *ramp-up period* within which to invest the funding raised in acquiring assets.
- Based on the risk attributes of the already ramped and to-be-ramped-up assets (say, adding up to $1 billion), we draw a probability distribution for the pool. Let us suppose the model comes up with a distribution suggesting that with a credit enhancement of 3%, it may be possible to get a rating of BBB, while a credit support of 6% may be enough to get an A rating. Similarly, the required enhancement levels for AA rating and AAA ratings are worked out as 9% and 12%, respectively.
- An SPV is created.
- The SPV raises cash worth $1 billion, of which 3% comes from the equity investors.
- A collateral manager is appointed to select the assets both at inception and on ongoing basis over time.
- With this cash, the collateral manager buys the pool worth $1 billion (inclusive of cash collateral).
- Since at inception the loans in the pool will obviously carry a weighted average interest that exceeds the weighted average fund-

ing cost of the transaction plus the collateral manager's fees and other expenses, there will be an excess spread. The excess spread will also be available to absorb expected losses in the pool.

The transaction structure is shown in Figure 12.3.

Legal Structure

Questions such as true sale that confront balance sheet cash transactions are not important in the case of arbitrage transactions. Quite obviously, the CDO is buying assets from the market, and not from the equity investors. There is no originator-enhancement in the transaction, nor is the originator controlling servicing or excess profits from the assets.

Underlying Assets

As the objective of an arbitrage transaction is to generate higher spreads, the selection of assets is done so as to capitalize on perceived

FIGURE 12.3 Arbitrage Cash CDO

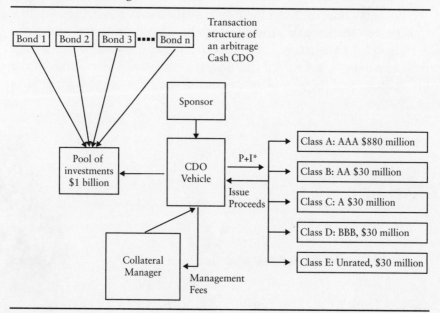

[a] P+I = Principal plus interest.

pricing inefficiencies. As discussed earlier, the motivation is clearly to select assets where, for a given rating, the returns are higher. To control the motivation of the manager to make investment decisions that would impair the quality of the portfolio, rating agencies put a limit on weighted average rating (as measured by a weighted average factor formula by a rating agency), weighted average spreads, and other actions of the manager.

Because the idea underlying an arbitrage CDOs is to maximize returns, there is a natural motivation to acquire positions in structured finance securities, particularly at lower rated levels which provided the opportunity to generate much higher spreads compared to like-rated corporate bonds. This resulted in the popularity of structured finance CDOs that we will discuss later in this chapter.

Reinvestment Period

Given the objective of an arbitrage CDO, it is quite obvious that the CDO will be a reinvesting transaction. The manager seeks not to distribute principal payments to investors in order to continue to use those funds to generate interest in excess of the funding cost.

For that reason, the reinvesting structure is the most common structure in the case of arbitrage CDOs. As is typical with any reinvesting-type transaction, there are tests to be satisfied before the manager may be permitted to reinvest—essentially asset coverage or OC trigger, and income or IC trigger. These tests are discussed later in Chapter 13.

Credit Enhancement Structure

The credit enhancement structure for arbitrage CDOs is similar to that of a balance sheet CDO, except that there is no originator-provided enhancement; instead, the juniormost class is commonly referred to as equity class.

Illustration of Potential Returns from Arbitrage CDOs

The illustration in Table 12.1 shows the returns on equity of a putative CDO. We have taken the size of the CDO as $500 million, invested in high-yield debt instruments yielding 10.5%. The liability

TABLE 12.1 Returns from a Hypothetical Arbitrage CDO

Arbitrage Conditions for CDO Equity Investment			
Assets	Size	Rate	Product
Portfolio of high-yield debt	500	10.50%	52.5
Liabilities			
AAA notes (assuming LIBOR = 5%)	350	5.45%	19.075
A notes	50	6.15%	3.075
BBB notes	25	7.15%	1.7875
BB notes	25	11%	2.75
Equity	50	0	0
Weighted average funding spread on liabilities			5.93%
Weighted average funding rate including equity			5.34%
Collateral yield			52.5
Less funding cost			26.6875
Less: base case losses and expenses		3.25%	16.25
Returns on equity			10.4375
Percentage return on equity of	50		20.88%

structure and the costs of the liabilities are obvious in the example. We have also assumed that there will be expenses and annual losses in the pool that add up to 3.25%. As can be seen in the table, the return on equity is 20.88% based on the assumptions made in the table.

Arbitrage Synthetic CDOs

While the purpose of arbitrage synthetic CDOs is the same as for an arbitrage cash CDO, the assets are acquired not in cash but in synthetic form.

Creating an Arbitrage Synthetic CDO

The steps in the creation of an arbitrage synthetic CDO are as follows:

- The assets of the CDO are synthetic assets. This means that protection is sold with respect to specific reference entities. As with a loan or a bond being a credit exposure to the obligor, the protection sold on a reference entity is an exposure to that entity and, therefore, economically equivalent to a long position is the reference entity. Each such protection sold with respect to a reference entity will have a notional value. For example, let us say we have 100 such credit default swaps, with a notional value of $10 million each, adding up to $1 billion. It is notable that typically the notional value for each reference entity in an arbitrage synthetic CDO will be the same. This allows ease of modeling.
- The process of lining up investors is the same as in case of an arbitrage cash CDO discussed earlier. However, most notably, the amount of actual funding needed on a notional pool of $1 billion, will only be a fraction, as discussed below.
- Based on the risk attributes of the notional pool, we draw a probability distribution for the pool. Let us suppose the model indicates that there is very little (say, 0.001%) probability of losses in the pool exceeding 12%. If so, the CDO may raise funding of only 12%, and enter into a super-senior swap for the balance of 88% on an unfunded basis.
- In the 12% funding size, we assume four classes of liabilities, each with a size of 3% with ratings of AAA, A, BBB, and unrated, respectively.
- An SPV is created.
- The SPV raises cash worth $120 million, which is reinvested in very high quality assets.
- A collateral manager is appointed to select the assets both at inception and on ongoing basis over time.
- During the ramp-up period, the collateral manager sells protection to one or more protection buyers (normally the sponsoring bank may be a protection buyer) with reference to the 100 reference entities.
- The income of the CDO will be (1) the premium earned from the selling of protection on the 100 credit default swaps; and (2) income on the investment in the collateral worth $ 120 million. This income should be enough to pay (1) the collateral manager's fees and other expenses of the CDO; (2) the super senior swap

FIGURE 12.4   Arbitrage Synthetic CDO

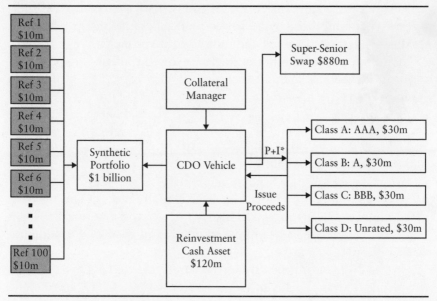

^a P+I = Principal plus interest.

    premium; and (3) weighted average coupons to the investors, including any differential returns for the equity investor.

- If there are losses on the credit default swaps, which require the CDO to pay compensation to the respective protection buyer, the CDO will sell the collateral to the extent required and would simultaneously write off Class D.

Figure 12.4 illustrates the transaction structure.

RESECURITIZATION OR STRUCTURED FINANCE CDOs

An interesting application of arbitrage CDOs is resecuritization: the securitization of securitization investments. These are called *structured product* CDOs or *resecuritizations*. The collateral for resecuritizations is mostly subordinate tranches of RMBS, CMBS, CDOs, and other ABS transactions.

    The genesis of structured finance CDOs is quite obvious—as arbitrage transactions search for assets which provide relatively higher rate of returns with a given rating, a structured finance security is an ideal choice. Quite often, the spreads on a BBB ABS are substantially higher than those on a BBB bond. Besides putting up structured finance, CDOs also served the motive of investment banks to have adequate supply of liquidity in the lower-rated tranches of securitization transactions.

Growth of Structured Product CDOs

In Chapter 11, we noted the sharp rate of growth in structured finance CDOs. From virtually zero in 1998, the structured product CDO market recorded a volume of about $10 billion in 2000, nearly 10% of the entire CDO market. In 2006, the percentage of structured finance CDOs zoomed to nearly 60% of the total market—out of a total volume of $549 billion, structured finance CDOs added to $312 billion.

In the 2007 subprime crisis, structured finance CDOs have been the prime victims. This is obviously because these CDOs have made substantial investments in subprime mortgage loan securitization transactions.

Assets of Structured Finance CDOs:

A structured finance CDO invests in:

- CMBS/REIT/RMBS
- Other CDOs
- ABS and real estate securities

The investment can be in cash or synthetic form.

The typical assets of structured finance CDOs are mezzanine (BBB or BB rated) ABS. Many CDOs have acquired investments in subprime mortgage securitizations.

A CDO^2, or CDO-squared, is a CDO (issuing CDO) that invests in other CDOs (sub-CDOs). Each sub-CDO is itself a pool of assets or entities. Quite often, there is an overlap in entities (i.e., common entities in the sub-CDOs).

In CDO^2 as well as other structured finance CDOs, there is obviously a high degree of correlation. In the case of CDO^2s, there is perfect correlation to the extent of common names. In the case of other structured finance CDOs, assuming a CDO invests in BBB tranches of 20 home equity securitizations, if the home equity sector starts exhibiting problems, each of those BBB investments might realize losses. Since the losses arise from a common source, that is, home equity sector, the issuing CDO realizes a leveraged impact of the losses.

INDEX TRADES AND INDEX TRACKING CDOs

If we think of an arbitrage synthetic CDO, it is a pool of synthetic exposure in a broad-based list of corporates or structured finance products. An investor investing in, say, a BBB tranche of this CDO is making a synthetic investment in the pool of assets of the CDO. Because the investor is taking a position in a subordinated tranche in the pool, the investor is effectively making a leveraged synthetic investment in the pool of entities comprised in the pool. The investor is therefore taking a view on the credit quality of the underlying names.

As synthetic CDOs grew, there emerged in the marketplace a need to offer an instrument whereby investors may express a view on a generalized pool of corporate names. For example, if someone wanted to express a view on the quality of Corporate America, this would not be possible in a single-tranche CDO (referred to as a *bespoke CDO*). Hence, structurers developed *indexes*. An index is a broad, standard list of names from a particular geography or particular sector—the movements in the index would represent movement in the whole spectrum of the geographical region or the sector in question.

There are various such indexes trading currently. CDX.NA is an index representing North American names. iTraxx is an index of corporate and noncorporate names from Europe and Asia. Each of these indices have subsets, such as index of investment-grade names (CDX.NA.IG), or index of below investment-grade names (CDX.NA.HY). They also have industry and geographical subsets.

An investor buying or selling protection on the index expresses a long or short view on the names comprised in the index. As one may buy or sell protection on the whole index, one may buy or sell protection on tranches of the index. Thus, the index is also a form of a standardized CDO.[7]

---

[7] For a detailed discussion of index trades, see Kothari (2008).

If pure index trades are like unfunded CDOs, there have been attempts to have funded, index-based CDOs. These CDOs exactly track the composition of an *on the run* index, and are often referred to as *tracker CDOs*.

KEY POINTS OF THE CHAPTER

➤ *Balance sheet CDOs apply the securitization technology to parcel out a portfolio of loans, usually low-rated loans or emerging market credits and below investment-grade bonds, held by large banks.*

➤ *Balance sheet CDOs may be either cash CDOs or synthetic CDOs.*

➤ *In cash flow balance sheet CDO transactions, the structure used is a true sale structure (i.e., the seller makes a legally perfected sale of the asset to the SPV).*

➤ *Correlation risk can be fatal to a CDO because the concept of creating different bond classes with varying probabilities of default is based on the diversification of the asset pool and, as a result, one of the important objectives of both balance sheet and arbitrage CDOs is to achieve diversification.*

➤ *Diversification is easier to attain in an arbitrage CDO transaction because the CDO manager selects assets to suit the objective of the transaction; in balance sheet transactions, the assets are being parcelled out of the balance sheet of the bank and, therefore, rating agencies and investors are more concerned about portfolio diversity.*

➤ *A CDO's enhancement structure will be based on the probability of default curve, with the default curve estimated using proprietary models of rating agencies.*

➤ *Cash CDOs are intended for raising liquidity; synthetic CDOs are intended for risk transfers.*

➤ *The advantages of synthetic CDOs over cash CDOs are related to the purpose of the originator.*

➤ *Synthetic CDOs have the following advantages over cash CDOs: (1) minimizes funding and reinvestment problems; (2) splits the funding and the risk transfer; (3) alleviates the problem related to true sale; (4) does not require artificial separation of origination and servicing functions; (5) lower legal costs; (6) no up-front taxation; (7) avoids double taxation of residual profits; (8) no accounting volatility; (9) does not reduce book size; (10) retains flexibility in customer service; and (11) allows for a bullet maturity profile for the notes.*

➤ *In arbitrage CDOs, the term* arbitrage *is used not in the traditional sense of arbitrage but rather to convey that via active management the spread between the return on assets and the funding may be captured.*

➤ *Unlike a balance sheet CDO, the purpose of an arbitrage CDO is not to liquidate the assets held on the balance sheet of the originator, but to accumulate assets from proceeds of the CDO in order to garner a so-called arbitrage profit.*

➤ *Issues such as true sale that confront balance sheet cash transactions are not important in the case of arbitrage transactions.*

➤ *Given that the objective of an arbitrage transaction is to generate higher spreads, the CDO manager must select assets so as to capitalize on perceived pricing inefficiencies.*

➤ *To control the motivation of the manager of an arbitrage CDO to acquire assets that would impair the portfolio's credit quality, rating agencies impose restrictions (in the form of tests) that must be satisfied by the portfolio's assets.*

➤ *There are tests (overcollateralization and interest coverage tests) that must be satisfied by the portfolio and if failed require the CDO manager to begin deleveraging the CDO by paying off the senior most bond classes until the tests are passed.*

➤ *The credit enhancement structure for arbitrage CDOs is similar to that of a balance sheet CDO, except that there is no originator-provided enhancement.*

➤ *The juniormost class is commonly referred to as the equity class.*

➤ *While the purpose of an arbitrage synthetic CDOs is the same as for an arbitrage cash CDO, the assets are acquired not in cash but in synthetic form.*

➤ *Since the idea of arbitrage CDOs is to maximize returns, CDO managers were motivated to include structured finance securities, which, particularly at lower-rated levels, offered the opportunity to realize a much higher spreads compared to like-rated corporate bonds.*

➤ *As the market for synthetic CDOs grew, there emerged in the marketplace a need to offer an instrument whereby investors may express a view on a generalized pool of corporate names and as a result structurers developed index products that allow a view to be expressed on a broad, standard list of names from a particular geography or particular sector.*

➤ *Via an index product, an investor could express a long or short view on the index by selling or buying the index.*

➤ *A standardized CDO allows an investor to buy or sell protection on particular tranches of an index.*

CHAPTER **13**

Structuring and Analysis of CDOs

In the two preceding chapters, we discussed the broad principles of CDOs, their economics, and their types. In this chapter, we take up a variety of issues concerning CDOs involving the structuring of CDOs and their analysis.

MEASURES OF POOL QUALITY

From the viewpoint of both CDO investors and the rating agencies that are assessing and monitoring pool assets, the quality of the CDO pool is important. This is true for both balance sheet and arbitrage transactions as well as for both cash and synthetic forms. In the case of managed pools, the quality is important not just at inception but through the CDOs' term, as the composition of the pool will change over time.

The checks on the pool are of two types: quality tests and diversity tests.

Asset Quality Tests

There are two asset quality tests: weighted average rating factor test and minimum and maximum weighted average coupon test.

Weighted Average Rating Factor

Since ratings are not numerical but alphabetical, rating agencies translate their ratings into numbers. These translated numericals are known as *rating factors*. The convention is that lower ratings are translated into a higher numerical. By weighting each asset in the portfolio by its rating factor and summing these products, a *weighted average rating factor* (WARF) is computed for the portfolio. The test involves monitoring the collateral so as to maintain a maximum WARF.

Minimum and Maximum Weighted Average Coupon

As the name of the test indicates, this test requires that the *weighted average coupon* (WAC) of the assets in the portfolio not fall below a specified minimum rate nor exceed a specified maximum rate. If a change in the composition of the assets allows the WAC to fall below a floor rate, the transaction might face negative excess spread. On the other hand, if the CDO manager constructs a portfolio with a bias towards assets carrying very high coupon rates, it might reflect inferior quality of the pool.

Diversity Tests

There are two types of diversity tests: concentration limits and diversity score.

Concentration Limits

Concentration limits impose limits on the percentage concentration in a particular asset, particular sector, cluster, geographical region, and so on. It is notable that while applying concentration limits per industry, rating agencies have their own definition of *industry clusters*. The industry clusters are so defined that industries within the cluster are correlated, but there is negligible intercluster correlation.

Diversity Score

Moody's has been using a kind of a rule of thumb to indicate the extent of diversity in a pool. Unlike other measures of concentration such as Herfindahl Index,[1] the *diversity score* is a back-of-the-envelope computation. The diversity score is determined as follows.

---

[1] The Herfindahl Index is used by economists as a measure of competition in a given industry.

TABLE 13.1   Moody's Diversity Score Table

Number of Firms in Same Industry	Diversity Score	Number of Firms in Same Industry	Diversity Score
1	1.0	6	3.0
2	1.5	7	3.2
3	2.0	8	3.5
4	2.3	9	3.7
5	2.6	10	4.0

First, the actual number of obligors in the pool is classified as per the industry clusters defined by the rating agency. Then, the number of obligors per industry is multiplied by a certain coefficient. The coefficient declines as there are more obligors per industry. For example, if there are two obligors in the *same* industry, they are multiplied by a coefficient of 0.75, to produce a score of 1.5. If there are three obligors, the coefficient is 0.667. Table 13.1 shows computation of the diversity score by applying the coefficients. The sum of the scores is the diversity score. Hence, now, the pool is taken to have a theoretical number of obligors equal to the diversity score. The higher the diversity score, the lower is the correlation in the pool. Consequently, to monitor the ongoing composition of the pool, a minimum diversity score is specified.

ASSET AND INCOME COVERAGE TESTS

We have referred to the OC and IC triggers several times in the preceding two chapters. The intuitive idea of the OC and IC trigger goes to the very root of commercial finance. For example, a bank giving a loan on a project would try to ensure a certain asset coverage or debt/equity ratio, and debt service coverage. Likewise, a CDO is allowed to maintain a certain leverage only as long as the OC and IC tests are satisfied. If the CDO manager continues to reinvest the cash flows of the CDO and maintains the liability structure, he is maintaining the leverage of the transaction. On the other hand, if the manager uses the cash flows to retire senior investors sequentially, he is reducing the leverage of the transaction, or *deleveraging* the transaction.

Hence, the OC and IC triggers serve as automatic deleverage triggers in the CDO.[2]

These are the tests that require regular adherence over the term of the CDO. As discussed below, there are two significant coverage tests, both in respect of the rated securities.

Overcollateralization Test

Since the liability structure of a CDO, like any structured finance vehicle, has various classes, the total amount of assets available to the seniormost class is in excess of the liability for the seniormost class. For example, if the assets in a pool are $100, and the seniormost class is $80, there is an overcollateralization of $20 if the seniormost class is looked at in isolation. The extent of overcollateralization is the asset coverage available to the seniormost class.

The availability of this asset coverage is imposed as a precondition for the CDO manager to continue to make reinvestments and hence maintain the leverage of the transaction. There are OC tests for various classes of rated liabilities. There is no OC test for the juniormost or unrated class.

In the example above, the overcollateralization for the seniormost class (say Class A) is 125% (100/80). For any class below Class A, the denominator in the formula includes the liability for the respective class as well as all senior liabilities since the claim at the respective class is subordinated to the senior liabilities. As for the numerator, the following is included (1) the principal amount of performing assets; (2) the lower of the fair market value or assumed recovery rate for defaulted assets; and, (3) cash and short-term investments, if any.

Note that for computing the value of the assets (numerator), we have taken the par value or book value in case of performing assets, not their market value. In the case of a type of CDOs called *market value CDOs*, the basis for the OC test will be the market value of assets.

---

[2] The use of automatic deleverage triggers has become almost universal in structured vehicles, such as structured investment vehicles, hedge funds, and CDOs. There is an apprehension that as these triggers require these vehicles a nondiscretionery, and hence, mindless liquidation of assets during a phase of market adversity, these triggers help intensify the cyclical effects of the downturn.

Below is an illustration of the working of the OC test for three tranches (A, B, and C) in a hypothetical CDO structure:

Tranche A OC test: CDO asset par/tranche A par
Tranche B OC test: CDO asset par/tranche A and B par
Tranche C OC test: CDO asset par/tranche A, B, and C par

Let us assume there are four classes of liabilities in a CDO of which the last one is unrated, adding up as:

	Par Value	Minimum OC	Present OC
Class A	50	1.5	2.2
Class B	30	1.2	1.375
Class C	15	1.1	1.157895
Class D	15	NA	
Total of liabilities	110		
Principal value of the assets	110		

Let us now suppose some of the assets in the portfolio default and the sum of the par value of the performing assets and recoverable value of nonperforming assets declines to 100. We can see in the table below that the OC test for class C is breached

	Par Value	Minimum OC	Present OC
Class A	50	1.5	2
Class B	30	1.2	1.25
Class C	15	1.1	1.052632 BREACH
Class D	15	NA	
Total of liabilities	110		
Principal value of the assets	100		

When the OC test is breached, the transaction would have to be deleveraged. This means that instead of reinvesting the cash flow, the manager must now pay off cash to the various classes sequentially as per their priority order until the OC test is passed. Assuming the waterfall structure does not allow any principal to be paid on a junior class before the senior class is fully redeemed (sequential pay-down structure), the position after deleverage will emerge as shown in revised the following table:

	Par Value	Minimum OC	Present OC	
Class A	5	1.5	11	
Class B	30	1.2	1.571429	
Class C	15	1.1	1.1	Pass
Class D	15	NA		
Total of liabilities	20			
Reduce asset worth	45			
Value of assets after default	55			

Interest Coverage Test

The other similar structural protection is the *interest coverage* (IC) test. The working of the IC test is substantially similar, but is based on an interest coverage ratio. That is, the interest receivable on the assets must cover the interest payable on a particular class in a certain proportion.

Below is an illustration of the working of the IC test for three tranches (A, B, and C) in a hypothetical CDO structure:

Tranche A IC test: CDO asset coupon/tranche A coupon
Tranche B IC test: CDO asset coupon/tranche A and B coupon
Tranche C IC test: CDO asset coupon/tranche A, B, and C coupon

A breach of this test will also lead to diversion of all interest to the senior classes to pay off principal until the interest coverage ratio is restored.

For market value CDOs, the working of the OC test will be based on the market value of the collateral instead of the par value. For assets where ready estimates of market value are not available, the CDO manager applies certain discounting factors to assess the market value.

RAMP-UP PERIOD

The ramp-up period is the period over which the CDO manager will be allowed to invest the proceeds of the issuance into assets as per the objectives of the CDO. While there is no need for a ramp-up period for balance sheet transactions, in arbitrage transactions, the CDO manager would need some time to line up the assets.

Ramp periods may be different for different transactions, allowing the CDO manager the right to select assets over a period of time. In market value deals, the ramp-up period can be typically between six months to one year; in some emerging market CDOs a ramp-up period of as long as two years is allowed. A longer ramp-up period means more risk and, therefore, rating agencies assign a lower rating for a transaction if the ramp-up period is long. The reason is that during the ramp-up period, the cash raised will be invested in liquid, permissible investments.

In addition to the ramp-up period, the CDO has a typical warehousing period, meaning a period prior to the issuance of the securities when the sponsor starts collecting the collateral. Reinvestment and amortization periods are the same as for traditional securitizations.

THE CDO MANAGER

The crucial agent in an arbitrage CDO is the manager of the portfolio of the CDO. The CDO manager may or may not be one of the equity investors in the CDO. Typically CDO managers are investment advisers and asset managers seeking to expand the amount of assets under their management. Their motivation is to increase their fee income, while having a negligible impact on the costs of their organization.

Qualities of the CDO Manager

Rating agencies look at experience, staffing, and financial and managerial resources of CDO managers when rating a CDO issue. The size of an organization has obviously been an important factor. Below are other important manager attributes that are considered by rating agencies.

Experience

CDO management requires skills that are unique. These skills are relative to the type of assets that the CDO would acquire. For instance, a CDO that would focus on high-yield corporate bonds would need a manager experienced in this asset class, and CDOs that focus on CMBS or REITs would require conversance with that market. However, as compared to generalized asset management, for instance, such as for mutual funds, managing a CDO portfolio has its own pulls and pressures. First, there are stringent rules imposed by rating agencies on portfolio composition. Moreover, there are asset-based triggers applicable. At the same time, in view of its liability structure, a CDO manager has to strike a balance between the needs of the equity investors (high returns) and those of the senior debt (safety). In the context of high-yield corporate CDOs, Moody's (2001, p. 3) notes:

> We recognize further that high-yield experience outside the CDO environment may not translate into skill with CDOs. We have found several cases of seasoned managers who were successful within a mutual fund or separate account context but who failed as CDO managers.

Highlighting the need for relevant experience, Standard and Poor's (2001) notes:

> The ability to analyze performance history in specific asset classes and performance within a structured credit vehicle (as opposed to a total return vehicle) is an important factor in the investment decision. As a result, repeat managers with solid performance records are gaining a strong advantage in the competition for fund management.

Staffing

The rating agencies insist that CDO management teams be adequately staffed. Too many assets per person are frowned upon. If the team is too thin, the rating agencies often insist on a "key man" provision whereby if a key person leaves the organization, it is treated as an event empowering noteholders to replace the key person.

Strong Internal Controls

Strong internal control systems are an essential part of the organization of CDO managers. Too much autonomy granted to any particular individual should be avoided. Periodic reviews by a credit committee, independent of the CDO yet understanding its business, is often considered desirable.

Technological Investments

As investment management gets more and more quantitative, CDO managers would find it advisable to invest in technology products that facilitate identification of investment proposals, compliance with asset and collateral tests, and other requirements and triggers.

Financial Resources

CDO managers need capital to be able to build a sound team and invest in technology.

Balancing between Equity Investors and Debt Investors

The CDO manager has to walk the tightrope of balancing between the needs of the noteholders and the equity holders. The equity holders are interested in value maximization while the noteholders are concerned about the regularity of payments. Their needs are conflicting. From the point of view of rating agencies, noteholder-friendly CDO managers are preferred; but the preference of rating agencies is understandable as they rate only the notes not the equity.

It is difficult to decipher and distinguish between CDO managers who are noteholder friendly or otherwise, but some have acquired a particular reputation over time. Here is Moody's (2001, p. 4) position:

> Moody's looks for the collateral manager to possess the core competencies that will enable him/her to make sound investment decisions that are consistent with the spirit and letter of the governing documents. In turn, we then analyze the transaction assuming nothing more (or less) than such capable and effective management.

In instances where the CDO manager owns equity in the CDO, the question of conflict becomes all the more glaring. Rating agencies have reviewed both the pros and cons of the CDO manager holding equity in the CDO. Among the advantages are the fact that the CDO manager does not have the pressure of having to account for external equity holders, while having the understanding and support of equity investors if the CDO manager has to strive to maintain the rating of the external notes.

At the same time, the cons are that the equity might have been sold with high-sounding promises and the temptation to give quick rewards to equity owners might conflict with the larger interest of the CDO, and therefore the ability to raise debt in the future. As Moody's (2001, p. 4) puts it:

> Collateral managers who fight the CDO structure to make immediate equity payments ("equity friendly"), while not trying to fix the deteriorating nature of their portfolios, ultimately harm the equity investor, the transaction and themselves. These managers may eventually turn off all payments to the equity investors with no reasonable chance of making any payments in the future. The short-sighted strategy of making immediate equity payments at the expense of a sound portfolio and structural integrity is very visible in the marketplace. Among the many ramifications to this approach is the difficulty, or impossibility, of raising debt at a reasonable cost for future deals. Basically, the CDO market may close for that manager.

The CDO Manager's Fees

The CDO manager's fees are among the first priorities in the waterfall. However, quite often the fees are broken into a *primary fee* and a *secondary fee*, with only the primary fee being senior to the noteholders and the secondary fee only payable out of the residual left after paying the noteholders.

The adequacy of fees from a marketplace perspective is necessary both as a motivation to the CDO manager to peform well, as well as looking at the possibility of inviting a backup servicer to take the task of servicing in the event of defaults by the primary servicer.

INVESTING IN CDOs

In this and the following section, we look at CDOs from the investor's perspective.

Investor Motivations

The CDO business has grown rapidly, as revealed by data in Chapter 11. Apart from sheer growth in the numbers of CDOs, the variety of investors who have invested in CDOs has also grown. Investors in senior, mezzanine, and equity classes come with different motivations.

Senior investors in CDOs are obviously driven by the diversification motive. The spreads at CDO AAA level are relatively higher than corporate AAAs, but the difference is not substantial. The IMF's *Global Financial Stability Report* of September 2007 gave some data about CDO (specifically, structured finance CDOs) investors. It appears that at senior level, hedge funds are major investors, followed by asset managers, banks, and insurance companies. At the equity level, banks, insurance companies, hedge funds, and asset managers, in that order, are the prime investors.

The following factors explain investor preference for CDOs:

1. *Strength and stability.* Compared to corporate debt, CDOs have had a historically lower default rate. However, being a highly leveraged instrument, CDOs are prone to cyclical changes. Once in a while, as the corporate debt scenario worsens, the CDO market gets some jitters. The subprime meltdown has caused substantial pains to the CDO sector, with several severe downgrades and some early amortizations.
2. *Diversification.* CDOs enable investors already active in traditional ABSs to diversify their portfolio as CDOs are a class of asset not correlated with traditional ABSs. For example, credit rating agencies consider traditional ABSs and CDOs as two separate sectors when they calculate a portfolio's diversity score. Investing in structured product CDOs indirectly allows investors to invest in a much more diversified pool.
3. *Standardization.* Though they are still a very young product, CDO methodology, rating devices, and structures have by and large been standardized. The credit enhancement levels, portfo-

lio composition, and diversity scores have been fairly uniformly been observed.

4. *Yield.* By far, yield has been a very significant motive as far as investment in lower tranches of CDOs goes. At the same rating, CDOs offer higher yields than traditional ABSs and so more than plain vanilla securities. Indicative BBB CDO spreads around January 2007, before the breakout of the subprime crisis, were between 300 and 400 basis points, whereas BBB corporate bonds would provide something like 250 basis points.

5. *Transparency.* The risk of each transaction is represented by a limited number of commercial debtors that can be analyzed on an issue-by-issue basis. In general, for investors in senior tranches, aggregate data suffice, but detailed information is given to investors in the more subordinated tranches who can fine-tune the monitoring of their investment carefully, or even model their risk profile themselves.

COLLATERAL AND STRUCTURAL RISKS IN CDO INVESTING

The collateral and structural risks when investing in CDOs include:

- Correlation risk
- Interest rate and basis mismatch
- Cross currency risk
- Ramp-up risks
- Reinvestment risks during the revolving period
- Lack of granularity:
- Asset risks

We discuss each risk next.

Correlation Risk

The quintessential risk in any CDO structure is the risk of correlation. CDOs are essentially correlation products; they create seemingly diversified asset pools and try to take advantage of minimal correlation by stretching the leverage. Needless to say, high degrees of leverage can never be sustained in the presence of high correlation.

So, if high correlation is present in the CDO, the structure becomes extremely fragile.

Armed with CDO evaluation models of the rating agencies, CDO structurers have the advantage of doing a mix and match of assets to try and contrive a structure that under rating agencies' assumptions, has minimal asset correlation. For example, if obligors from different industry clusters are selected as per the rating agencies' definitions, the correlation is presumed to be either zero or minimal.[3]

In situations of economic downturn, most often there are widespread intersector disturbances that cause generic losses to several segments. In adverse business cycles, the absence of correlations among industries will not hold, leading to a basic assumption being questioned.

Interest Rate and Basis Mismatch

One of the primary interest rate risks in CDO collateral arises out of mismatch; that is, interest rates on liabilities often have a floating rate, while that on the debt instruments may either be fixed or floating linked to a different reference interest rate. While hedge agreements are often used to alleviate interest rate risk mismatch, the CDO manager must ensure that the hedge counterparty complies with the conditions set by the rating agencies in order to assign a AAA rating to the senior tranches.

Connected mismatches are mismatches in payment dates and payment periodicity. Managing a CDO, to an extent, is like managing an operating financial intermediation business and these mismatches are unavoidable. The mismatch spells a risk either way. If the assets repay more frequently than the liabilities, the transaction suffers from negative carry; if the assets repay less frequently than the liabilities, the transaction runs into liquidity problems. One possible solution is to enter into a total return swap receiving payments matching those on liabilities; however, the costs of the swap as well as the rating of the swap counterparty may both be issues of concern. If the swap counterparty is the issuer or an affiliate of the issuer, the swap will surely create problems of consolidation on bankruptcy.

---

[3] The rating agencies' correlation assumptions have been critically reviewed in Fender and Kiff (2004).

High-yield transactions also suffer from *spread compression* risk, the risk of higher yielding investments either being called back or defaulting, while the reinvestment is in less yielding debt and thus reducing the arbitrage spread. This is partly mitigated by the fact the coupon on the liabilities is also a floating rate.

Cross-Currency Risk

When a CDO transaction is comprised of debt or loans from various countries, particularly emerging markets, there is cross currency risk. Such risk is mostly hedged on a customized basis. Here again, the rating agencies' stipulation to the rating of the hedge counterparty is important.

Liquidity Risk

Liquidity risk arises in part from mismatches in coupon receipts and payments but more significantly may arise due to delays and defaults. The cash flow models that have been developed to analyze the default risk of a CDO do not capture the liquidity risk because it is essentially an intraperiod risk (e.g., the availability of cash during the half-year). The OC and IC tests also do not capture liquidity risks.

One of the ways usually adopted to minimize the liquidity problem is to ensure that when collateral is sold, the accrued interest portion inherent in the sale proceeds is not available for reinvestment but is retained for coupon payments. A certain minimum liquidity reserve may also be necessary.

Ramp-Up Risks

The ramp-up period may be anywhere between three to six months. In structured product CDOs, the ramp-up period is even longer. There is a much smaller ramp-up period in balance sheet CDOs.

The risks during the ramp-up period include the following:

- Negative carry because the short-term investments in which the CDO manager invests during this period carry much lower coupon than the liabilities.

- The risk of bonds or assets not being available, referred to as origination risk.
- Concentration risk during the ramp-up period.
- Adverse interest rate changes during the ramp-up period.

Arbitrage transactions where ramp-up risks are significant use various methods to mitigate those risks. Among these are a staggered ramp-up period in which the aggregate ramp-up is divided into smaller segments each with a target ramp-up period. This is done so that if the ramp up is not achieved during that period, the excess must be returned.

Reinvestment Risks during the Revolving Period

CDOs almost universally allow reinvestment by the CDO manager during a long enough period, usually during the first four to six years. The 100% reinvestment period is the period ending one year before the repayment begins, and thereafter, a proportion of the cash collected is reinvested. The reinvestment option granted to the CDO manager is supposedly quite useful. Standard & Poor's (2002) notes:

> Reinvestment of collateral cash receipts during this time has several advantages. Reinvestment can be used to maintain collateral quality and portfolio diversification, as rating changes, or as maturities, amortization, prepayments, or defaults reconfigure the pool. In addition, if prepayments during the revolving period are reinvested in eligible collateral, they may preserve yield for investors. The revolving period also enables a transaction to profit purely from limited trading activities, that is, buying and selling bonds and/or loans.

On the other hand, reinvestment option introduces several risks. These risks are redressed by introducing the collateral tests (such as, OC, IC, and weighted average coupon tests) discussed earlier. Moreover, stringent criteria for selection of eligible collateral is followed which is also subject to authorization and surveillance of the trustees.

Lack of Granularity

Most CDOs invest in a limited number of assets, which is by definition matched with the arbitrage objective. One cannot think of generating arbitrage profits investing in a very broad cross-section of assets. The asset pool of a typical CDO will consist of 80 to 120 names. If there are 80 assets in the pool, default of any one asset means 1.25% of the assets defaulting. The asset pool is nongranular, so it exposes the structure risk.

Asset Risks

The risks inherent in the collateral portfolio differ based on the composition of the portfolio. Essentially, a portfolio of bonds or loans, apart from carrying the most basic and common risk—credit risk—carries the risk of interest rate volatility, callability, convertibility, and exchangeability.

Increasingly in CDOs, CDO managers have made substantial investments in nonprime or illiquid assets. In periods of stress, when deleverage triggers have been applied, some of these CDOs have wound up with substantial losses.

KEY POINTS OF THE CHAPTER

> *For all CDOs (balance sheet, arbitrage, cash, and synthetic), investors and rating agencies must assess and monitor the quality of the asset pool.*

> *The quality of the asset pool is measured by two types of tests: asset quality tests and diversity tests.*

> *Asset quality tests include (1) weighted average rating factor test and (2) minimum and maximum weighted average coupon test.*

> *The weighted average rating factor (WARF) is a numerical score developed by rating agencies as a measure of the rating quality of the asset pool.*

> *The weighted average coupon (WAC) test requires that the assets in the portfolio not fall below a specified minimum rate nor exceed a specified maximum rate.*

➤ *Diversity tests include (1) concentration limits and (2) minimum diversity score.*

➤ *Concentration limits impose limits on the percentage concentration in a particular asset, particular sector, cluster, geographical region, and so on.*

➤ *The diversity score is a measure developed by Moody's to quantify the extent of diversity in a pool.*

➤ *Asset and income coverage tests involve overcollateralization and interest coverage triggers that serve as automatic deleverage triggers for a CDO.*

➤ *Minimum asset coverage test is provided by the* overcollateralization *(OC) test, which is imposed as a precondition for the CDO manager to continue to make reinvestments and hence maintain the leverage of the transaction.*

➤ *There are OC tests for various bond classes of rated liabilities, but no OC test for the juniormost or unrated bond class.*

➤ *The interest coverage (IC) test requires that the interest receivable on the assets must cover the interest payable on particular bond classes by a specified proportion.*

➤ *The ramp-up period is the period over which the CDO manager will be allowed to invest the proceeds of the issuance in assets as per the objectives of the CDO and the length of time for the ramp-up period differs by the type of transaction.*

➤ *CDO managers are typically investment advisers and asset managers seeking to expand the amount of assets under management and they may or may not be one of the equity investors in the CDO.*

➤ *The fee income received by a CDO manager is typically broken into a primary fee which is senior to the payment to the noteholders and a secondary fee which is paid out of the residual after paying the noteholders.*

➤ *The key attributes of a CDO manager looked at by rating agencies is (1) experience in the asset class managed; (2) staffing; (3) strong internal controls; (4) technological investments; (5) finan-*

cial resources; and (6) conflicts when there is manager-owned equity in the CDO and noteholders.

➤ *The reasons for investing in CDOs include (1) for certain asset classes CDOs are financially stronger and more stable in terms of historical defaults than the asset classes themselves; (2) diversification can be obtained; (3) standardization; (4) yield enhancement; and (5) transparency.*

➤ *The collateral and structural risks when investing in CDOs include (1) correlation risk; (2) interest rate and basis mismatch; (3) cross-currency risk; (4) ramp-up risks; (5) reinvestment risks during the revolving period; (6) lack of granularity; and (7) asset risks.*

Implications for
Financial Markets

Benefits of Securitization to Financial Markets and Economies

In this last part of the book, we will look at securitization's economic impact. At the time of this writing, there are questions about the contribution of securitization to financial markets and to an economy because of the now well-documented problems of the securitization of one asset class: subprime mortgages. The disastrous economic consequences of this sector of the securitization market started out as a credit risk concern regarding subprime mortgage borrowers in July 2007, spread to credit concerns in other lending markets, and by fall 2007 raised issues regarding liquidity. By late 2007, there were concerns about the impact of the subprime mortgage crisis on the global economy.

The root of this crisis was the lax underwriting standards used by aggressive mortgage originators. There are at least three developments that might have lead to the lax underwriting standards. First, housing prices had been rising since the early 1970s, increasing borrowers' equity in mortgaged houses and resulting in lower default rates. Second, the Federal Reserve brought down interest rates to historically low levels in the 2001–2002 period, thereby providing the right economic environment to not only approve loans but in the creation of mortgage designs that make it easier for subprime borrowers to qualify for loans such as fixed-rated interest-only mortgages, pay option adjustable-rate mortgages,[1] and stated income (no documen-

---

[1] A pay option adjustable-rate mortgage allows the borrower to select the payment method: fully amortizing over 15 years or 30 years, interest-only payments, or a payment based on a below market rate that results in negative amortization.

tation) loans. Third, these mortgages did not choke the balance sheet of originators because securitization markets provided an excellent distribution engine. When lenders start competing to lend funds, loan quality invariably suffers. Consequently, when these loans were securitized, it was garbage-out, as it was garbage-in. Commentators have found fault with securitization markets despite the fact that it is nothing more than a tool to transform loans to securities. However, there are important lessons to be learned. We discuss these in the next chapter. However, consider the following statements made in February 2008 regarding the role and future of securitization.

In a speech by Robert Steel, Under Secretary of the U.S. Department of the Treasury, before the American Securitization forum in February 5, 2008,[2] he stated:

> The securitization market is an example of how this incredible pace of innovation has changed financial markets. Secretary Paulson and I have been very clear—we believe that the benefits of securitization are significant. It enables investors to improve their risk management, achieve better risk adjusted returns and access more liquidity.
>
> While being an advocate for the benefits of your industry, it is also important for me to be straight forward. We must be honest and admit some degree of malfeasance. It is clear that in some instances market participants acted inappropriately. Secretary Paulson has indicated that certain adjustments to the mortgage process, such as licensing standards for mortgage originators, would help in weeding out the bad actors. Common sense licensing standards would take into account prior fraudulent or criminal activity, and should require initial and ongoing education.

Mr. Steel further remarked:

> Secretary Paulson is leading the President's Working Group to evaluate broad, long-term lessons-learned from current challenges, and where appropriate make recommendations. Securitization can remain a strong market in the future, but

---

[2] http://www.ustreas.gov/press/releases/hp808.htm

market participants must accept some degree of responsibility and commit to lessons-learned.

In a September 20, 2007 article in the *Economist*, "When it goes wrong . . .," the following comment was made regarding securitization

But do not expect a rush back to the ways of the 1960s. Securitisation has become far too important for that. Indeed, it has not yet fulfilled its promise. Wall Street eggheads may be licking their wounds at present, but they will soon be coming up with even more products. And, given time, there will no doubt be another wave of buying. More importantly, the transformation of sticky debt into something more tradable, for all its imperfections, has forged hugely beneficial links between individual borrowers and vast capital markets that were previously out of reach. As it comes under scrutiny, the debate should be about how this system can be improved, not dismantled.

In this chapter, we look at the benefits of securitization on a country's financial markets and economy while in the next chapter our focus is on the concerns with securitization. With respect to benefits, we discuss three aspects of securitization: (1) impact on funding costs for borrowers; (2) impact on financial disintermediation; and (3) impact on an economy.

SECURITIZATION AND FUNDING COSTS

In Chapter 2 we stated that one of the motivations for securitization is the potential reduction in funding costs. In this section, we will discuss this issue further. Modigliani and Miller (1958) addressed an important economic issue about firm valuation: Does the breaking up of the financial claims of a firm alter the firm's value? They concluded that in a world with no taxes and no market frictions, the capital structure of a firm is irrelevant. That is, the splitting of the claims between creditors and equity owners will not change the firm's value. Later, Modigliani and Miller (1961) corrected their position to take into account the economic benefits of the interest tax shield provided by debt financing. In the presence of taxes, the firm's optimal capital structure is one in which it is 100% debt financed.

Over the 50 years following the original Modigliani and Miller paper, several theories have been put proposed to explain why we observe less than 100% debt financing by firms. The leading explanation is that firms do not engage in 100% debt financing because of the costs of financial distress. A company that has difficulty making payments to its creditors is in financial distress. Not all companies in financial distress ultimately enter into the legal status of bankruptcy. However, extreme financial distress may very well lead to bankruptcy.[3] The relationship between financial distress and capital structure is straightforward: As more debt financing is employed, fixed legal obligations increase (interest and principal payments), and the ability of the firm to satisfy these increasing fixed payments decreases. Consequently, the probability of financial distress and then bankruptcy increases as more debt financing is employed. So, as the debt ratio increases, the present value of the costs of financial distress increase, reducing some of the value gained from the use of tax deductibility of interest expense.

The same type of question is being asked of asset securitization: Does asset securitization increase a firm's value? Effectively, asset securitization breaks up a company into a set of various financial assets or cash flow streams. Some of those various subsets of financial assets are isolated from the general creditors of the originator and benefit solely the investors in the asset-backed securities issued. In a world without asset securitization each investor has a risk in the unclassified, composite company as a whole. There are, of course, secured lenders whose claims are backed by specific collateral, but such collateral value is also liable to be eaten up by the generic business risks of the entity. Does the decomposition of the company's cash flow and granting specific debt holders a position of priority over other debt holders serve an economic purpose? If there is any advantage for this special category of debt holders with priority on

---

[3] While bankruptcy is often a result of financial difficulties arising from problems in paying creditors, some bankruptcy filings are made prior to distress, when a large claim is made on assets (for example, class action liability suit).

the claims of designated financial assets, is it at the cost of the other investors in the firm, and, therefore, the aggregation of the risk-return profile of these different types of investors just the sum of a firm's value without securitization?

Structural Arbitrage Argument

Asset securitization rests on the essential principle that there is an arbitrage in risk-reward tranching of the cash flows and, as a result, the sum of the parts is different from the whole. Participants in financial markets include investors with different needs to satisfy their investment objectives and hence different risk-reward appetites. Consequently, the carving up of different exposures to credit risk and interest rate risk by giving preferences for different investors that is done through structuring in a securitization makes economic sense. Essentially, the capital structure of the firm is itself evidence of the efficiency of the structural arbitrage—if there was no efficiency in creating corporate claims with different priorities, we will have a generic common claim on the assets of the corporation. If the stacking order of priorities in the capital structure itself has an economic value, securitization simply carries that idea further.

Arbitrage activity is the most apparent example of the alchemy of securitization. An arbitrage vehicle acquires financial assets and funds the acquisition by issuing asset-backed securities, thereby making an arbitrage profit in the process. While there is no reason for the weighted average cost of the funding to be lower than the weighted average return from the assets acquired, the market proves that there is an arbitrage involved in stratifying the risks in the asset portfolio.

The principle of structural arbitrage is one of the principles in securitization. While this has been disputed by theorists, it has been observed quite clearly in the market. Schwarz (2002) argues that securitization does reduce funding costs and therefore is not a zero-sum game. His arguments are based on the economic rationale for secured lending: Because secured lending by definition puts the secured lender at priority to the unsecured one, costs are lowered. Schwarz also argues that securitization allows a firm to enter the capital market directly and certainly capital market funding is more efficient than funding by financial intermediaries. While financial intermediaries play an important function in terms of credit creation and capital allocation, funding should come from where it eventually comes—households.

Increased Financial Leverage Argument

There was an increased focus on securitization following the bank-ruptcy of Enron in 2001 due to the role played by special purpose ve-hicles that it used. Moody's published its view in *Moody's Perspective 1987–2002: Securitization and its Effect on the Credit Strength of Companies*. In this paper, Moody's posed the question as to whether securitization provides access to low-cost funding and provided the following response:

> Not really. Many in the market believe that securitization of-fers "cheap funding" because the pricing on the debt issued in a securitization transaction is typically lower than pricing on the company's unsecured borrowings. However, the secu-ritization debt is generally backed by high-quality assets, cash held in reserve funds, and may be overcollateralized. This means that the relatively lower pricing comes at the expense of providing credit enhancement to support the securitization debt.

While it may be true that credit enhancement using overcollater-alization or some other mechanism is an inherent cost for the secu-ritization transaction, what is important to understand is the nature of credit enhancement. In typical corporate funding, because equity investors are a firm's first-loss capital, equity is the credit enhance-ment for the lenders to a firm. The extent of such credit enhancement in typical corporate funds, that is the appropriate leverage ratios for the firm, is in general extraneously specified either by lending prac-tices or in the case of regulated entities such as banks, regulatory requirements. This may force a firm to require much higher credit enhancements in the form of equity than warranted. In contrast, in a securitization, the required credit enhancement is linked directly to the expected losses in the portfolio and, therefore, the risks of the portfolio of financial assets.

If it is accepted as true that equity is a costlier funding source than debt funding, the higher leverage requirements attributable to traditional lending to firms in an industry or by regulatory capital requirements imposing higher weighted average funding costs on the firm. Greater financial leverage is permitted by employing securitization and, therefore, a lower funding cost or correspondingly higher returns on equity are attainable. This is achieved not from more efficient operations but from higher leverage.

A rating arbitrage argument has been offered as to why one would expect securitization to result in lower weighted average costs. *Rating arbitrage* occurs because securitization allows the corporate ratings of the originator to remain unaffected and the transaction to be rated solely on the strength of its assets and the credit enhancement mechanisms in the structure. The auto industry provides an excellent example. When the U.S. automakers General Motors and Ford were downgraded, they did not reduce their securitization volume. In fact, the evidence as cited earlier indicates the opposite. Volumes not only increased, but the asset-backed securities received a triple-A rating. Moreover, the existing asset-backed securities outstanding prior to May 2005 were in fact upgraded to the triple-A level, essentially because of an increase in credit support levels.

SECURITIZATION AND FINANCIAL INTERMEDIATION

Let us take a closer look at the notion that securitization has resulted in *financial disintermediation* and there are benefits to an economy that result from financial disintermediation. The argument is that corporate borrowers can obtain funds directly from the capital market rather than from financial intermediaries such as banks. Assume a financial market that does not have a public debt market. That is, there is no market for corporate borrowing via the issuance of bonds. While our focus will be on the U.S. financial market, in some countries there still exists a very limited public market and in other countries public debt markets are relatively recent developments.

In the absence of a public debt market, all financial transactions involving corporate borrowing are done directly with a lender. Let us further assume that the potential lenders are individual investors and there are no financial intermediaries. In this scenario, there will be a direct lender-borrower relationship between the individual investor and the corporate borrower. The individual investor must have the ability to analyze the financial condition of the corporate borrower, prepare the legal documentation for the loan, service the loan, and, if the borrower fails to perform, institute legal proceedings against the borrower to recover the outstanding principal and unpaid interest for the loan. More than likely, an individual investor will not have the capability of performing these services and must therefore engage third parties to undertake these activities, paying a fee for these services. Moreover, the lender must have sufficient funds to provide the full amount of the funds requested by the borrower and agree to accept the entire credit risk. Of course, the lender could ask other individuals to participate as part of a lending group to obtain a larger pool of funds that can be lent, as well as spread the credit risk and other costs associated with the loan among the members of the group.

Basically, there are at least three problems in a world without public debt markets and financial intermediaries: transactional difficulty, informational difficulty, and perceived risk. Transactional difficulty arises because an individual investor may not have sufficient funds to satisfy the amount needed by the borrower, nor might the tenure of the loan sought by the borrower match what the individual investor is willing to grant. There is informational difficulty because the individual investor may not be capable of assessing the creditworthiness of the borrower. Finally, the individual investor's perception of the risk associated with a loan will be based on only the credit risk of the borrower with no opportunity to diversify that risk over other borrowers.

It is because of these disadvantages associated with individual investors lending to corporations, as well as lending to other individuals, that gives rise to the need for financial intermediaries. A financial intermediary raises funds from individual investors and then uses those funds to lend to corporations and individuals. Consequently, it can accommodate the demand for a larger amount of funds than a typical individual investor. Financial intermediaries provide one or more of the following three economic functions: (1) providing maturity intermediation; (2) reducing risk via diversification; and (3) reducing the costs of contracting and information processing. Let us look at each of these.

A financial intermediary such as a bank can provide loans for a length of time that can accommodate the needs of a borrower. This is difficult for an individual investor to do. A financial intermediary makes loans with a range of maturities despite the fact that the claims it issues on itself can be short-term. For example, a bank can borrow funds by issuing certificates of deposit that have maturities from six months to five years and yet manage its duration risk exposure so as to be able to issue bank loans from three months to say 10 years. This role performed by financial intermediaries, referred to as maturity intermediation, has two implications for financial markets. First, it offers borrowers more choices for the maturity for their loans and investors with more choices for the maturity of their investments and borrowers have more choices for the length of their debt obligations. Second, it lowers borrowing costs because while an individual investor may be reluctant to commit funds for a long period of time and thereby charge borrowers a higher cost to extend maturity, a financial intermediary is willing to make longer-term loans at a lower cost to the borrower. Hence, borrowing costs are reduced.

Individual investors who have a small sum to invest would find it difficult to achieve diversification. Yet by investing in a financial intermediary, individual investors can attain cost-effective diversification.

Financial intermediaries maintain staffs to handle the tasks associated with granting a loan. These associated costs, referred to as information processing costs, can be done more efficiently by financial intermediaries than by individual investors. The costs of writing loan contracts and enforcing the terms of the loan agreement, referred to as contracting costs, can also be done more cost effectively by financial intermediaries compared to individual investors. This reduces the cost of borrowing for those seeking funds.

Let us see how securitization can fulfill these roles. Consider first maturity intermediation. As we have explained, a pool of assets can be used to create asset-backed securities with different maturity ranges. For example, a pool of 30-year residential mortgage loans can be used to create securities with maturities that are short, intermediate, and long term. Diversification within an asset type is accomplished because of the large number of loans in a typical securitization. Finally, the costs of contracting and information processing are provided in asset securitization. The contracting costs are provided by the originator of the loans. Information processing is provided at two levels. The first is when a loan is originated. The second is when a rating agency rates the individual asset-backed securities in the transaction.

There is one activity that is performed by some financial intermediaries that is not replaced by securitization. The asset-backed securities created from a securitization transaction must still be distributed to the public and a secondary market maintained. Technically, the distribution of securities and the maintaining of secondary markets is not a role of a fund-based financial intermediary. Rather, it is the role played by investment bankers. As more corporations shift from borrowing from financial intermediaries, the role of underwriting by investment banks will increase while their role as lenders will decline. This trend is reinforced from both the asset side and the liability side of the balance sheet of financial intermediaries. More money is moving from traditional deposits into institutional modes of savings such as mutual funds. Therefore, financial intermediaries are originating and distributing more assets than holding them on their balance sheet.

Thus, with a securitization, the types of fees generated by financial intermediaries will change. Fee income from loans and the corresponding costs charged in granting those loans (which are embedded in the loan rate) will be replaced by fees for servicing, distributing, and market making.

BENEFITS OF SECURITIZATION IN AN ECONOMY

Securitization is as necessary to any economy as organized financial markets. The end result of a properly structured securitization is the creation of tradable securities with better liquidity for financial claims that would otherwise have remained bilateral deals and been highly illiquid. For example, very few individuals would be willing to invest in residential mortgage loans, corporate loans, or automobile loans. Yet they would be willing to invest in a security backed by these loan types. By making financial assets tradable in this way, securitization (1) reduces agency costs thereby making financial markets more efficient and (2) improves liquidity for the underlying financial claims thereby reducing liquidity risk in the financial system.

A number of researchers have found that the securitization of residential mortgages has lowered rates paid by borrowers. See, for example, Hendershott and Shilling (1989), Sirmans and Benjamin (1990), and Jameson, Dewan, and Sirmans (1992). Lucas, Goodman, and Fabozzi (2007) have reported that the securitization of commercial and industrial loans for collateralized loans obligations has helped not only fuel the growth of the institutional loan market but has diminished the role of banks as holders.

The Case of the U.S. Housing Finance Market

To appreciate this important contribution to an economy, consider the origins of securitization.[4] In the first decades of the post-World War II period, the bulk of residential mortgage loans was originated and retained in the portfolio of depository institutions (and, to a lesser extent, portfolios of insurance companies). By 1950, depository institutions held nearly 50% of these loans, of which *savings and loan associations* (S&Ls) held 20%; by the mid-1970s the share of depository institutions had grown to 64%, of which S&Ls held 37%.

The supply of funds to the residential mortgage market was therefore dependent on the ability of depository institutions, particularly S&Ls, to raise funds and hold the residential mortgage loans they originated in their loan portfolio. However, depository institutions were encouraged by legislation and regulation to confine deposit-seeking and lending activities to their local housing market. Under such constraints, a poor allocation of resources that could be committed to the residential mortgage market developed, as some regions had an excess supply of funds and low mortgage rates and others had shortages and high mortgage rates.

Enter a new participant—the mortgage banker. Unlike thrift and commercial bankers, mortgage bankers did not provide funds from deposit taking. Instead, they originated mortgages and sold them, not just to insurance companies, but to thrifts in other parts of the country looking for mortgage investments—in essence providing a brokerage function. This seemed like an adequate market, bringing mortgage rates throughout the country closer together and reducing the shortage of mortgage money in high-demand regions of the country.

---

[4] For a further discussion, see Fabozzi and Modigliani (1992).

The mortgage market operated this way through the late 1960s, but it had a major flaw—it was dependent on the availability of funds from thrifts and banks, whether local or national. However, in the late 1960s—an economic period characterized by high and fluctuating inflation and interest rates—disintermediation (i.e., the withdrawing of funds from depository institutions), induced by ceilings on interest rates imposed on depository institutions, led to a reduction in funds available to all depository institutions. To counter (or at least mitigate this problem), the country needed a residential mortgage market that was not dependent on deposit-taking institutions. This could only be accomplished by developing a strong secondary mortgage market in which investment groups other than deposit-taking institutions and insurance companies would find it attractive to supply funds.

The problem was that as an investment vehicle, residential mortgage loans were unappealing for three reasons. First, they were illiquid. Second, holding only a few residential mortgage loans and not allowing diversification exposed an investor to substantial credit risk. Third, holding aside credit risk and liquidity risk, due to the uncertainty about the cash flows attributable to prepayment risk, residential mortgage loans were unappealing to financial institutions from an asset/liability perspective.

Given that residential mortgage debt is the largest debt market in the world, and given the highly undesirable investment property of long-term, fixed rate residential mortgage loans for U.S. and non-U.S. institutional investors (even in the absence of credit risk and liquidity risk), the challenge was to create a more appealing investment product. This was done by taking the individual residential mortgage loan and using it to create various mortgage-backed security products. The two major products are pass-through securities and collateralized mortgage obligations.

A pass-through security is created when one or more holders of mortgage loans form a collection (pool) of mortgage loans and sell shares or participation certificates in the pool. A pool may consist of several thousand or only a few mortgage loans. Every month, a certificate holder is entitled to a pro rata share of the cash flow generated by the pool of mortgage loans. The first mortgage-backed pass-through security was created by Ginnie Mae in 1968. Because

Ginnie Mae MBS are backed by the full faith and credit of the United States government, investors need not be concerned with credit risk.

Investors prefer investing in a fraction of a pool of mortgage loans to investing in a single residential mortgage loan, just as investors prefer to hold a diversified portfolio of stocks rather than an individual stock. Individual residential mortgage loans expose an investor to unique (or unsystematic) risk and systematic risk. The risks are that the homeowner will prepay the mortgage loan when interest rates decline and/or that the borrower may default on the loan.

Unsystematic prepayment risk is the risk of an adverse change in the speed at which prepayments are made that is not attributable to a change in mortgage interest rates. Systematic prepayment risk is an unfavorable change in prepayments attributable to a change in mortgage interest rates. Systematic risk in the case of default rates represents widespread default rates, perhaps because of severe economic recession. Investing in a diversified pool of residential mortgage loans in the form of a pass-through security reduces most unsystematic risk, leaving only systematic risk. Another important advantage of a pass-through security is that it is considerably more liquid than an individual mortgage loan or an unsecuritized pool of mortgage loans.

By reducing liquidity risk and eliminating credit risk, Ginnie Mae made investing in the mortgage sector of the bond market attractive to investors. The creators of broad-based bond market indexes—Lehman Brothers, Salomon Smith Barney, and Merrill Lynch—fostered the demand for pass-through securities because these securities constituted the mortgage sector of the broad-based bond market indexes. Thus, even though an asset manager does not have an exposure to liabilities but manages a portfolio whose benchmark is a broad-based bond market index, that asset manager would effectively be required to invest in the mortgage market or face the risk of being mismatched against the benchmark.

Even after reducing liquidity risk and eliminating credit risk, there was still one risk to deal with when the pool of residential mortgage loans are long-term fixed-rate mortgage loans—prepayment risk (contraction risk and extension risk). When investing in pass-through securities in which the underlying pools are comprised of long-term, fixed rate residential mortgage loans, some institutional investors are concerned with extension risk while others must deal with contraction risk. As explained in Chapter 3, these issues were mitigated for certain institutional investors by (1) pooling pass-through securities; and (2) redirecting the cash flows of a pool of pass-through securities to different bond classes to create securities with different exposure to prepayment risk and interest rate risk (i.e., bond classes in a CMO). These securities would therefore have different risk/return patterns than the pass-through securities from which they were created.

The creation of a CMO did not eliminate prepayment risk; it only distributed the various forms of this risk among different classes of bondholders. As explained in Chapter 3, the CMO's major financial innovation was that the bond classes created were more appealing to global bond investors because (1) certain bond classes more closely satisfy the asset/liability needs of investors and (2) certain bond classes are more efficient for investors seeking to take an aggressive position in the mortgage market by taking advantage of anticipated movements in interest rates and prepayments. The bottom line is that the bond classes created in a CMO broadened the appeal of mortgage-backed products to traditional fixed income investors.

The key role that securitization played in the development of the American housing finance market is clear. Via the process of securitization, an attractive financing instrument for homebuyers (i.e., the long-term, fixed rate mortgage loan) was used to create securities that appeal to institutional investors throughout the world. The economic fortunes of the previous major investors in the mortgage market—depository institutions, including S&Ls—no longer play the same role. While at one time the investor in a mortgage-related product was the local S&L, today it is just as likely to be a non-U.S. institutional investor.

KEY POINTS OF THE CHAPTER

➤ *Securitization has an impact on a country's financial markets and economy.*

➤ *While questions about the contribution of securitization have been tainted by the subprime mortgage crisis that is clearly attributable to lax underwriting standards, securitization remains an important process for corporations, municipalities, and government entities seeking funding.*

➤ *With respect to reducing funding costs, the same theoretical issues about the relevance of a firm's capital structure that were first addressed by Modigliani and Miller are being asked in securitizations.*

➤ *Asset securitization has the potential for reducing funding costs by breaking up a company into a set of various financial assets or cash flow streams with some of those various subsets of financial assets being isolated from the general creditors of the originator and benefit only the investors in the asset-backed securities issued.*

➤ *The question in a securitization is if the benefits accruing to the holders of the asset-backed securities come at the expense of the firm's other creditors.*

➤ *There are two arguments proffered as to why this is not the case: structural arbitrage argument and increased financial leverage argument.*

➤ *The principle of structural arbitrage asserts that there is an arbitrage in risk-reward tranching of the cash flows for different market participants and, as a result, the sum of the parts is different from the whole.*

➤ *It is argued that greater financial leverage is permitted by employing securitization and, therefore, a lower funding cost or correspondingly higher returns on equity are attainable that is achieved not from more efficient operations but from higher leverage.*

➤ *A "rating arbitrage" argument has been offered as to why one would expect securitization to result in lower weighted average costs.*

➤ *Rating arbitrage occurs because securitization allows the corporate ratings of the originator to remain unaffected and the transaction to be rated solely on the strength of its assets and the credit enhancement mechanisms in the structure.*

➤ *It has been argued that securitization activities results in financial disintermediation and there are benefits to an economy that result from financial disintermediation.*

➤ *The disintermediation benefit argument is that corporate borrowers can benefit via lower funding costs by raising funds directly from the capital market rather than from financial intermediaries such as banks.*

➤ *The benefits to an economy of securitization is that it makes financial assets tradable and as a result (1) reduces agency costs making financial markets more efficient and (2) improves liquidity for the underlying financial claims which reduces liquidity risk in the financial system.*

CHAPTER 15

Concerns with Securitization's Impact on Financial Markets and Economies

In the previous chapter, we reviewed the benefits of securitization to financial markets and economies. In this chapter, we describe the concerns that have been identified by regulators and economists with securitization. These concerns are:

- Reduces the effectiveness of monetary policy.
- Adverse impact on banks.
- Lax underwriting standards and poorly designed securities.
- Increases opaqueness of bank risk.

REDUCES THE EFFECTIVES OF MONETARY POLICY

In 1992, the Bank for International Settlements (1992) while recognizing the potential advantages of securitization also expressed concerns that could potentially offset those benefits. These concerns are beyond those the Bank for International Settlements identified as regulatory concerns. A major concern was that making credit available by allowing borrowers direct access to end lenders of funds could lead to the reduced role of banks in the financial intermediation process and less financial assets and liabilities held at banks. This could make it more difficult for monetary authorities to implement monetary policy. Thus, during periods of tight monetary policy, for example, banks can originate loans and then securitize the loans rather than holding them in their portfolio. This avoids the need for banks to fund the loans originated.

At a theoretical level, there are various theories that economists have proffered to explain securitization's influence on monetary policy. Bernanke and Gertler (1995) identify two channels through which securitization can influence monetary policy: the bank lending channel and the balance sheet channel. Both theories are based on the effect of cyclical changes on the suppliers and demanders of credit. The bank lending channel theory is based on cyclical changes in the ability of banks to intermediate credit while the balance sheet channel theory is based on cyclical changes in the financial condition of borrowers. The more obvious and direct link to securitization is the bank lending channel theory which is the one noted already.

Several empirical studies provide support for the thesis that securitization has weakened monetary policy. Loutskina and Strahan (2006) show how securitization has weakened the link from bank funding conditions to credit supply in the aggregate and as a result has mitigated the real effects of monetary policy. Frame and White (2004) and the Bank for International Settlements (2003) have shown that the mortgage hedging activities of the two government-sponsored entities, Fannie Mae and Freddie Mac, have at times moved Treasury rates. Two empirical studies by Federal Reserve economists support the view that based on mortgage loans, securitization has had a significant impact on monetary policy (see Estrella, 2002 and Kuttner, 2000).

If the regulatory control of the financial supervisor is based on assets that are held on the balance sheet of regulated institutions, such control has been rendered highly ineffective as banks and financial intermediaries throughout the world today operate on an originate-and-distribute model. They originate assets that do not necessarily rest on the balance sheet of the originator: they are distributed in various ways, of which securitization is only one. Several controls of traditional monetary theory are based on assets held on the balance sheet—for example, liquidity ratios imposed on banks.

In the present day model of financial intermediaries, financial supervisors have to learn to impose regulations that do not differentiate assets based on where they ultimately stay—the balance sheet of the bank or that of some conduit or off-balance-sheet entity.

ADVERSE IMPACT ON BANKS

The Bank for International Settlements (1992) expressed concern that because nonbank financial institutions are exempt from capital requirements, they will have a competitive advantage in investing in securitized assets. This could lead to some pressure on the profitability of banks.

In addition, because asset securitization enables banks to lend beyond the constraints of the capital base of the banking system, there is the potential for a decline in the total capital employed in the banking system. This would increase the financial fragility of not only a country's financial system, but also the financial fragility of the global financial system because a smaller capital base could not absorb substantial credit losses by the banking system. While this concern may not be applicable in all countries, it would be in countries where banks have traditionally been the dominant financial intermediary.

There have been several studies that have investigated the impact of risk-transfer that takes place as a result of a securitization by a bank. The findings are mixed. While some researchers find that risk is reduced (see, for example, Greenbaum and Thakor, 1987), others find that because the assets remaining on a bank's balance sheet may be lower quality after a securitization, the risk is increased (see, for example, Wolfe, 2000 and Murray, 2005). An argument put forth by Cantor and Rouyer (2000) is that a bank employing securitization successfully shifts credit risk on a net basis to investors in asset-backed securities when the riskiness of the bond classes sold exceeds the riskiness of the issuer prior to the securitization. If this condition is not satisfied, a securitization transaction may increase the net exposure of the bank to the credit risk of its assets.

The concerns as to inadequacy of the risk-capital of banks have been answered, to a large part, by the new capital standards Basel II. Basel II is a risk-sensitive capital standard, and computes capital based on the riskiness of asset pools, whether such pools are on the balance sheet or off-balance sheet. For instance, if a bank securitizes a pool but continues to be exposed to the credit risk by way of a retained interest, Basel II requires capital to the extent of the losses that the bank may be liable to absorb. Possibilities of regulatory arbitrage, at least as far as capital requirements are concerned, have greatly been reduced due to Basel II.

LAX UNDERWRITING STANDARDS AND
POORLY DESIGNED SECURITIES

With lenders able to remove assets that they originate from their balance sheet and therefore transfer credit risk via securitization, a major concern is that this process has motivated lenders to originate loans with bad credits. Given the ability of lenders to pass along loans into the capital market via credit enhancement (a large part of which is just the excess spread), lenders have been viewed by critics of securitization as abandoning their responsibility of evaluating the creditworthiness of potential borrowers.

This practice has been followed by banks who have securitized their subprime lending portfolios. For example, in an article in the online edition of the October 7, 2002 issue of *Business Week* ("The Breakdown in Banking") the following appeared:

> By selling off their loans, banks were able to lend to yet more borrowers because they could reuse their capital over and over. But it also meant that they made lending decisions based on what the market wanted rather than on their own credit judgments. The wholesale offloading of risk made the banking system less of a buffer and more of a highly streamlined transmitter of the whims of the market.

Banking regulators are well aware of this issue. On July 11, 1997, the U.S. Division of Banking Supervision and Regulation of the Board of Governors of the Federal Reserve System sent a letter to the officer in charge of supervision at each Federal Reserve Bank cautioning:

> The heightened need for management attention to these risks is underscored by reports from examiners, senior lending officer surveys, and discussions with trade and advisory groups that have indicated that competitive conditions over the past few years have encouraged an easing of credit terms and conditions in both commercial and consumer lending.[1]

The concern that high credit risk loans were being packaged and shipped to the capital markets via securitization increased in 2004

---

[1] SR 97-21 (SUP), July 11, 1997.

and 2005 as banks designed mortgage loans with features such as optional adjustability, negative amortization, and interest-only payment that increased credit risk to holder of such loans. In 2006, as subprime lending activity reached a new pitch, there were record volumes of securitization of home equity loans. Going into 2007, with a declining housing price index and generally deteriorating consumer credit, the mortgages originated and securitized in 2006 witnessed far higher rates of default than estimated at the time of the issuance of the securities.

In its *Financial Stability Report of April 2007*, the Bank of England has also commented on the risk that, in the originate-and-distribute model on which most larger financial intermediaries work today, there might be relaxed underwriting norms and generally reduced motivation to maintain credit quality. There have been numerous contentions that the originate-to-distribute model has weakened the quality of credits being originated.

On the face of it, the argument can easily be countered. The first counter-argument is that originate-to-distribute is the very basis of our economic system. If a shoemaker stitches a poor quality shoe because he is making it to distribute, and not making it to hold, every shoe in the market will be of poor quality. The key issue is, if we ignore the cosmetics of accounting, every banker who originates a loan does so with other peoples' money, and not his. Whether the bank refinances itself with loans, or covered bonds, or deposits, or mortgage backed securities, or loan syndications, invariably the bank is doing a mere intermediation function. As originate-to-distribute is what a financial intermediary is meant to do, it is not the balance sheet treatment of the mode of funding that makes or mars the banker's underwriting standards.

It is also to be noted that if the loan is originated by the bank, the origination desk and the structured finance desk do not have any practical nexus. The loan originator does not even know, at the time of origination, whether the loan will stay on the balance sheet of the bank or not.

One common argument that is advanced is that securitization is responsible for subprime lending since the originators have a limited first-loss risk. One cannot ignore the fact that apart from first-loss risk, originators also have something much more valuable at stake—

their reputation. Technical documentation might make a securitization look like an offering of an obscure SPV, but the investors in the market invariably lay blame for a bad transaction on the originator. For example, in the Goldman Sachs subprime mortgage transaction we discuss later in this Chapter, Goldman Sachs is merely a repackager of the transaction, but as the financial press discovered problems in the transaction, it was Goldman Sachs that was blamed.

There is nothing to establish that if securitization markets did not exist, there will not be phases in banking when banks would take more risks than they ought to. One of the basic rules of continuity is cyclicality. Risk appetite, and consequently, risk premiums also demonstrate a cyclical behavior. A look at the credit spreads from 1970 to March 2008 gives a clear indication of this cyclicality. Prolonged periods of benign credit dims our vision towards risk—everyone joins the party from the originators, to investors, to analysts and rating agencies. This is more so as the average age of the people manning the financial world has constantly come down.

Moving from the origination of loans to the securitizing of them, there is the related concern that the securities issued to the public will be poorly designed and too complicated to be understood by investors. Because of the complexity of such securities, the concern is then that there will be an over reliance on the ratings assigned by the rating agencies. The rating agencies in turn employ models that may be the best at the time of the analysis, but as with all models they may be flawed. This is particularly the case when such models utilize data over time periods that do not reflect the full range of potential outcomes under different economic and interest rate scenarios. For example, in the case of securities backed by automobile loans, there are extensive historical databases on the performance of such loans under different economic and interest rate scenarios. The same could not be said for the historical databases used in assigning ratings for securities backed by subprime mortgage loans.

Trite response to a problem as massive as the subprime crisis is the making of new regulations, as if it is a lack of law that led to the so-called lax underwriting standards. At the time of this writing, there have been solutions proposed to deal with the issue of lax standards in the underwriting process in the mortgage sector. In testimony before the Committee on Oversight and Government Reform,

Subcommittee on Domestic Policy (U.S. House of Representatives) on May 21, 2007, Alex Pollock of the American Enterprise Institute notes that:

> I believe that in an ideal mortgage finance system, the loan originator should always maintain a significant credit risk position in the loan, which creates a superior alignment of incentives. This is always my advice to developing countries as they consider housing finance ideas. As it did in the sub-prime mortgage boom, securitization typically breaks the link between the originator of the loan and who actually bears the credit risk. This can lead to less careful lending.

Moody's (2007) proposes several enhancements to help investors differentiate the quality of underwriting standards by originators and the reliability of the information provided by issuers. These include (1) a third-party oversight to verify the accuracy of the loan data underlying the transaction; (2) making loan level data available to investors; (3) stronger and more uniform representations by issuers regarding loan information; and (4) a third-party responsible to monitor and enforce those representations and warranties. The President's Working Group has also suggested legislative changes that would lay responsibility on mortgage originators and repackagers.

Andrew Davidson (2008, p. 2) has proposed an updated form of representation and warranties, what he calls an "origination certificate." Specifically, his proposal is as follows:

> An origination certificate would be a guaranty or surety bond issued by the originating lender and broker. The certificate would verify that the loan was originated in accordance with law, that the underwriting data was accurate, and that the loan met all required underwriting requirements. This certificate would be backed by a guarantee from the originating firm or other financially responsible company.
>
> The origination certificate would travel with the loan, over the life of the loan. By clearly tying the loan to its originators, the market would gain a better pathway to measure the performance of originators and a better means of enforcing violations.

Borrowers would also have a clear understanding of whom to approach for redress of misrepresentations and fraud.

While risk arising from economic uncertainty can be managed and hedged over the life of the loan, the risks associated with poor underwriting and fraud can only be addressed at the initiation of the loan. Such risks should not be transferred to subsequent investors, but should be borne by those who are responsible for the origination process.

Legislative initiatives to curb predatory mortgage lending would hold the different parties to a securitization responsible. In November 2007, the U.S. House of Representatives passed legislation that would make companies that sell mortgage-backed securities responsible for such loans responsible. A bill introduced by Senator Christopher Dodd of Connecticut in December 2007 would hold the investors in mortgage-backed securities responsible for bad loans (i.e., assignee liability). If this bill became law, think of the implications. If a mutual fund purchases in the secondary market a mortgage-backed security containing such loans, shareholders of the mutual fund would be responsible for such loans. Moreover, since state and local pension funds invest in mortgage-backed securities, these pension funds would have to absorb the losses. The central banks of other countries are investors in these securities and they would face the same consequences. The origination certification proposal by Davidson described earlier is clearly superior to the assignee-liability suggested by this proposed legislation.

However, there are two limitations to any proposal for fixing liabilities on the originator. There are two aspects of originator liability—legal liability and reputational liability. As for legal liability, every loan that is sold by an originator is sold with some basic "representations and warranties," and some disclosures. No originator carries more liabilities than the representations or warranties it makes, and no originator can be held responsible for the risks that it had explicitly disclosed to the buyer. MBS issuance documentation gives voluminous data, along with a brief summary of the risks that the paper carries. For instance, in the Goldman Sachs transaction that we discuss next, it is clearly evident that almost all the loans had loan-to-value ratios exceeding 80%.

The other issue is reputational loss, which is there irrespective of the origination certificate.

A Case Study

The now-classic example of lax standards and a poorly designed security structure in the mortgage area is that of a subprime mortgage deal by Goldman Sachs: Goldman Sachs Alternative Mortgage Product (GSAMP) Trust 2006-S3. This deal, sold in April 2006, was dissected by Allan Sloan (2007) in a *Fortune Magazine* article. According to Sloan, he placed this deal under his investigative microscope after asking professionals in the mortgage area to select the worst deal that they knew of that was issued by a top-tier firm. The GSAMP Trust 2006-S3 was a $493 million deal and was one of 83 mortgage deals by Goldman Sachs in 2006.

The collateral was 8,724 second-lien mortgages originated by Fremont Investment & Loan, Long Beach Mortgage Co., as well as other originators. A summary of the collateral characteristics follows:

- A third of the loans were in California.
- The average loan-to-value ratio was 99.29%.
- About 68% of the loans were no documentation or low documentation.

Basically, the average borrower had no equity in the home and for about two thirds of the borrowers, the verification of income was either not documented or had minimal documentation. Remember, these are second-lien mortgages. That is, lenders are not repaid until the first-lien mortgage holders are repaid.

There were 13 bond classes in the deal, with the senior classes (A-1, A-2, and A-3) being $336 million of the $494 million and receiving a rating of triple A. There were seven mezzanine classes making up $123 million of the deal and two noninvestment-grade bond classes of $21 million sold to two institutional funds. The mezzanine classes received investment-grade ratings (double A to triple B minus). Thus, 93% of the deal received an investment-grade rating by the two rating agencies that rated the deal, Moody's and Standard & Poor's. The first-loss bond class of $13 million was either retained by Goldman Sachs or sold off to some investor. In assigning ratings to the bond classes in the structure, while it is unknown as to what default assumption was made by Standard & Poor's, Sloan reports that Moody's projected that less than 10% of the loans would eventually default.[2]

In February 2007, less than one year after issuance, both rating agencies downgraded the bond classes in the deal. The triple-A rating assigned to the senior classes was reduced to triple BBB, resulting in a loss in the market value of the tranches. One month later, GSAMP Trust 2006-S3 was defaulting on its obligations to bond classes with 18% of the loans defaulting by September 2007. As a result, the two B-bond classes and the bottom four mezzanine bond classes lost all of their value.

As for the rating agencies role in this transaction, Sloan (2007) writes the following based on a discussion with a representative of Moody's:

"[In hindsight,] I think we would not have rated it" had Moody's realized what was going on in the junk-mortgage market, says Nicolas Weill, the firm's chief credit officer for structured finance. Low credit scores and high loan-to-value ratios were taken into account in Moody's original analysis, of course, but the firm now thinks there were things it didn't know about.

INCREASES OPAQUENESS OF BANK RISK

Another major concern with securitization is that it masks the risks to which a bank is exposed when assets are securitized but there are significant retained risks. The retained risks are not easily identified by an examination of the bank's balance sheet. Rather these retained risks are reflected in the economic value of retained or residual interests in the bank's securitization transactions.

After a securitization is completed, a bank retains the risk/reward profile associated with the residual cash flow (i.e., the cash flow after making payments to the investors in the asset-backed securities and ongoing fees associated with the securitization). The residual interest

---

[2] S&P had projected a cumulative loss of 14.84% [see http://www2.standardandpoors.com/spf/pdf/media/Teleconference_final_072507.pdf]

appears on the balance sheet of the securitizer but must be marked to market. There is no market where the value of the residual interest can be obtained. Rather, the determination of the value of the residual interest, both at the time of the securitization and thereafter, is estimated using the standard discounted cash flow analysis based on several assumptions. This can result in material differences in the value of the residual interest depending on the assumptions used. The failures of at least three U.S. banks—Superior Bank, First National Bank of Keystone, and Pacific Thrift and Loan—were caused by the alleged improper valuation of the residual interests or, equivalently, the improper appreciation of the risk on securitized assets.[3]

Consider for example the case of Superior Bank of Hinsdale, Illinois that was closed in July 2001. In 1993, the bank started originating and then securitizing subprime home mortgages in large volumes. It eventually expanded into securitizing its subprime automobile loans. Its securitizations were being supported by both residual interests and overcollateralization. By June 30, 1995, the bank's residual interests were almost 100% of Tier-1 capital; five years later it represented 348% of Tier-1 capital, meaning that the risk on the asset side was 3.5 times the risk on the liability side. As noted earlier, the first-loss risk retained by the bank in a securitization transaction is effectively the equity in a corporation. More to the point, if Superior Bank's Tier 1 capital is the first-loss support, the bank's equity holders effectively agreed to absorb the first-loss risk of $1, and correspondingly, the bank went out in the market to bear first-loss risk to the extent of $3.48. Further masking this risk was that Superior Bank was able to book profits on the sale of subprime loans under generally accepted accounting principles. Unfortunately, regulators did not see the financial difficulties with Superior Bank for quite sometime when regulators were required the bank to revalue its residual interests.[4]

---

[3] The bankruptcy filing by New Century in April 2007 was also under investigation for securitization accounting practices, including gain-on-sale accounting and overvalued residual interests. New Century was one of the major subprime lenders in the U.S. market.

[4] For further details see the investigation report of the Inspector General, *FDIC: Issues Relating to the Failure of Superior Bank 6th*, Febuary 2002, at http://www.fdicig.gov/reports02/02-005.pdf.

The Superior Bank case not only demonstrated the concern that bank risk could be masked, but it also highlighted the concerns with subprime lending. In a hearing before the Committee on Banking, Housing, and Urban Affairs of the U.S. Senate in February 2002 regarding the failure of Superior Bank, Thomas McCool, Managing Director of Financial Markets and Community Investment, stated:

> Superior's practice of targeting subprime borrowers increased its risk. By targeting borrowers with low credit quality, Superior was able to originate loans with interest rates that were higher than market averages. The high interest rates reflected, at least in part, the relatively high credit risk associated with these loans. When these loans were then pooled and securitized, their high interest rates relative to the interest rates paid on the resulting securities, together with the high valuation of the retained interest, enabled Superior to record gains on the securitization transactions that drove its apparently high earnings and high capital. A significant amount of Superior's revenue was from the sale of loans in these transactions, yet more cash was going out rather than coming in from these activities.[5]

KEY POINTS OF THE CHAPTER

➤ *The concerns with securitization are (1) potential reduction in the effectiveness of monetary policy; (2) potential adverse impact on banks; (3) lax underwriting standards and poorly designed securities; and (4) increased opaqueness of bank risk.*

➤ *A major concern about securitization is that by allowing borrowers direct access to end lenders of funds could lead to the reduced role of banks in the financial intermediation process and less financial assets and liabilities held at banks such that it is more difficult for monetary authorities to implement monetary policy.*

---

[5] United States Gerneral Accounting Office, *Analysis of the Failure of Superior Bank, FSB*, Hinsdale, Illinois, Statement of Thomas J. McCool, February 7, 2002, pp. 7–8.

➤ Bank regulators have expressed the concern that because non-bank financial institutions are exempt from capital requirements, securitization will give them a competitive advantage in investing in securitized assets, leading to some pressure on the profitability of banks.

➤ Regulators have expressed concern that because securitization enables banks to lend beyond the constraints of the capital base of the banking system, there is the potential for a decline in the total capital employed in the banking system that would increase the financial fragility of not only a country's financial system but also the financial fragility of the global financial system.

➤ There is a concern that the ability of lenders to pass along loans into the capital market via securitization has resulted in the abandonment of sound lending policies and motivating lenders to originate loans with bad credits.

➤ A related concern is that the securities issued to the public will be poorly designed and too complicated to be understood by investors resulting in an over reliance on the ratings assigned by the rating agencies.

➤ There are concerns that securitization hides the risks to which banks are exposed to the residual risks associated with a securitization, particularly when the valuation of any retained interest in a securitization is difficult to estimate.

Basics of Credit Derivatives

Credit derivatives are derivative contracts that seek to transfer defined credit risks in a credit product or bunch of credit products to the counterparty to the derivative contract. The counterparty to the derivative contract could either be a market participant, or could be the capital market through the process of securitization. The credit product might either be exposure inherent in a credit asset such as a loan, or might be generic credit risk such as bankruptcy risk of an entity. As the risks and rewards commensurate with the risks are transferred to the counterparty, the counterparty assumes the position of a virtual or synthetic holder of the credit asset.

The counterparty to a credit derivative product that acquires exposure to the risk synthetically acquires exposure to the entity whose risk is being traded by the credit derivative product. Thus, the credit derivative trade allows investors to trade in the generic credit risk of the entity without having to trade in a credit asset such as a loan or a bond. Given the fact that the synthetic market does not have several of the limitations or constraints of the market for cash bonds or loans, credit derivatives have become an alternative parallel trading instrument that is linked to the value of a firm—similar to equities and bonds.

When coupled with the device of securitization, credit derivatives have been transformed into investment products. Thus, investors may invest in credit-linked notes and gain credit exposure to an entity, or a bunch of entities. Securitization linked with credit derivatives has led to the commoditization of credit risk. Apart from commoditization of credit risk by securitization, there are two other developments that seem to have contributed to the exponential growth of credit derivatives—index products and structured credit trading.

In the market for equities and bonds, investors may acquire exposure to either a single entity's stocks or bonds, or to a broad-based index. The logical outcome of the increasing popularity of credit derivatives was credit derivatives indexes. Thus, instead of gaining or selling exposure to the credit risk of a single entity, one may buy or sell exposure to a broad-based index or subindexes, implying risk in a generalized, diversified index of names.

The idea of tranching or structured credit trading is essentially similar to that of seniority in the bond market—one may have senior bonds, *pari passu* bonds, or junior bonds. In the credit derivatives market, this idea has been carried to a much more intensive level with tranches representing risk of different levels. These principles have been borrowed from the structured finance market. Thus, on a bunch of 100 names, one may take either the first 3% risk, or the 3% to 7% slice of the risk, or the 7% to 10% slice, and so on.

The combination of tranching with the indexes leads to trades in tranches of indexes, opening doors for a wide range of strategies or views to take on credit risk. Traders may trade on the generic risk of default in the pool of names, or may trade on correlation in the pool, or the way the different tranches are expected to behave with a generic upside or downside movement in the credit spreads, or the movement of the credit curve over time, and so on.

In Part Four of this book, we discussed synthetic *collateralized debt obligations* (CDOs). The instrument used to create a synthetic CDO is a credit derivative. Credit derivatives are credit default swaps, total return swaps, and credit-linked notes. In this appendix, we provide the basics of credit derivatives focusing only on credit default swaps, total return swaps, and credit-linked notes. Credit derivatives also include portfolio synthetic trades structured either as bespoke collateralized CDOs or as index trades referenced to standardized baskets of entities or asset backed securities. We describe these in Chapter 13.

ELEMENTS OF A CREDIT DERIVATIVE TRANSACTION

The subject matter of a credit derivative transaction is a credit asset, that is to say, an asset or contract that gives rise to a relationship between a creditor and debtor. However, credit derivatives are usually not related to a specific credit asset but trade in the generic risk of default of a particular entity. The entity whose risk of default is being traded in is commonly referred to as the *reference entity*. There are cases where the credit derivative is linked not to the general default of the reference entity but the default of specific asset or portfolio of assets. This is called the *reference obligation, reference asset,* or the *reference portfolio.*

The party that wants to transfer the credit risks is called the *protection buyer* and the party that provides protection against the risks is called the *protection seller.* The two are mutually referred to as the counterparties. Protection buyer and protection seller may alternatively be referred to as the *risk seller* and the *risk buyer,* respectively.

We have mentioned above that it is not necessary for the protection buyer to actually own the reference asset: He might either be using the credit derivative deal as a proxy to transfer the risk of something else that he holds or may be doing so for trading or arbitrage reasons. Irrespective of the motive, a credit derivative deal does not necessitate the holding of the reference asset by either of the counterparties, by which it is also obvious that the protection buyer need not hold the reference asset of the same value or for the same tenure for which the credit derivative deal is written.

Therefore, like most other derivatives, credit derivatives are written for a notional value, usually in denominations of $1 million. The premium paid by the protection buyer and the protection payment provided by the protection seller are both computed with reference to this notional value. For the same reason, the tenure of the credit derivative does not have to coincide with the tenure of the credit asset.

Since the derivative deal focuses on the credit risk, it is necessary to define the credit risk. This is done by defining *credit events.* Credit events are the specific events upon the occurrence of which protection payments will be made by the protection seller to the protection buyer. Parties may define their credit events; in *over-the-counter* (OTC) transactions taking place under the standard documentation of the International Swap and Derivatives Association (ISDA) standard documentation, credit events are chosen from a list of credit events specified by the ISDA. In the case of a total rate of return swap, a type of a credit derivative discussed later, the entire credit risk of volatility of returns from a credit asset, without reference to the reasons therefore, is transferred to the protection seller, and hence the definition of credit events is relevant only for termination of the swap on its occurrence.

The *premium* is what the protection buyer pays to the protection seller over the tenure of the credit derivative. If there is no credit event during the tenure of the deal, the protection buyer pays the premium, and at the time of expiration, the deal is terminated. If there is a credit event, there will be a protection payment due by the protection seller to the protection buyer, and the deal is terminated without waiting for the tenure to be over. The *protection payments* or *credit event payments* are what the protection seller has to pay to the protection buyer should the credit event happen. The protection payment is either the outstanding par value plus accrued interest (computed with reference to the notional value) of the reference asset, or the difference between such par value plus accrued interest and the postcredit-event market value of the reference asset. In the former case, the protection buyer delivers the reference asset to the protection seller (called *physical settlement*) and in the latter case, there is no transfer of the credit asset (called *cash settlement*) as the protection seller merely compensates the protection buyer for the losses suffered due to the credit event.

In either case, the protection payments are not connected with the actual losses suffered by the protection buyer.

In case the terms between the parties have fixed physical settlement as the mode, the protection buyer shall be required to deliver a defaulted obligation of the reference entity on default. Generally, the definition of such defaulted obligations is broad enough to allow the protection buyer to select from several available obligations of the reference entity to deliver. Such obligations are called *deliverable obligations*. Both reference obligations and deliverable obligations are defined usually by characteristics. Hence, any obligation of the reference entity that satisfies the characteristics listed will be a deliverable obligation. Quite obviously, the protection buyer will have the motivation to deliver the *cheapest-to-deliver obligation*.

For example, let us suppose a bank has an outstanding secured loan facility of $65 million, payable after seven years, given to a certain corporation, say X Corp. The bank wants to shed a part of the risk of the said facility, say $50 million, and enters into a credit derivative deal with a counterparty (the protection seller). The bank is the protection buyer in this deal. The derivative deal is done for a notional value of $50 million for X Corp. as the reference entity and say with a tenure of five years. The reference obligation is "senior unsecured loans or bonds of the reference entity." Parties agree to physical settlement. In this deal, the bank will pay a premium of 80 basis points to the protection seller during the full term of the contract, that is, five years if a credit event does not occur. If a credit event occurs, the bank stops making payments up to the date of the credit event and seeks a protection payment.

The type of credit derivative described in this illustration is called a *credit default* swap or simply *default swap* and is the most common form of a credit derivative.

In our example, the bank is buying protection basically for hedging purposes. However, it may be noted that there are mismatches between the actual loan held by the bank and the derivative. The amount of the loan is $65 million, whereas the notional value of the derivative is only $50 million. The actual loan is a secured loan facility, while the reference asset for the credit derivative is a senior unsecured loan. The term of the loan is seven years, while the term of the derivative is five years. We emphasize that there may be a complete disconnect between the actual credit asset, if at all held by the protection buyer, and the credit derivative. For the purpose of our discussion, it would be all the same if the protection buyer did not have any loan given to X Corp., and was simply trying to buy protection hoping to make a profit when the premium for buying protection against X Corp. went above 80 basis points (bps).

Since a credit derivative is referenced to "senior unsecured loans or bonds of X Corp.," the credit events (as defined by the parties) will be triggered if there is such an event on any of the obligations of X Corp. that satisfy the characteristics listed for the reference obligations. Generally speaking, if there is a default on any of the loans or bonds of X Corp., or if X Corp. files for bankruptcy, it would trigger a credit event.

The obvious purpose of the party buying protection in this case is to partially hedge against the risk of default of the exposure held by the protection buyer. The protection buyer, the bank in our example, actually holds a secured loan, but buys protection for a senior unsecured loan for two reasons. First, since the market trades in general risk of default of X Corp., the defaults are typically defined with reference to unsecured loans as they are more likely to default than secured loans. Second, for the protection buyer, the protection is stronger when it is referenced to an inferior asset than the one actually held by the bank in our example.

The protection seller is earning a premium of 80 bps by selling protection. This party, of course, is exposed to the risk of default of X Corp. In the normal course, to create the same exposure, the protection seller would have to lend out money to X Corp. In this case, the protection seller has acquired the exposure without any initial investment (see this discussion later in this appendix about funded derivatives). The objective of the protection seller might be simply to create and hold this exposure as a proxy for a credit asset to X Corp. Alternatively, the protection seller might also be viewing the transaction as a trade: this party would stand to gain if the cost of buying protection against X Corp. declines to below 80 bps. The protection seller may encash this gain either by buying protection at the reduced price, or by other means.

If the credit event does not happen over the five-year term of the contract, the derivative expires with the protection buyer having made periodic premium payments to the protection seller. If the credit event does happen, the protection buyer may choose to make a physical settlement. In that case, the protection buyer may well deliver an unsecured bond of X Corp., as evidently, the possible recovery on the secured loan that X Corp. is holding will be better than the market price of the unsecured bonds of X Corp. Thus, if the protection buyer purchases such bonds at a price of 30%, he would stand to make 70% of the notional value because the protection seller will be obligated to pay to the protection buyer the par value of the defaulted assets that satisfy the characteristics of the deliverable obligations. The protection buyer may continue to hold the secured loan and recover it through enforcement of security interests or otherwise.

BILATERAL DEALS AND CAPITAL MARKET DEALS

A credit derivative may be a transaction between two counterparties, or may be a capital market transaction. Bilateral transactions between parties or dealers are normally referred to as OTC deals, since they take place between parties on an OTC basis as opposed to exchange-traded derivatives. The other possible format of a credit derivative deal is embedding the derivative into some capital market instrument and offering such instrument to investors in the capital market.

The most basic distinction between capital market deals and counterparty or OTC deals is based on who the counterparty is. Obviously, the counterparty for any credit derivative deal is a specific party and it is impossible to envisage a credit derivative where the "capital market" is the counterparty. However, capital market transactions intend to transfer the exposure to the capital market instruments by interposing *special purpose vehicles* (SPVs). In a capital market transaction, the risk is first transferred by the protection buyer to the SPV, which is turn transmits the risk into the market by issuing securities which carry an embedded derivative feature.

A credit derivative deal might either be linked with a single reference entity, called a *single-name default swap*, or a portfolio of entities, called a *portfolio default swap*. Since the market is essentially OTC, it is intermediated by dealers and brokers. For well-known reference entities, the market is quite liquid and bid-ask spreads are quite fine. Another very liquid part of the market is standardized index trades, which are discussed later.

Sometimes, credit derivative deals are embedded into capital market securities to make it an investment product. This takes the form of CDOs that we cover in Part Four of this book. CDOs might relate either to a pool of assets sitting on the balance sheet of a bank (i.e., balance sheet CDO) or a bunch of reference entities drawn from the market (i.e., arbitrage CDO).

REFERENCE ASSET OR PORTFOLIO

From the viewpoint of obligor specification, there are two types of credit derivatives: a *single-obligor derivative* or (*single-name derivative*), and a *portfolio derivative*. As implied by the name, a single-obligor credit derivative refers to an obligation of a specific named obligor, whereas a portfolio trade refers to specific obligations of a portfolio of obligors.

In either case, the reference is to obligations of the reference entity, such as an unsecured loan or unsecured bond of the obligor. Parties may define the obligation either by making it specific such as a particular loan or a particular bond issue, or give a broad generic description such as any loan, or any bond, etc. Most of the OTC transactions are referenced to a generic senior unsecured loan of the reference entity, which is primarily chosen as representative of the risk of default, mostly leading to a bankruptcy, of an obligor on a plain unstructured credit.

In case of portfolio default swaps, the portfolio may be a *static portfolio* or a *dynamic portfolio*. As implied by name, a static portfolio is one where the constituents of the obligor portfolio remain fixed and known over time. In the case of a dynamic portfolio, though the total value of the reference portfolio remains fixed, its actual composition may change over time as new obligors may be introduced into the pool, usually for those that have been repaid or prepaid, or those that have been removed due to failure to comply with certain conditions. It is obvious that the selection of the names forming part of the dynamic portfolio will be based on definite selection criteria, elaborately laid down in the transaction documents, so as to ensure that the reinstatement of obligors over time does not change the portfolio risk.

STRUCTURED PORTFOLIO TRADE

Where the credit derivative deal relates to a portfolio, it is possible to create tranches of the risk arising out of it. We have earlier briefly discussed the concept of tranches. Hence, it is possible for the protection buyer to come up with several tranches—junior, mezzanine, and senior tranche or a 0%–4%, 4%–8% tranche, and so on. The protection buyer may either buy protection on all these tranches, or one or more than one of these. Such trades are called *structured credit trades*, or *structured portfolio trades*. The word "structured" puts such trades in line with other segments of structured finance such as securitization. The word "structured" also implies that the number and sizing of the tranches are structured to suit investors' appetite for risk and urge for returns.

Basket Trades

Another common variety of a structured credit derivatives prevailing in the market is called a *basket derivative*, where the reference asset is a basket of obligations, and the credit event is n-*th to default in a basket*. For example, consider a first-to-default in a basket of 10 obligors. The deal is referenced to a basket of 10 defined obligors, each with a uniform notional value, and when any one out of the basket becomes the first to default, the protection payments will be triggered; thereafter, the deal is terminated. Effectively, this might be a very efficient way of buying protection against a portfolio of 10 assets while paying a much smaller premium. This is because the joint probability of more than one obligor defaulting in a basket of 10 obligors is very small; while the probability of any one of the 10 defaulting is much higher. So, the losses of the protection seller are limited to only one of the 10 obligors, while at the same time providing needed protection against a larger portfolio to the protection buyer.

At times, parties might even transact a basket deal where protection is bought for second-to-default obligor. The intent here is that the first or threshold risk will be borne by the protection buyer, but any subsequent loss after the first default will be transferred to the protection seller. Conceptually, the protection buyer has limited losses to the first default in the portfolio, seeking protection from the protection seller for the second default. The third or subsequent default in the portfolio is unprotected, but that is only a theoretical risk as the probability of three defaults in an uncorrelated portfolio is nominal. Likewise, one may think of an *n*-th to default basket swap.

Basket default swaps, like all portfolio trades, are structured with the parties taking a view on the inherent correlation in the basket. Higher the correlation in the basket, the risk of the first-to-default protection seller comes down while that of the second-to-default protection seller goes up.

Index-Based Credit Derivative Trades

The idea of portfolio credit trades, structured or otherwise, was carried further with the introduction of the index trades and gained tremendous popularity. A single-name credit derivative allows the parties to trade in credit risk of a particular entity. A portfolio derivative allows parties to transact trade in the credit of a broad-based portfolio—let us say, a portfolio of 125 U.S. corporates. The selection of these 125 U.S. corporates may be done by the person who structures the transaction. However, to allow parties to trade on a common portfolio, index trades construct a standard pool of N number of names (or securities), and allows various traders to trade in such common portfolio. The common portfolio is known as the *index*, in line with indexes of equities, bonds, and other similar securities. The advantage of index trades is that they allow the carrying out of structured trades in a generalized portfolio so capital market participants may take views on the general corporate credit environment in a specific country or region or sector. In view of their advantage over bespoke portfolio trades (i.e., portfolios of names selected by the structuter), index trades have quickly grown to become a very large component of the credit derivatives market.

Protection Buyer

The protection buyer is the entity that seeks protection against the risk of default of the reference obligation. The protection buyer is usually a bank or financial intermediary which has exposure to credit assets, funded or unfunded. In such a case, the primary objective of a protection buyer is to hedge against the credit risks inherent in credit assets. The credit assets in case of OTC transactions are mostly corporations, or sovereigns, primarily emerging market sovereigns. In the case of several CDOs, the assets can be diversified obligor pools representing a broad cross-section of exposure in various industries. There have been several cases where risks on a portfolio of a very large number of obligors have been transferred through derivatives, for example, *small and medium enterprises* (SME) loans, auto leases, and so on.

At times, dealers could be buying protection for shorting credit assets for the purpose of arbitraging by selling protection or otherwise gaining by way of a widening of credit spreads on the reference entity. Buying protection is the same as going short on a bond. The protection buyer gains if the credit quality of the reference entity worsens. One may also visualize that usually, between the bond market, equity market, and the credit derivatives market, there is a degree of correlation. Hence, the protection buyer shorts exposure on the entity by buying protection.

Buying of protection is also seen by the market as a convenient way of synthetically transferring the loan while avoiding the problems associated with actual loan sales. Sale or securitization of loans involves various problems, depending on the jurisdiction concerned, relating to obligor notification, partial transfers, transfer of security interests, further lending to the same borrower, and so on. (Apart from the procedural issues related to transfer of loan portfolios, a major legal risk in a loan sale is generically referred to as the "true sale" risk, that is, the possibility that the sale of the loans will either be disregarded by a court or rendered unfructuous by a consolidation of the transferee with the transferor. For a detailed discussion on the true sale problems, see Kothari (2006).) Synthetic transfers, in contrast, avoid all of these problems as the reference asset continues to stay with the originator.

In credit derivatives documentation, the protection buyer is also referred to as the *fixed rate payer*. Perhaps this term is the remnant of the interest rate swap documentation.

Protection Seller

We have discussed briefly the motivations of the protection seller earlier. To reiterate, the protection seller is mainly motivated by yield enhancement, or getting to earn credit spreads from synthetic exposures where direct creation of loan portfolios is either not possible or not feasible. In OTC transactions, the major protection sellers are insurance companies, banks, hedge funds, equity funds, and investment companies. In the case of CDOs, the protection sold is embedded in securities which are mostly rated, and the investors acquire these securities based on their respective investment objectives.

The protection seller may also be taking a trading view and expecting the credit quality of the reference entity to improve. Selling protection is equivalent of going long on a bond—as the quality of the underlying entity improves, the protection seller stands to gain.

In credit derivatives documentation, the protection seller is also referred to as the *floating rate payer*.

Funded and Unfunded Credit Derivatives

Typically, a credit derivative implies an undertaking by the protection seller to make protection payments on the occurrence of a credit event. Until the credit event happens, there is no financial investment by the protection seller. In this sense, a credit derivative is an unfunded contract.

However, quite often, for various reasons, parties may convert a credit derivative into a funded product. This may take various forms, such as:

- The protection seller prepays some kind of estimate of protection payments to the protection buyer, to be adjusted against the protection payments, if any, or else, returned to the protection seller.
- The protection seller places a deposit or cash collateral with the protection buyer, which the latter has a right to appropriate in case of protection payments.
- The protection buyer issues a bond or note that the protection seller buys with a contingent repayment clause entitling the protection buyer to adjust the protection payments from the principal, interest, or both, payable on the bond or note.

The purpose of converting an unfunded derivative into a funded form may vary: it could either be a simple collateralization device for the protection buyer, or may be the creation of a funded product which features a derivative and is therefore a restructured form of the original obligation with reference to which the derivative was initially written. When the funded derivative takes the form of a bond or note, it is referred to as a *credit-linked security* or *credit-linked note*, which implies that a credit derivative has been embedded in a security.

Credit Event

Credit event or events are the contingencies or the risk of which is being transferred in a credit derivative transaction. There are certain credit derivatives, such as total rate of return swaps, where the reference to credit event is merely for closing out the transacton because the cash flows are swapped regularly; but most credit derivative deals refer to an event or events upon the happening of which protection payments will be triggered.

ISDA's standard documentation lists and elaborates different credit events for different types of credit derivative deals. For standard credit derivatives, there are six credit events: bankruptcy, failure to pay, obligation default, obligation acceleration, repudiation or moratorium, and restructuring. Parties are free to choose one or more credit events. If the parties use a non-ISDA document, they can define their own credit events as well. In most capital market transactions, credit events are given a structured meaning by the parties.

In OTC trades, the most common credit events are bankruptcy, failure to pay, and restructuring. *Restructuring* as a credit event has had a controversial history in the credit derivatives business. This is because a mere restructuring is not a case of default in common banking or credit parlance, and yet triggers protection payments in the case of credit derivatives. If a protection buyer holds a loan that gets restructured, say, with the borrower seeking extension of maturity by something like two years, theoretically, the protection buyer has not lost much money (except may be on account of impairment of credit of the borrower). Yet, under restructuring the protection buyer still seek compensation by delivering a cheapest-to-deliver asset of the reference entity that he may acquire from the market. To put reasonable curbs on what may be delivered pursuant to a restructuring event, ISDA documentation gives certain options to parties, essentially in the form of maturity limitations of the deliverable obligations.

It is quite possible for credit derivatives trades to not include restructuring as a credit event at all. For example, index trades do not include restructuring.

There are credit default swaps on asset-backed securities. The *dealer template* for transacting credit default swaps on subprime mortgage bonds was first published by the ISDA in June 2005 and the *user* or *monoline* template was published soon thereafter.[1] In the case of credit derivatives on asset-backed securities, the generic definitions of *bankruptcy* and *failure to pay* would obviously not be applicable. For example, while all of a corporation's senior unsecured debt is

---

[1] CDS on subprime mortgage bonds and other asset-based securities had been around in one-off and specialized documentation since 1998.

impacted in the same way by the corporation's bankruptcy, for an asset-backed security each bond class in the structure has its own individual credit quality. Moreover, while a corporation's failure to make an interest payment is significant, for an asset-backed security transaction missed payments might be small and furthermore might be reversed in the future. Hence, there are unique credit events that the ISDA has established for credit default swaps on asset-backed securities.[2]

Notional Value

We have discussed above the relevance of notional value in a derivative deal. Credit derivatives also refer to a notional value as the reference value for computing both the premium and the protection payments. Notional values are generally standardized into denominations of $1 million. However, capital market transactions can use their own nonstandard notional values.

There are certain derivatives where the notional value is not fixed—it declines over time. This is where the derivative is linked with an amortizing loan or an asset-backed security where the underlying asset pool consists of amortizing assets.

Premium

The premium is the consideration for purchasing protection that the protection buyer pays to the protection seller over time. The premium is normally expressed in terms of basis points. For example, a premium of 85 bps will mean on a notional value of $1 million, the protection buyer will pay to the protection seller $8,500 as the annual premium. The premium is normally settled on a quarterly basis but typically accrues on a daily basis.

The premium may not be constant over time—there might be a step-up feature, meaning the premium increases after a certain date. This might be either to reflect the term structure of credit risk or simply for a perfunctory regulatory compliance reason as discussed next.

---

[2] For a discussion of these credit events and the ISDA template, see Chapter 6 in Goodman, Li, Lucas, Zimmerman, and Fabozzi (2008).

Tenure

The tenure is the term over which the derivative deal will run. The tenure comes to an end either by the passage of time or upon happening of the credit event, whichever is earlier. For portfolio derivatives, the credit event on one of the obligors may not lead to termination of the derivative.

As we discussed earlier, the tenure of the credit derivative need not coincide with the maturity of the actual exposure of the protection buyer. However, for regulatory purposes, conditions for capital relief curtail the benefit of capital relief where there is a maturity mismatch between the tenure of the underlying credit asset and that of the credit derivative. So, the common practice in transactions where the protection buyer intends to seek capital relief, but where the protection seller wants to give protection only for three years while the underlying exposure is for five years, is to quote a rate for three years with a step-up after year three, with an option to terminate with the protection buyer. The protection buyer will terminate the transaction due to the step-up feature, effectively getting protection only for three years, while theoretically for regulatory purposes the exposure is fully covered for five years.

Loss Computation

If a credit event takes place, the protection seller must make compensatory loss payments to the protection buyer, as in the case of a standard insurance contract. However, the significant difference between a standard insurance contract and a credit derivative is that for the latter, it is not important that the protection buyer must actually suffer losses; nor is the amount of actual loss relevant. Losses of the protection seller are also known as the protection payment.

The loss computation and the payments required to be made by the protection seller are a part of the settlement of the contract. Obviously, the losses of the protection seller will depend on the settlement method—physical or cash. Where the terms of settlement are cash, the contract will provide for the manner of computing losses. Here, the loss is the difference between the par value of the reference asset (that is to say, the notional value, plus accrued interest as per terms of the credit), less the fair value on the valuation date. Most of the reference assets will not have any deterministic market values as such. Consequently, the method of computing the fair value is described in the contract in detail. If the reference asset is something like a senior unsecured loan, the market value may be determined by taking an average of the quotes given by several independent dealers. Typically, the quotes are taken on more than one date and, therefore, there are various *valuation methods* applicable such as highest or average highest.

As significant as specifying the valuation method is the specification of the valuation date. Usually, a cooling off period is allowed between the actual date of happening of a credit event and the valuation date. This is to allow for the knee-jerk reaction of the market values to be mitigated, and more rational pricing of the defaulted credit asset to take place.

Computation of losses is not required for a type of derivative called *binary swaps* or *fixed recovery swaps* where the protection seller is required to pay a particular amount to the protection buyer, irrespective of the actual losses or valuation.

Threshold Risk or Loss Materiality Provisions

Credit derivative contracts may sometimes provide for a threshold risk, up to which the losses will be borne by the protection buyer, and it is only when the losses exceed the threshold limit that a claim will lie against the protection seller. This is also called a *materiality loss provision*, under the understanding that only material losses will be transferred to the protection seller, even though the threshold limit may be quite high and not necessarily prevent immaterial losses from being claimed from the protection seller. In such cases, the more appropriate term is *first-loss risk*—where the first-loss risk up to the specified amount is borne by the protection buyer and it is only losses above the first-loss amount that are transferred to the protection seller.

Cash and Physical Settlement

Settlement arises when a credit event takes place. The terms of settlement could be either cash settlement or physical settlement. In the case of cash settlement, the losses computed as discussed above are paid by the protection seller to the protection buyer; there is no transfer of the reference asset by the protection buyer. With physical settlement, the protection buyer physically delivers (i.e., transfers an asset of the reference entity that satisfies the criteria for a deliverable obligation), and gets paid the par value of the delivered asset, limited, of course, to the notional value of the transaction. The concept of deliverable obligation in a credit derivative is critical as the derivative is not necessarily connected with a particular loan or bond. Being a transaction linked with generic default risk, the protection buyer may deliver any of the defaulted obligations of the reference entity. However, to prevent against something like equity or other contingent securities from being delivered, transaction documents typically specify the characteristics of the deliverable obligations.

The general belief in the credit derivatives market is that losses of the protection seller are less in the case of a physical settlement than in the case of cash. This belief is quite logical, since the quotes in the case of cash settlement are made by potential buyers of defaulted assets who also hope to make a profit in buying the defaulted asset. Physical settlement is more common where the counterparty is a bank or financial intermediary who can hold and take the defaulted asset through the bankruptcy process, or resolve the defaulted asset. Physicaly settlement is, however, quite problematic where there are plenty of outstanding transactions referenced to an entity. This situation is almost certain to arise in the case of entities included in popular indexes. When several protection buyers scout the market for buying defaulted assets, there might be a *short squeeze* in the market, and an artificial inflation in the price of the defaulted security. In appreciation of these difficulties, the market has of late started moving in the direction of cash settlements or fixed recovery trades.

TYPES OF CREDIT DERIVATIVES

In this secton, we provide a brief introduction to the various types of credit derivatives.

Credit Default Swap

A *credit default swap* can literally be defined as an option to swap a credit asset for cash should the credit asset trigger a credit event. It is an option bought by the protection buyer and written by the protection seller. The strike price of the option is the par value of the reference asset. Unlike a capital market option, the option under a credit default swap can be exercised only when a credit event takes place.

In a credit default swap if a credit event takes place, depending upon the settlement terms the protection buyer at his option may swap the reference asset or any other deliverable obligation of the reference obligor for either cash equal to the par value of the reference asset or receive compensation to the extent of the difference between the par value and market value of the reference asset.

Credit default swaps are the most important type of credit derivative in use in the market.

Total Return Swap

A credit default swap protects the protection buyer against losses when a credit event happens. However, a credit event is a rare event. The holder of a credit asset is not merely concerned with losses in the event of default, but mark-to-market losses because they are more frequent. A credit asset might continue to give mark-to-market losses for quite some time before it actually ripens into a default.

As the name implies, a *total rate of return swap* or *total return swap* is a swap of the total return out of a credit asset swapped against a contracted prefixed return. The idea in a total rate of return swap is to protect the protection buyer against mark-to-market losses as well. Hence, the parties swap the total return from the reference credit asset or pool of assets. The total return out of a credit asset is reflected by the actual interest realized from the reference asset plus the actual appreciation, minus depreciation in its price over time. The total returns from a credit asset may be affected by various factors, some of which may be quite extraneous to the asset in question, such as interest rate movements. Nevertheless, the protection seller in a total return swap guarantees a prefixed spread to the protection buyer, who in turn, agrees to pass on the actual collections and actual variations in prices on the credit asset to the protection seller.

So periodically, the protection buyer swaps the actual return on a notional value of the reference asset for a certain spread on a reference rate, say LIBOR + 60 bps.

Credit-Linked Notes

A *credit-linked note* (CLN) is a securitized form of credit derivative that converts a credit derivative into a funded form. Here, the protection buyer issues notes or bonds which implicitly carries a credit derivative. The buyer of the CLN sells protection and prefunds the protection sold by way of subscribing to the CLN. Should there be a credit event payment due from the protection seller, the amounts due on the notes or bonds, on account of credit events, will be appropriated against the same and the net, if any, will be paid to the CLN holder. A CLN carries a coupon which represents the interest on the funding and the credit risk premium on the protection sold; that is to say, the protection inherently sold via the CLN is compensated in the form of the coupon on the CLN. Obviously, the maximum amount of protection that the CLN holder provides is the amount of principal invested in the CLN.

Valuing Mortgage-Backed and Asset-Backed Securities

In this appendix, we will explain the methodology for valuing *asset-backed securities* (ABS) and *mortgage-backed securities* (MBS) and measures of relative value. We begin by reviewing cash flow yield analysis and the limitations of the spread measure that is a result of that analysis—the nominal spread. We then look at a better spread measure called the zero-volatility spread, but point out its limitation as a measure of relative value for MBS products because of the borrower's prepayment option and for ABS products where the prepayment option has value. Finally, we look at the methodology for valuing MBS and for ABS products where the prepayment option has value—the Monte Carlo simulation model. A byproduct of this model is a spread measure called the *option-adjusted spread* (OAS). This measure is superior to the nominal spread and the zero-volatility spread for ABS products where the prepayment option has a value because it takes into account how cash flows may change when interest rates change. That is, it recognizes the borrower's prepayment option and how that affects prepayments when interest rates may change in the future. While the OAS is superior to the two other spread measures, it is based on assumptions that must be understood by an investor and the sensitivity of the security's value and OAS to changes in those assumptions must be investigated.

CASH FLOW YIELD ANALYSIS

The yield on any financial instrument is the interest rate that makes the present value of the expected cash flow equal to its market price plus accrued interest. For ABS and MBS, the yield calculated is called a *cash flow yield*. The problem in calculating the cash flow yield of MBS and ABS is that because of prepayments the cash flow is unknown. A prepayment is the amount of the payment made by the obligor in the loan pool that is in excess of the scheduled principal payment. Prepayments can be voluntary such as for refinancing the loan or involuntary such as for a default by the obligor. Consequently, to determine a cash flow yield some assumption about the prepayment rate and recovery rate in the case of defaults must be made.

The cash flow for MBS and ABS is typically monthly. The convention is to compare the yield on MBS and ABS to that of a Treasury coupon security by calculating the security's bond-equivalent yield. bond-equivalent yield for a coupon security is found by doubling the semiannual yield. However, it is incorrect to do this for MBS and ABS because the investor has the opportunity to generate greater interest by reinvesting the more frequent cash flows. The market practice is to calculate a yield so as to make it comparable to the yield to maturity on a bond-equivalent yield basis. The formula for annualizing the monthly cash flow yield for MBS and ABS is as follows:

$$\text{Bond-equivalent yield} = 2[(1 + i_M)^6 - 1]$$

where i_M is the monthly interest rate that will equate the present value of the projected monthly cash flow to the market price (plus accrued interest) of the security.

All yield measures suffer from problems that limit their use in assessing a security's potential return. The yield to maturity for a Treasury, agency, or corporate bond has two major shortcomings as a measure of a bond's potential return. To realize the stated yield to maturity, the investor must: (1) reinvest the coupon payments at a rate equal to the yield to maturity and (2) hold the bond to the maturity date. The reinvestment of the coupon payments is critical and for long-term bonds can comprise as much as 80% of the bond's return. The risk of having to reinvest the interest payments at less than the computed yield is called *reinvestment risk*. The risk associated with a decline in the value of a security due to a rise in interest rates is called *interest rate risk* and in practice is quantified by computing the security's duration and convexity.

These shortcomings are equally applicable to the cash flow yield measure for ABS and MBS: (1) the projected cash flows are assumed to be reinvested at the computed cash flow yield and (2) the security is assumed to be held until the final payout based on some prepayment assumption. The importance of reinvestment risk, the risk that the cash flow will be reinvested at a rate less than the calculated cash flow yield, is particularly important for amortizing MBS and ABS products, because payments are monthly and both interest and principal must be reinvested. Moreover, an additional assumption is that the projected cash flow is actually realized. If the prepayment experience and the recovery rate realized differ from that assumed, the cash flow yield will not be realized.

Given the computed cash flow yield and the average life for a security based on some prepayment assumption and default/recovery assumption, the next step is to compare the yield to the yield for a comparable Treasury security. *Comparable* is typically defined as a Treasury security with the same maturity as the (weighted) average life or the duration of the security. The difference between the cash flow yield and the yield on a comparable security is called the *nominal spread*.

Unfortunately, it is the nominal spread that investors will too often use as a measure of relative value for ABS and MBS. However, this spread masks the fact that a portion of the nominal spread may be compensation for accepting prepayment risk. Instead of nominal spread, investors need a measure that indicates the compensation after adjusting for prepayment risk for all MBS and for ABS where the prepayment option has value. This measure is called the option-adjusted spread. Before discussing this measure, we describe another spread measure commonly quoted for MBS and ABS called the zero-volatility spread. This measure takes into account another problem with the nominal spread. Specifically, the nominal spread is computed assuming that all the cash flows for a security should be discounted at only one interest rate. That is, it fails to recognize the term structure of interest rates.

ZERO-VOLATILITY SPREAD

The proper procedure to compare ABS and MBS to a Treasury is to compare it to a portfolio of Treasury securities that have the same cash flow. The value of the security is then equal to the present value of all of the cash flows. The security's value, assuming the cash flows are default-free, will equal the present value of the replicating portfolio of Treasury securities. In turn, these cash flows are valued at the Treasury spot rates.

The *zero-volatility spread* is a measure of the spread that the investor would realize over the entire Treasury spot rate curve if the security being analyzed is held to maturity. It is not a spread off one point on the Treasury yield curve, as is the nominal spread. The zero-volatility spread (also called the *Z-spread* and the *static spread*) is the spread that makes the present value of the cash flows from the security when discounted at the spot rate plus the spread equal to the market price of the security plus accrued interest. A trial-and-error procedure (or search algorithm) is required to determine the zero-volatility spread.

In general, the shorter the average life of the security, the less the zero-volatility spread will deviate from the nominal spread. The magnitude of the difference between the nominal spread and the zero-volatility spread also depends on the shape of the yield curve. steeper the yield curve, the greater the difference.

If borrowers in the underlying loan pool have the right to prepay but do not typically take advantage of a decline in interest rates below the loan's rate to refinance, then the zero-volatility spread is the appropriate measure of relative value and it should be using in valuing cash flows to determine the value of ABS. This is the case, for example, for automobile loan ABS. While borrowers have the right to refinance when rates decline below the loan rate, they typically do not. In contrast, for standard residential mortgage loans, home equity loan ABS, and manufactured housing the borrowers in the underlying pool do refinance when interest rates decline below the loan rate. next methodology and spread measure are used for products with this characteristic. Basically, they are used for all residential MBS and mortgage-related ABS.

VALUATION USING MONTE CARLO SIMULATION AND OAS ANALYSIS

In fixed income valuation modeling, there are two methodologies commonly used to value securities with embedded options—the Monte Carlo simulation model and the lattice model. The Monte

Carlo simulation model involves simulating a large number of potential interest rate paths in order to assess the value of a security on those different paths.[1] This model is the most flexible of the two valuation methodologies for valuing interest rate sensitive instruments where the history of interest rates is important. MBS and mortgage-related ABS are commonly valued using this model. As explained below, a byproduct of this valuation model is the OAS.[2]

A lattice model is used to value callable agency debentures and corporate bonds.[3] This valuation model accommodates securities in which the decision to exercise a call option is not dependent on how interest rates evolved over time. That is, the decision of an issuer to call a bond will depend on the prevailing interest rate at which the issue can be refunded relative to the issue's coupon rate and the costs associated with refunding, and not the path interest rates took to get to that rate. MBS and mortgage related ABS which allow prepayments have periodic cash flows that are interest rate path-dependent. This means that the cash flow received in one period is determined not only by the current interest rate level, but also by the path that interest rates took to get to the current level. Prepayments for MBS and mortgage-related are interest rate path-dependent because this month's prepayment rate depends on whether there have been prior opportunities to refinance since the underlying loans were originated. Moreover, the cash flows to be received in the current month by investors in a bond class of an MBS and mortgage-related ABS transaction depends on the outstanding balances of the other bond classes in the transaction. For example, in the case of a *planned amortization class* (PAC) bond in a collateralized mortgage obligation structure, all prepayments from the time the security was issued up to the valuation date affect the amount of the support bond's outstanding and therefore the cash flow at the valuation date for the PAC bond. Thus, we need the history of prepayments to calculate the balances of bond classes in a structure.

---

[1] For a more detailed discussion of the use of Monte Carlo simulation for valuing MBS and ABS with illustrations, see Fabozzi, Ramamurthy, and Gauthier (2000) and Levin and Davidson (2008).

[2] An alternative model for valuing agency passthrough securities that does not require a prepayment model is provided in Kalotay, Yang, and Fabozzi (2004).

[3] The lattice model for the valuation of corporate bonds is found in Kalotay, Williams, and Fabozzi (1993).

Conceptually, valuation using the Monte Carlo simulation model is simple. In practice, however, it is very complex. The simulation involves generating a set of cash flows based on simulated future refinancing rates, which in turn imply simulated prepayment and default/recovery rates. The objective is to figure out how the value of the collateral gets transmitted to the bond classes in the structure. More specifically, modeling is used to identify where the value in a transaction has been allocated and where the risk (prepayment risk and credit risk) has been distributed in order to identify the bond classes with low risk and high value.

Simulating Interest Rate Paths and Cash Flows

Monte Carlo simulation is a management science/operations research technique that is commonly employed in finance. The purpose of Monte Carlo simulation is to generate a probability distribution for the outcome of some random variable of interest. In its application to valuing securities, it is used to generate interest rate paths so that potential cash flows on those paths can be determined and then each path is valued. (In the parlance of simulation, an interest rate path is referred to as a trial.) The value for the security on each of those interest rate paths is then one value in determining the estimated probability distribution for the security's value.

The procedure for generating the interest rate paths begins with a benchmark term structure of interest rates and associated with this benchmark are market prices for benchmark securities. Given the benchmark term structure of interest rates, the interest rate paths are adjusted (i.e., calibrated) so that the average price produced by the model for each benchmark security will equal the market price for the benchmark security.

Most models use the on-the-run Treasury issues in this calibration process. Other model developers use off-the-run Treasury issues as well. The argument for using off-the-run Treasury issues is that the price/yield of on-the-run Treasury issues will not reflect their true economic value because the market price reflects their value for financing purposes (i.e., an issue may be on special in the repo market). Some models use the LIBOR curve instead of the Treasury curve. The reason is that some investors are interested in spreads that they can earn relative to their funding costs and LIBOR for many investors is a better proxy for that cost than Treasury rates.

To generate the interest rate paths, an assumption about the evolution of future interest rates is required. There are various types of interest rate models. Most Monte Carlo simulation models use some form of one-factor interest rate model. The one factor used is the short-term interest rate. When using a particular one-factor interest rate model, several further assumptions must be made. The first, and the most important, is the assumption about the volatility of the short-term interest rate. The volatility assumption determines the dispersion of future interest rates in the simulation. Many model developers do not use one volatility number for the yield volatility of all maturities for the benchmark curve. Instead, they use either a short/long yield volatility or a term structure of yield volatility. A short/long yield volatility means that volatility is specified for maturities up to a certain number of years (short yield volatility) and a different yield volatility for greater maturities (long yield volatility). The short yield volatility is assumed to be greater than the long yield volatility. A term structure of yield volatilities means that a yield volatility is assumed for each maturity. (In practice, interest rate volatility is extracted from interest rate cap market prices.) From these prices, a term structure of yield volatility is obtained. Differences in the assumption about volatility of short-term interest rates can have a material impact on the resulting value derived for the security.

Another assumption relates to the speed of mean-reversion of the short-term interest rate. Mean-revision in an interest rate model has to do with not allowing interest rates to fall below a lower barrier and not exceed an upper barrier before rates revert back to some average interest rate specified by the model developer or user.

The random paths of interest rates should be generated from an arbitrage-free model of the future term structure of interest rates. By arbitrage free it is meant that the model replicates today's term structure of interest rates, an input of the model, and that for all future dates there is no possible arbitrage within the model.

The simulation works by generating many scenarios of future interest rate paths. In each month of a given scenario (i.e., path), a monthly interest rate and a refinancing rate are generated. The monthly interest rates are used to discount the projected cash flows in the scenario. The refinancing rate is needed to determine the cash flows because it represents the opportunity cost the borrower is facing at that time.

If the refinancing rates are high relative to the borrower's loan rate, the borrower will have no incentive to refinance. For MBS and mortgage-related ABS, there is a disincentive to prepay (i.e., the homeowner may avoid moving in order to avoid refinancing). If the refinancing rate is low relative to the borrower's loan rate, the borrower has an incentive to refinance.

Prepayments (voluntary and involuntary) and recoveries are projected by feeding the refinancing rate and loan characteristics into a prepayment model and default model. (In the case of agency MBS (Ginnie Mae, Fannie Mae, and Freddie Mac) no assumption about defaults and defaults are required.) Given the projected prepayments, the cash flows along an interest rate path can be determined. To be able to do this, the entire deal must be reverse engineered. That is, the deal's waterfall (i.e., the rules for distribution of interest, principal repayment, and loss allocation) must be specified so that the cash flow for the bond class being valued can be determined. Model developers do not reverse engineer the deals. Rather, there are vendors who provide the waterfall for deals that are used in conjunction with the Monte Carlo simulation model.

To make this more concrete, consider a newly issued loan pool with a maturity of M months that is the collateral for an MBS or mortgage-related ABS. Table B.1 shows N simulated interest rate path scenarios. Each scenario consists of a path of M simulated one-month future interest rates.[4] So, the first assumption made to generate the short-term interest rate paths in Table B.1 is the volatility of short-term interest rates.

Table B.2 shows the paths of simulated refinancing rates corresponding to the scenarios shown in B.1. In going from B.1 to B.2, an assumption must be made about the relationship between the benchmark short-term interest rate and the refinancing rate. The assumption is that there is a constant spread relationship between the refinancing rate and the interest rate for a maturity that is the best proxy for the borrowing rate. Typically, it is the 10-year rate that is used as a proxy.

---

[4] The determination of the number of paths generated is based on a variance-reduction method.

TABLE B.1 Simulated Paths of One-Month Future Interest Rates

Month	Interest Rate Path Number						
	1	**2**	**3**	**...**	**n**	**...**	**N**
1	$f_1(1)$	$f_1(2)$	$f_1(3)$	...	$f_1(n)$	...	$f_1(N)$
2	$f_2(1)$	$f_2(2)$	$f_2(3)$	...	$f_2(n)$	...	$f_2(N)$
3	$f_3(1)$	$f_3(2)$	$f_3(3)$	...	$f_3(n)$	...	$f_3(N)$
...	...	...	...	...	...	...	...
t	$f_t(1)$	$f_t(2)$	$f_t(3)$	...	$f_t(n)$	...	$f_t(N)$
...	...	...	...	...	...	...	...
M–2	$f_{M-2}(1)$	$f_{M-2}(2)$	$f_{M-2}(3)$	...	$f_{M-2}(n)$	...	$f_{M-2}(N)$
M–1	$f_{M-1}(1)$	$f_{M-1}(2)$	$f_{M-1}(3)$	...	$f_{M-1}(n)$	...	$f_{M-1}(N)$
M	$f_M(1)$	$f_M(2)$	$f_M(3)$	...	$f_M(n)$	...	$f_M(N)$

Notation: $f_t(n)$ = 1-month future interest rate for month t on path n; N = total number of interest rate paths; M = number of months for the loan pool.

TABLE B.2 Simulated Paths of Refinancing Rates

Month	Interest Rate Path Number						
	1	**2**	**3**	**...**	**n**	**...**	**N**
1	$r_1(1)$	$r_1(2)$	$r_1(3)$	...	$r_1(n)$	...	$r_1(N)$
2	$r_2(1)$	$r_2(2)$	$r_2(3)$	...	$r_2(n)$	...	$r_2(N)$
3	$r_3(1)$	$r_3(2)$	$r_3(3)$	...	$r_3(n)$	...	$r_3(N)$
...	...	...	...	...	...	...	...
t	$r_t(1)$	$r_t(2)$	$r_t(3)$	...	$r_t(n)$	...	$r_t(N)$
...	...	...	...	...	...	...	...
M–2	$C_{M-2}(1)$	$C_{M-2}(2)$	$C_{M-2}(3)$	...	$C_{M-2}(n)$	...	$C_{M-2}(N)$
M–1	$C_{M-1}(1)$	$C_{M-1}(2)$	$C_{M-1}(3)$	...	$C_{M-1}(n)$	...	$C_{M-1}(N)$
M	$C_M(1)$	$C_M(2)$	$C_M(3)$	...	$C_M(n)$	...	$C_M(N)$

Notation: $r_t(n)$ = refinancing rate for month t on path n; N = total number of interest rate paths; M = number of months for the loan pool.

TABLE B.3   Simulated Cash Flows for the Loan Pool

| Month | Interest Rate Path Number | | | | | | |
	1	2	3	...	n	...	N
1	$C_1(1)$	$C_1(2)$	$C_1(3)$	...	$C_1(n)$	...	$C_1(N)$
2	$C_2(1)$	$C_2(2)$	$C_2(3)$	...	$C_2(n)$	...	$C_2(N)$
3	$C_3(1)$	$C_3(2)$	$C_3(3)$	...	$C_3(n)$	...	$C_3(N)$
...	...	...	...	...	...	...	...
t	$C_t(1)$	$C_t(2)$	$C_t(3)$	...	$C_t(n)$	...	$C_t(N)$
...	...	...	...	...	...	...	...
M–2	$C_{M-2}(1)$	$C_{M-2}(2)$	$C_{M-2}(3)$	...	$C_{M-2}(n)$	...	$C_{M-2}(N)$
M–1	$C_{M-1}(1)$	$C_{M-1}(2)$	$C_{M-1}(3)$	...	$C_{M-1}(n)$	...	$C_{M-1}(N)$
M	$C_M(1)$	$C_M(2)$	$C_M(3)$	...	$C_M(n)$	...	$C_M(N)$

Notation: $C_t(n)$ = loan pool's cash flow for month t on path n; N = total number of interest rate paths; M = number of months for the loan pool.

Given the refinancing rates, the collateral's cash flows on each interest rate path can be generated. This requires a prepayment and default/recovery model. So our next assumption is that the prepayment and default/recovery models used to generate the loan pool's cash flows are correct. The resulting cash flows are depicted in Table B.3.

Given the loan pool's cash flow for each month on each interest rate path, the next step is to use the waterfall for the structure to determine how the cash flow is distributed to the bond class being valued. Let us use BCC to denote the cash flow for that bond class. Table B.4 shows the simulated cash flows on each of the interest rate paths for the bond class being valued.

Calculating the Present Value of a Bond Class for a Scenario Interest Rate Path

Given the cash flows for the bond class on an interest rate path, the path's present value can be calculated. The discount rate for determining the present value is the simulated spot rate for each month on the interest rate path plus an appropriate spread. The spot rate on a path can be determined from the simulated future monthly rates. The relationship that holds between the simulated spot rate for month t on path n and the simulated future one-month rates is

TABLE B.4 Simulated Cash Flows for the Bond Class Being Valued

Month	Interest Rate Path Number						
	1	2	3	...	n	...	N
1	$BCC_1(1)$	$BCC_1(2)$	$BCC_1(3)$	... $BCC_1(n)$		... $BCC_1(N)$	
2	$BCC_2(1)$	$BCC_2(2)$	$BCC_2(3)$	... $BCC_2(n)$		... $BCC_2(N)$	
3	$BCC_3(1)$	$BCC_3(2)$	$BCC_3(3)$	... $BCC_3(n)$		... $BCC_3(N)$	
...	...	...	...	... ...		... ...	
t	$BCC_t(1)$	$BCC_t(2)$	$BCC_t(3)$	... $BCC_t(n)$		... $BCC_t(N)$	
...	...	...	...	... ...		... ...	
M–2	$BCC_{M-2}(1)$	$BCC_{M-2}(2)$	$BCC_{M-2}(3)$	... $BCC_{M-2}(n)$		... $BCC_{M-2}(N)$	
M–1	$BCC_{M-1}(1)$	$BCC_{M-1}(2)$	$BCC_{M-1}(3)$	... $BCC_{M-1}(n)$		... $BCC_{M-1}(N)$	
M	$BCC_M(1)$	$BCC_M(2)$	$BCC_M(3)$	... $BCC_M(n)$		... $BCC_M(N)$	

Notation: $BCCt(n)$ = bond class's cash flow for month t on path n; N = total number of interest rate paths; M = number of months for the loan pool.

$$z_t(n) = \{[1 + f_1(n)][1 + f_2(n)]. . .[1 + f_t(n)]\}^{1/t} - 1$$

where

$z_t(n)$ = simulated spot rate for month t on path n.
$f_j(n)$ = simulated future 1-month rate for month j on path n.

Consequently, the interest rate path for the simulated future one-month rates can be converted to the interest rate path for the simulated monthly spot rates as shown in Table B.5. Therefore, the present value of the cash flows for month t on interest rate path n discounted at the simulated spot rate for month t plus some spread is

$$PV[BCC_t(n)] = \frac{BCC_t(n)}{[1 + z_t(n) + K]^t}$$

where

$PV[BCC_t(n)]$ = present value of the cash flow for the bond class for month t on path n.
$BCC_t(n)$ = cash flow for the bond class for month t on path n.

TABLE B.5 Simulated Paths of Monthly Spot Rates

Month	Interest Rate Path Number					
	1	2	3	...	n	...
1	$z_1(1)$	$z_1(2)$	$z_1(3)$	...	$z_1(n)$	... $z_1(N)$
2	$z_2(1)$	$z_2(2)$	$z_2(3)$	...	$z_2(n)$	... $z_2(N)$
3	$z_3(1)$	$z_3(2)$	$z_3(3)$	...	$z_3(n)$	... $z_3(N)$
...	...	...	...	...	...	... ...
t	$z_t(1)$	$z_t(2)$	$z_t(3)$	...	$z_t(n)$	... $z_t(N)$
...	...	...	...	...	...	... ...
M–2	$z_{M-2}(1)$	$z_{M-2}(2)$	$z_{M-2}(3)$	...	$z_{M-2}(n)$	... $z_{M-2}(N)$
M–1	$z_{M-1}(1)$	$z_{M-1}(2)$	$z_{M-1}(3)$	...	$z_{M-1}(n)$	... $z_{M-1}(N)$
M	$z_M(1)$	$z_M(2)$	$z_M(3)$	...	$z_M(n)$	... $z_M(N)$

Notation: $z_t(n)$ = spot rate for month t on path n; N = total number of interest rate paths; M = number of months for the loan pool.

$z_t(n)$ = spot rate for month t on path n.

K = spread.

The present value for path n is the sum of the present value of the cash flows for each month on path n. That is,

$$PV[\text{Path}(n)] = PV[BCC_1(n)] + PV[BCC_2(n)] + \ldots + PV[BCC_M(n)]$$

where $PV[\text{Path}(n)]$ is the present value of interest rate path n.

Determining the Theoretical Value

The present value of a given interest rate path is treated as the theoretical value of a bond class if that path is realized. The theoretical value of the bond class using the Monte Carlo simulation model is determined by calculating the average of the theoretical values of all the interest rate paths. That is, the theoretical value is equal to

$$\text{Theoretical value} = \frac{PV[\text{Path}(1) + \ldots + PV[\text{Path}(N)]}{N} \qquad (B.1)$$

where N is the number of interest rate paths.

Notice that the results of the Monte Carlo simulation model produce one value, the average value, and that value is taken as the theoretical value. However, as noted earlier, the purpose of a Monte Carlo simulation model is to estimate the probability distribution for the variable of interest. While a probability distribution can easily be obtained from the values for each path and summary information in addition to the mean such as dispersion and skewness measures can be computed, it is rare if that information is provided. Basically, the reason is that investors rarely seek that information because too often they do not understand the Monte Carlo simulation process.

Moreover, it should be apparent how the Monte Carlo simulation model is driven by assumptions. Hence, a user of a model such as the one described here is subject to *modeling risk*. To mitigate modeling risk, an investor can test the sensitivity of the value produced by the model to alternative assumptions. For example, for the volatility assumption, the model can be rerun assuming a proportionality lower and higher volatility than initially assumed. The sensitivity to prepayments can be analyzed in the same way. From the sensitivity analysis, an investor can determine which assumptions appear to be more important for the security being considered for purchase.

Option-Adjusted Spread

Thus far we have seen how the theoretical value of a security can be determined using the Monte Carlo simulation model. Recall that in the model, a spread (K) is added to the monthly spot rates on all the interest rate paths in Table B.5 in order to determine the discount rate used for calculating the present value of the cash flows. The spread should reflect the risk associated with the security as required by the market. However, the reverse can be done. Given (1) the cash flows in Table B.4 for the bond class being valued, (2) the spot rates in Table B.5, and (3) the market price of the security being valued, one can determine the spread that will make the average value for the interest rate paths equal to the market price (plus accrued interest). That spread is what is referred to as the *option-adjusted spread* (OAS).

$$\text{Market price} + \text{Accrued interest}$$
$$= \frac{PV[Path(1)] + \ldots + PV[Path(N)]}{N} \tag{B.2}$$

where N is the number of interest rate paths.

Basically, the OAS is used to reconcile the model's value (i.e, the value determined by the Monte Carlo simulation model given by equation (B.1)) with the market price. On the left-hand side of equation (B.2) is the market's valuation of the security as represented by the market price. On the right-hand side of equation (B.2) is the model's evaluation of the security (i.e., the theoretical value), which is the average present value over all the interest rate paths. Basically, the OAS was developed as a measure of the spread that can be used to convert dollar differences between model value and market price. But what is it a "spread" over? In describing the model above, we can see that the OAS is measuring the average spread over the benchmark spot rate. It is an average spread since the OAS is found by averaging over the interest rate paths for the possible future benchmark spot rate curves.

This spread measure is superior to the nominal spread which gives no recognition to the prepayment risk. The OAS is "option adjusted" because the cash flows on the interest rate paths are adjusted for the option of the borrowers to prepay.

Option Cost

The implied cost of the option embedded in a security can be obtained by calculating the difference between the OAS and the zero-volatility spread. That is,

$$\text{Option cost} = \text{Zero-volatility spread} - \text{OAS}$$

The option cost measures the prepayment (or option) risk embedded in MBS and ABS. Note that the cost of the option is a byproduct of the OAS analysis, not valued explicitly with some option pricing model.

When the option cost is zero because the borrower tends not to exercise the prepayment option when interest rates decline below the loan rate or when there is no prepayment option, then substituting zero for the OAS in the previous equation and solving for the zero-volatility spread, we get

$$\text{Zero-volatility spread} = \text{OAS}$$

Consequently, when the value of the option is zero (i.e., the option cost is zero) for a particular ABS, simply computing the zero-volatility spread for relative value purposes or for valuing that ABS is sufficient. Even if there is a small value for the option, the zero-volatility spread should be adequate rather than calculating an OAS using the Monte Carlo simulation model.

Simulated Average Life

The average life of a security when using the Monte Carlo simulation model is the weighted average time to receipt of principal payments (scheduled payments and projected prepayments). The average life reported in a Monte Carlo model is the average of the average lives along the interest rate paths. That is, for each interest rate path, there is an average life. The average of these average lives is the average life reported by the model.

Additional information is conveyed by the distribution of the average life. The greater the range and standard deviation of the average life, the more uncertainty there is about the security's average life.

MEASURING INTEREST RISK

There are two measures of interest rate risk that are commonly used: duration and convexity. *Duration* is a first approximation as to how the value of an individual security or the value of a portfolio will change when interest rates change. *Convexity* measures the change in the value of a security or portfolio that is not explained by duration. How these measures are computed when using the Monte Carlo simulation model is described in this section.

Duration

The most obvious way to measure a bond's price sensitivity as a percentage of its current price to changes in interest rates is to change rates by a small number of basis points and calculate how its price will change. To do this, we introduce the following notation. Let

V_0 = initial value or price of the security.

Δy = change in the yield of the security (in decimal).

V_- = the estimated value of the security if the yield is decreased by Δy.

V_+ = the estimated value of the security if the yield is increased by Δy.

There are two key points to keep in mind in the foregoing discussion. First, the change in yield referred to above is the same change in yield for all maturities. This assumption is commonly referred to as a "parallel yield curve shift assumption." Thus, the foregoing discussion about the price sensitivity of a security to interest rate changes is limited to parallel shifts in the yield curve. Second, the notation refers to the estimated value of the security. This value is obtained from a valuation model. Consequently, the resulting measure of the price sensitivity of a security to interest rate changes is only as good as the valuation model employed to obtain the estimated value of the security.

Now let us focus on the measure of interest. We are interested in the percentage change in the price of a security when interest rates change. This measure is referred to as duration. It can be demonstrated that duration can be estimated using the following formula:

$$\text{Duration} = \frac{V_- - V_+}{2V_0(\Delta y)} \tag{B.3}$$

The duration of a security can be interpreted as the approximate percentage change in price for a 100 basis point parallel shift in the yield curve. Thus a bond with a duration of five will change by approximately 5% for a 100 basis point parallel shift in the yield curve. For a 50 basis point parallel shift in the yield curve, the bond's price will change by approximately 2.5%; for a 25 basis point parallel shift in the yield curve, 1.25%, and so on.

What this means is that in calculating the values of V_- and V_+ in the duration formula, the same cash flows used to calculate V_0 are used. Therefore, the change in the bond's price when the yield curve is shifted by a small number of basis points is due solely to discounting at the new yields. This assumption makes sense for option-free bonds such as Treasury securities and nonmortgage ABS such as credit card ABS and auto loan-backed ABS. However, the same cannot be said for MBS and mortgage-related ABS because for these products the cash flows are sensitive to changes in interest rates. Rather, for these products a change in yield will alter the expected cash flows because it will change expected prepayments.

The Monte Carlo simulation model takes into account how parallel shifts in the yield curve will affect the cash flows. Thus, when V_- and V_+ are the values produced from the valuation model, the resulting duration takes into account both the discounting at different interest rates and how the cash flows can change. When duration is calculated in this manner, it is referred to as *effective duration* or *option-adjusted duration*.

To calculate effective duration, the value of the security must be estimated when interest rates are shocked (i.e., changed) up and down a given number of basis points. In terms of the Monte Carlo simulation model, the yield curve used is shocked up and down and the new curve is used to generate the values to be used in equation (B.3) to obtain the effective duration.

There are two important aspects of this process of generating the values when the rates are shocked that are critical to understand. First, the assumption is that the relationships assumed do not change when rates are shocked up and down. Specifically, (1) the interest rate volatility is assumed to be unchanged to derive the new interest rate paths for a given shock (i.e., the new Table B.1), as well as the other assumptions made to generate the new Table B.2 from the newly constructed Table B.1, and (2) the OAS is assumed to be constant. The constancy of the OAS comes into play because when discounting the new cash flows (i.e., the cash flows in the new Table B.4), the current OAS that was computed is assumed to be the same and is added to the new rates in the new Table B.1.

Convexity

The duration measure indicates that regardless of whether interest rates increase or decrease, the approximate percentage price change is the same. However, this does not agree with the price volatility property of a bond. Specifically, while for small changes in yield the percentage price change will be the same for an increase or decrease in yield, for large changes in yield this is not true. This suggests that duration is only a good approximation of the percentage price change for a small change in yield.

The reason for this result is that duration is in fact a first approximation for a small change in yield. The approximation can be improved by using a second approximation. This approximation is referred to as convexity. (The use of this term in the industry is unfortunate since the term convexity is also used to describe the shape or curvature of the price/yield relationship.) The convexity measure of a security can be used to approximate the change in price that is not explained by duration.

The convexity measure of a bond can be approximated using the following formula:

$$\text{Convexity measure} = \frac{V_+ + V_- - 2V_0}{2V_0(\Delta y)^2} \qquad \text{(B.4)}$$

where the notation is the same as used earlier for duration. When the values for the inputs in the convexity measure as given in equation (B.4) are obtained from a Monte Carlo simulation model, the resulting convexity is referred to as *effective convexity*. Note that dealers often quote convexity by dividing the convexity measure by 100. When the convexity measure is positive, we have the situation where the gain is greater than the loss for a given large change in rates. That is, the security exhibits positive convexity. Most nonmortgage ABS have *positive convexity*. However, if the convexity measure is negative, we have the situation where the loss will be greater than the gain. A security with this characteristic is said to have *negative convexity* and it occurs with MBS and mortgage-related ABS.

References

Bank for International Settlements (1992). "Asset Transfers and Securitization." Working paper, Basle, September.

Bernanke, Ben S., and Mark Gertler (1995). "Inside the Black Box: The Credit Channel of Monetary Policy Transmission." *Journal of Economic Perspectives* 9, no. 4 (Autumn): 27–48.

Blum, Len, and Chris DiAngelo (1998). "Structuring Efficient Asset-Backed Securities." Chapter 2 in Frank J. Fabozzi (ed.), *Issuer Perspectives on Securitization*. Hoboken, NJ: John Wiley & Sons.

Cantor, Richard, and Stanislas Rouyer (2000). "Another Perspective on Credit Risk Transfer and Assets Securitization." *Journal of Risk Finance* 1, no. 2 (Winter): 37–47.

Davidson, Andrew (2008). "Reinventing Securitization." *The Pipeline* published by Andrew Davidson & Co., Inc. (February).

Estrella, Arturo (2002). "Securitization and the Efficacy of Monetary Policy." *Federal Reserve Bank of New York Economic Policy Review* 8, no. 1 (May): 241–255.

Fabozzi, Frank J. (2006). *Fixed Income Mathematics: Analytical and Statistical Techniques-Fourth Edition*. New York: McGraw-Hill.

Fabozzi, Frank J., Anand K. Bhattacharya, and William S. Berliner (2007). *Mortgage-Backed Securities: Products, Structuring, and Analytical Techniques*. Hoboken, NJ: John Wiley & Sons.

Fabozzi, Frank J., Harold Davis, and Moorad Choudhry (2006). *Introduction to Structured Finance*. Hoboken, NJ: John Wiley & Sons.

Fabozzi, Frank J., and Franco Modigliani (1992). *Mortgage and Mortgage-Backed Securities Market*. Boston: Harvard Business School Press.

Fabozzi, Frank J., Raymond Morel, and Brian D. Grow (2005). "Use of Interest Rate Derivatives in Securitization Transactions." *Journal of Structured Finance* (Summer): 22-27.

Fabozzi, Frank J., Shrikant Ramamurthy, and Laurent Gauthier (2000). "Analysis of MBS." Chapter 29 in Frank J. Fabozzi (ed.), *Investing in Asset-Backed Securities*. Hoboken, NJ: John Wiley & Sons.

Fender, Ingo and John Kiff (2005). "CDO Rating Methodology: Some Thoughts on Model Risk and Its Implications." *Journal of Credit Risk* 1, no. 3 (Summer): 53–60.

Fender, Ingo, and Janet Mitchell (2005). "Structured Finance: Complexity, Risk and the Use of Ratings." *BIS Quarterly Review* (June): 67–79.

Fitch Ratings (2004). "Criteria for Whole Business Securitization." January 28.

Frame, W. Scott, and L. J. White (2004). "Fussing and Fuming over Fannie and Freddie: How Much Smoke, How Much Fire? *Federal Reserve Bank of Atlanta Working Paper Series,* Working paper 2004-26.

Goodman, Laurie S., Shumin Li, Douglas J. Lucas, Thomas A. Zimmerman, and Frank J. Fabozzi (2008). *Subprime Mortgage Credit Derivatives*. Hoboken, NJ: John Wiley & Sons.

Greenbaum, Stuart I., and Anjan V. Thakor (1987). "Bank Funding Modes: Securitization versus Deposits." *Journal of Banking and Finance* 11, no. 3 (September): 379–401.

Harris, Gus (2001). *"Responses to Frequently Asked CDO Questions (Second of Series)." Structured Finance Special Report, Moody's Investor Service,* July 20.

Hendershott, Patric H., and James D. Shilling (1989). "The Impact of Agencies on Conventional Fixed-Rate Mortgage Yields." *Journal of Real Estate Finance and Economics* 2, no. 2 (June): 101–115.

Jameson, Mel, S. Dewan, and C. F. Sirmans (1992). 'Measuring Welfare Effects of "Unbundling" Financial Innovations: The Case of Collateralized Mortgage Obligations." *Journal of Urban Economics* 31, no. 1: 1–13.

Jorion, Philippe (1995). *Big Bets Gone Bad*. San Diego, CA: Academic Press.

Kalotay, Andrew J., Williams, George O., and Fabozzi, Frank J. (1993). "A Model for the Valuation of Bonds and Embedded Options." *Financial Analysts Journal* 49, no. 3 (May–June): 5–46.

Kalotay, Andrew J., Yang, Deane, and Fabozzi, Frank J. (2004). "An Option-Theoretic Prepayment Model for Mortgages and Mortgage-Backed Securities." *International Journal of Theoretical and Applied Finance* 7, no. 8: 949–978.

Kendall, Leon T., and Michael J. Fishman (eds.) (1996). *A Primer on Securitization*. Cambridge, MA: MIT Press.

Kotecha, Mahesh K. (1998). "The Role Financial Guarantees in Asset-Backed Securities." Chapter 6 in Frank J. Fabozzi (ed.), *Issuer Perspectives on Securitization*. Hoboken, NJ: John Wiley & Sons.

Kothari, Vinod (1996). *Lease Financing and Hire-Purchase*, 4th ed. New Delhi: Wadhwa & Company.

——— (2006). *Securitization: The Financial Instrument of the Future*, 3rd ed. Singapore: John Wiley & Sons.

——— (2008). *Credit Derivatives and Structured Credit Trading*. Singapore: John Wiley & Sons.

Kuttner, Kenneth (2000). "Securitization and Monetary Policy." Unpublished paper, Federal Reserve Bank of New York.

Loutskina, Elena, and Philip E. Strahan (2006). "Securitization and the Declining Impact of Bank Finance on Loan Supply: Evidence from Mortgage Acceptance Rates." NBER Working paper No. 11983.

Levin, Alexander, and Andrew Davidson (2008). "The Concept of Credit OAS in valuation of MBS," *Journal of Portfolio Management* 34, no. 3 (Spring): 41–44.

Lucas, Douglas J., Laurie S. Goodman, and Frank J. Fabozzi (2006). *Collateralized Debt Obligations: Structures and Analysis,* 2nd ed. Hoboken, NJ: John Wiley & Sons.

Lumpkin, Stephen (1999). "Trends and Developments in Securitization." *Financial Market Trends* 74: 25–57.

Mason, Howard K., and Rick L. Biggs (2002). "Credit Card Securitization: A Quick Primer." Bernstein Research, Sanford C. Bernstein & Co., May.

Meckling, William H. (1977). "Financial Markets, Default, and Bankruptcy." *Law and Contemporary Problems* 41, no. 4 (Autumn): 124–177.

Miller, Merton H. (1977). "The Wealth Transfers of Bankruptcy: Some Illustrative Examples." *Law and Contemporary Problems* 41, no. 4 (Autumn): 39–46.

Modigliani, Franco, and Merton H. Miller (1958). "The Cost of Capital, Corporation Finance and the Theory of Investment." *American Economic Review* 48 (June): 261–297.

Modigliani, Franco and Merton H. Miller (1963). "Corporate Income Taxes and the Cost of Capital: A Correction." *American Economic Review* 53 (June): 433–443.

Moody's (2007). "Moody's Proposes Enhancements to Non-Prime RMBS Securitization." Press release, Moody's Investors Services, September 26.

Mortgage Bankers Association (2000). The Standard Roles and Responsibilities of the Master and Sub-servicers in CMBS Transactions. White paper, June 22.

Murray, A. P. (2001). "Has Securitization Increased Risk to the Financial System?" *Business Economics* 36, no. 1: 63–72.

Pfister, Benedicte (2002). "Whole Business Securitizations: A Unique Opportunity for U.K. Assets." International Structured Finance Special Report, Moody's Investor Service, October 19.

Rutan, Everett, and Berthelon, Sophie (2007). "Moody's Update on Bank-Sponsored ABCP Conduit Programs: A Review of Credit and Liquidity Issues." *International Structured Finance*, Moody's Investors Service, September 12.

Schwarcz, Steven (2002). *Structured Finance: A Guide to the Principles of Asset Securitization*, 3rd ed. New York: Practicing Law Institute.

Silver, Andrew A. (2000). "Rating Asset-Backed Securities." Chapter 2 in Frank J. Fabozzi (ed.), *Investing in Asset-Backed Securities*. Hoboken, NJ: John Wiley & Sons.

Sirmans, C. F., and John D. Benjamin (1990). "Pricing Fixed Rate Mortgages: Some Empirical Evidence." *Journal of Financial Services Research* 4, no. 3: 191–202.

Sloan, Allan (2007). "Junk Mortgages Under the Microscope," *Fortune Magazine*, October 16.

Standard & Poor's (2001). "Cash Flow CDOs: Continued Growth Despite Economic Risks." *Commentary: Structured Finance*, August 7.

———— (2002). "Global CBO/CLO Rating Criteria." *Structured Finance Ratings*, April.

———— (2004). "Servicer Evaluation Rankings Criteria." *Structured Finance Ratings*, September 21.

———— (2005a). "Structured Finance Market Opinion Survey Confirms Operational Risk Remains A Serious Concern For Securitization Professionals." *Structured Finance*, February 24.

———— (2005b). "Backup Servicer Plays Vital Role in Non-commodified-Asset Securitizations." *Structured Finance*, June 20.

———— (2005c). "Global ABCP Criteria." *Structured Finance*, September 29.

Tadie, Patrick (2005). "Trustees and Technology in Securitization." Supplement to *The 2005 Guide to Structured Finance*. New York: International Financial Law Review.

Wolfe, Simon (2000). "Structural Effects of Asset-Backed Securitization." *European Journal of Finance* 6, no. 4 (December): 353–369.

Index